Teaching, Assessing and Evaluation for Clinical Competence

A practical guide for practitioners and teachers

Mary Neary
PhD, BEd (Hons), Cert Ed (FE), RNT, RCNT, RGN, RMN, RNMH

Cardiff University School of Social Sciences
Glamorgan Building
King Edward VII Avenue
Cardiff CF10 3WA

First published in 2000 by:
Stanley Thornes (Publishers) Ltd

Reprinted in 2001 by:
Nelson Thornes Ltd
Delta Place
27 Bath Road
CHELTENHAM
GL53 7TH
United Kingdom

08 09 10/10 9 8 7

A catalogue record for this book is available from the British Library.

ISBN 978 0 7487 4417 6

Page make-up by Acorn Bookwork

Printed and bound in Spain by Graficas Cems

Contents

ACKNOWLEDGEMENTS

I express my thanks and appreciation for the help and use of documents given to me by the following: Donna Young, Charles Frears College of Nursing & Midwifery and De Monfort University, Leicester; Jo North, Sheffield College of Nursing and Midwifery; Jim Richardson, College of Medicine, University of Wales, Cardiff; Malcolm Goodwin, College of Nursing & Midwifery, Bangor University; nursing staff and ward managers at L.R.I. Leicester; Jenny Moon, School of Social Sciences, University of Wales, Cardiff; Thomas Moore, Welsh National Board (WNB), Wales; teaching staff at the Teacher Training and Education Department, Huddersfield University; and the PGCE tutorial staff at the School of Social Sciences, University of Wales, Cardiff.

Dedication

To my beloved Aunt, Muriel Howe. My mentor.

INTRODUCTION

THE AIM AND PURPOSE OF THIS BOOK

The aim of this book is to lay the foundations of knowledge and understanding necessary to allow practitioners to take on the role of facilitator, assessor and mentor. This book is intended to be used by lecturers and tutors involved in teaching and assessing and mentor/preceptor courses.

This book is suitable for anyone working in a clinical environment who has responsibility for health-care students during their clinical practice placements. The book is based on the philosophy that:

> *The competent mentor and/or assessor should also be a competent facilitator of learning and evaluator of students' learning. (Neary, 1996, p.146)*

Each section contains exercises which readers are encouraged to undertake as part of a self-directed approach to their own learning and development as facilitators and assessors.

The United Kingdom Central Council for Nursing, Midwifery and Health Visiting (UKCC) report *Fitness for Practice* has highlighted the need to refocus the teaching and assessment of competence and states:

> *The assessment of competence cannot be reduced solely to an assessment of a student's ability to carry out certain tasks. Outcome-based standards for theory and practice and different assessment strategies are required to achieve greater congruence between what is learned in the classroom and on practical placements and to ensure fitness for practice. We conclude that assessment strategies need to be improved if they are to measure students' competence to practise effectively. (UKCC, 1999, p.36).*

This book has been designed to facilitate that purpose and to involve practitioners in how to 'do' and how to learn from their practical experience. Responsible practitioners need to be able to integrate theory and practice, and to make sense of their own experiences and those of their students.

Most practitioners will have considerable clinical experience and some formal education on teaching, assessing and evaluating students' practice. Thus the focus will be on 'knowledge for use' and 'learning by doing'. The role of practitioner as assessor consists of identifying a process for making judgements and decisions as well as focusing upon outcomes.

The following statements are designed to provoke critical thinking as part of the teaching, assessing and evaluating process.

1 Decisions are made on the basis of habit, common sense and use of intuitive knowledge (Benner, 1984).
2 Habitual patterns provide a considerable measure of efficiency and enable individuals to do more than would be possible if one made every decision with a conscious mind.
3 When the situation is 'new' or 'difficult' the need for something other than habitual patterns becomes apparent.
4 Action is determined by a goal or objective.
5 Evaluation is usually tied to measuring how closely stated goals have been achieved.
6 Failure to achieve a goal leads to:
   - loss of confidence
   - anger
   - sense of worthlessness
   - disbelief.
7 A belief in doing the 'right thing' can help in motivating or generating action.
8 Recognizing the need for change, when already under the stress of many changes.
9 People and organizations resist change. The resistance may be particularly great when people feel that they have some investment in the original design and when their response has become a habit.
10 Conditions (physical characteristics, culture, resources, available structure, relationships, etc.) and stance (attitudes, values, belief, expectations and assumptions) will change over time.
11 Evaluation is built in from the beginning, whereas learning outcomes can be modified as a result of education.
12 An unanticipated outcome is not necessarily a failure.
13 There are always some intended or expected outcomes and some unintended, unpredictable or unexpected outcomes. Both provide for new learning and new action.

Questions to ask yourself

1 What is the relationship of the above statements to my preparation as a practitioner and/or mentor.
2 How do the above statements help me to become a:
   - competent practitioner?
   - critical thinker?
   - effective decision maker?
   - effective facilitator?

In answer consider Schön's statement:

> *We need to have a stable process rather than a fixed outcome.*
> *(Schön, 1971)*

The statements, data and models on which this book is based are derived from evidence collected during the following three major research projects.

1 The practitioner-teacher: a study on the introduction of mentors in the preregistration nurse education programme in Wales (Davies *et al.*, 1994).

2 An investigation: continuous assessment of students' clinical competence in CFP (Neary, 1996).

3 Fitness for practice: the UKCC Commission for Nursing and Midwifery Education (UKCC, 1999).

FOCUSING ON GENERAL ISSUES

The book begins by focusing on the general issues pertinent to any practitioner who undertakes the teaching, mentoring and assessing of preregistration health-care students. It then covers the specific roles and responsibilities of teaching for clinical competence and clinical assessment within the pre-registration nursing programmes. It is hoped that practitioners will then begin to appreciate the wider applications of the practical assessment process and also gain an insight into the demands of the teaching and assessing role. The self-directed activities in each section will facilitate this process. Users will be referred to as practitioners throughout.

It is imperative that the changing role of a practitioner as a mentor and assessor is appreciated. Practitioners are offered the following learning outcomes with individual responsibility for updating.

1 Describe the general principles of teaching, learning and assessing, i.e. validity, reliability, etc. and use examples from your own practical experiences.

2 Discuss the purpose of facilitating, learning and assessing for clinical competence.

3 Explore the issues involved in:
- the moral/ethical/legal aspects of teaching and assessing for clinical competence
- subjectivity and self-awareness in assessment
- minimizing the 'observer effects' in practical assessment
- devising a list of criteria for use in teaching and assessing in clinical practice.

4 Outline briefly the national events which had a bearing upon the development of nurse education. Describe how this is being developed in the practical and clinical setting (practice placements for students).

5 Describe the purpose and process of the educational audit for clinical placements; explore the implications of this.

6 Discuss the structure, philosophy and major themes inherent in the educational programmes. Describe how these are integrated within the assessment tool for clinical competence.

7 Describe in detail the process of practical assessment in pre-registration nursing and midwifery programmes, including:
- how the activity statements may be operationalized through the development of learning opportunities

- how learning opportunities may be structured within an action plan developed for a student
- the roles and responsibilities of practitioners in teaching and assessing students
- the regulations and process through which a student may use the right of appeal within the assessment process
- the role of mentoring.

8 Analyse the strengths and weaknesses in both giving and receiving constructive feedback.

9 Identify the criteria for entry onto a teaching/assessing course, for example:
- a first-level registered nurse or a senior second-level nurse
- must have been qualified for no less than one year
- must have been in a post, part time or full time, for no less than one year.

THE PHILOSOPHY OF TEACHING AND LEARNING

Nursing and other health-care professions are practice disciplines and therefore learning is primarily in clinical settings with qualified practitioners acting as role models. Professional skills and values are projected largely subconsciously by qualified professionals as they go about their routine activities; in the same way, these skills and values are learned largely subconsciously by students as they too go about their everyday duties. The relationship means that teaching students (as well as teaching patients/clients) is an integral part of the qualified professional's role.

Teaching is an open, complex skill composed of a combination of cognitive, interpersonal and motor skills which are in turn a function of the overlap of insight and action (Tomlinson, 1988). Like all skills, teaching skills can be deliberately taught and learned if certain conditions are met (Fitts and Posner, 1969).

The social environment in which the skills will be exercised must be conducive to their development and use (Gelatly, 1987). Students need to be furnished with adequate opportunities to apply and incorporate relevant insights from contributory disciplines to teaching and learning situations within practice placements. Students need also to be provided with constructive and informative feedback, soon enough after the practice attempts to be meaningful (Tomlinson, 1988). Such structuring will facilitate the creation of a positive learning environment for practitioners and students to experience; hopefully they will learn that such an environment is crucial to the acceptance of constructive feedback and the development of the skills required to constructively criticize the work of others. Importantly for their own professional development and performance, they will become skilful in the art of self-monitoring and self-assessment and learn to be reflective practitioners.

Teaching is undertaken in the pursuit of aims or purposes and reflects some mental representation or 'idea' of those purposes and aims in the minds of teachers and facilitators of learning. These representations are not necessarily consciously held, however, and may not be consistent or readily modified. Irrespective of their consciousness or clarity, they finally emerge in practice (Schön and Argyris, 1977). Therefore meaningful learning begins by rendering conscious, where possible, a person's subconscious representations and ideas and then examining them against formal insights from relevant disciplines and practical realities.

The mutual exploration and examination of subconscious ideas and images encourages and facilitates the cross-fertilization of ideas that is central to adult learning (we need to remind ourselves that our students are adult learners). It also encourages an open, critical approach to new knowledge and ideas which in turn underpins the deep and elaborate mental processing of information upon which meaningful learning depends. In addition, and importantly for the professional development of practitioners, students will learn to appreciate the value of theory in professional practice, which will motivate them to keep up to date with developments in their own areas of clinical expertise and professional education.

Follow-up workshops and/or discussion groups

Once practitioners have gained practice in teaching and assessing students under the supervision of a mentor, it is advisable to attend follow-up study days in the form of workshops, discussion groups and debriefing sessions. You may even want to create a mentor/assessor support group (Neary, 1996) (see Appendix 1 for example).

The aims of such workshops are to:

- share individual teaching and learning strategies
- share worries about assessment
- define some performance indicator for 'high-quality' teaching and assessment
- define staff development needs in the area of teaching and assessments
- pinpoint the weakness in teaching, assessment priorities and devices
- explore alternative ways of facilitating, learning and assessing
- enhance the learning which can be derived from assessments
- produce agreed standards of teaching and facilitating learning
- produce 'quality criteria' for assessing
- collect facts and information from experience gained while enacting the role of teacher and assessor
- evaluate your own role as teacher and assessor
- advise the curriculum planning and moderating team on assessment procedures and processes
- encourage group learning
- share knowledge which will help others to become reflective practitioners
- share ways in which chance in practice can be effective and fulfilling

- share any misunderstanding over the dual or even triple roles of mentoring, teaching and assessing.

ASSESSING AT DIFFERING LEVELS

There has been much discussion relating to the assessing of students in clinical practice at the various levels. However, very little is written about qualified practitioners' assessments of their own clinical practice, and yet they are expected to assess students' clinical competence. One key issue to emerge from a study by Neary (1996) was the shortage of available devices for assessing practitioners. Assumptions are made about practitioners' abilities to assess levels of standards and performance because they are already qualified registered practitioners. A further study (Davies *et al.*, 1994) showed that practitioners acting as mentors and assessors to students had not had their own 'clinical competence' or teaching and assessing skills assessed since they qualified. Both studies suggested there was a need for practitioners to be properly prepared and assessed for their roles as teachers, assessors and evaluators of learning.

With the move of nurse education and other health professions into higher education, tutors need to be able to convince their university colleagues that because many clinical practitioners operate at a very high level, an assessment strategy needs to be developed by both tutorial and service staff within a partnership model to determine the practitioner's ability to:

- facilitate learning
- teach and assess students
- provide feedback to students
- demonstrate a progression of achievement
- develop their own personal and professional competence
- develop their own skills in becoming a reflective practitioner
- demonstrate fitness for practice.

CREATING A LEARNING ENVIRONMENT

This book has its focus on the 'individual practitioner' which has led to the design of its self-directed learning approach. The purpose is to ensure that theory is being integrated into and developed through clinical practice and ultimately reflected in the quality of teaching and assessing of student clinical competence. If practitioners are able to integrate theory into practice this in turn develops a positive learning environment and the relationship between practitioner, student and health-care manager will be that of "partners in learning". Additionally, if the practitioners are effectively prepared and regularly update their own professional competence, this will invariably lead to improvement in the quality of care given to every person who is in receipt of health care (Neary, 1996). This updating, if it is carefully planned and effective, can lead to higher morale among practitioners, with a concomitant lowering of anxiety. Brockfield (1986) reminds us, however, that adult students must be helped to become self-directed and self-motivating.

To create a self-directed, self-motivating environment, we need a well-structured programme of learning – the curriculum. A well-planned curriculum will help to shape and give guidance to a programme of learning in which practitioners, teachers, assessors, mentors and students become partners in the learning process. Having an understanding of how the curriculum is structured, designed and implemented will, I believe, encourage practitioners to become aware of the need for professional development for both themselves and their students.

An example of a curriculum can be found in Appendix 2. However, all practitioners should obtain a personal copy of their own from their local college of nursing and health studies.

NOVICE TO EXPERT: THEORY AND PRACTICE

Box 1.1

Stage 1	Novice	Beginners have had no experience of the situation in which they are expected to perform.
Stage 2	Advanced beginner	Students can demonstrate marginally acceptable performance.
Stage 3	Competent	Typified by the student who has been on the job in the same or similar situations. Competence develops when the student begins to see his or her actions in terms of long-range goals and is consciously aware.
Stage 4	Proficient	The proficient performer perceives situations as a whole rather than in terms of aspects and performance is guided by maxims. Perception is the key word here.
Stage 5	Expert	The expert performer no longer relies on the analytic principle (rule, guideline) to connect his or her understanding of the situation to an appropriate action.

Work by Benner (1984) (Box 1.1) emphasizes the differences between theory and practice.

The model outlined by Dreyfus and Dreyfus (1980), and quoted within Benner's work, suggests that there are five levels of proficiency: novice, advanced beginner, competent, proficient and expert.

Analysing practitioner descriptions of their experience was a central method in Benner's work. In her view, nursing had failed to articulate the uniqueness and richness of the knowledge embedded in expert clinical practice. She utilized the Dreyfus and Dreyfus (1980) model of skill acquisition to frame the movement from novice to expert:

a movement from a reliance on abstract principles and rules to use of past, concrete experience. (Benner, 1984, p.4)

Practitioners claimed that they based their actions on previous experience that became progressively more significant as they developed expertise. Expertise develops when preconceived notions and expectations are challenged, refined or altered by the actual practical situation. This appeared to support the argument that continuing education and staff development programmes should be designed to help them use such experience in developing their teacher and assessor role and that of mentor if required.

Benner (1984) asserted that nursing practice had been studied primarily from a sociological perspective and that the profession had learned much about role relationships, socialization and acculturation in nursing practice. She argued that we have learned less about the knowledge embodied in actual nursing practice, the knowledge that accrues over time in the practice of an applied discipline. Carper (1978) echoed the same sentiments when she stated that such knowledge has gone uncharted and unstudied because the differences between practical and theoretical knowledge have been misunderstood. Benner (1984; Benner and Tanner, 1987) also relied on the writings of Polyani (1958), who developed Ryle's (1949) distinction that 'knowing how' consisted of two kinds of knowledge. They pointed out that we have many skills (know-how) that are acquired without 'knowing what' and, further, that we cannot always theoretically account for our own know-how in many common activities.

It is my belief that effective teaching, assessing and evaluating would help practitioners and students to develop the 'know how' and the 'know what' in a more effective, efficient and realistic way. One way to develop this process could be through the appropriate preparation of all practitioners for their role as facilitators of learning.

The content of this book relies in part upon the above principles. Particular models are offered as they enable the demonstration of teaching and assessing and for some mentoring skills to be identified at novice to expert levels. This will clearly demonstrate a progression along a spiral of increasing complexity of cognitive skills, integrated into practice, at the same time acknowledging that much learning occurs while the practitioner is giving care to the consumer of health-care provision and assessing students' progress. An important part of any professional education is personal and professional growth. A prerequisite of both a product and process model of learning is a revisiting and enhancing of concepts, which can be considered as the spiral element (Neary, 1993).

Encouragement to reflect on previous practice, identification of learning needs and implementation of what has been learned are seen as essential. Each practitioner is therefore expected to use reflective skills and to develop their own potential in becoming 'reflective practitioners'.

CONCLUSIONS

The models chosen for the facilitation of learning of theory and practice must be explored by each professional practitioner on any learning programme. All mentors and assessors should be familiar with their contents, their role within the models and how they are expected to augment the assessment of theory with that of assessing clinical practice (Appendices 3, 4 and 5 offer examples).

If professional practitioners are to become competent facilitators of learning and assessors of students' clinical competence, then creative ways must be developed for assessing how this has been fully incorporated into the students' normal everyday clinical practice, commensurate with the level of academic achievement. The route to perfecting assessment tools for both students and practitioners is long and arduous but will ultimately be beneficial to all involved, not least the patient or client receiving the intervention from the professionals.

2 STRATEGY FOR LEARNING

INTRODUCTION

The reflective practitioner

Before going on to teaching and learning strategies, this section introduces the concepts of reflection, mentorship, adult learning, competencies and learning outcomes, learning contracts and contract assignments. The purpose of this section is to help the reader to become an effective and competent facilitator of learning, to understand his or her role in the assessment process, and develop the skills of reflective practice.

REFLECTION

Becoming a reflective practitioner

Much has been written about reflection and it is not the intention here to go into the theories that surround reflection. For the interested reader a list of further reading is given at the end of the chapter.

The intention is to encourage you to reflect on your own experiences and perhaps keep a learning journal as part of your own professional development. Many students are expected to keep a journal and will need help and guidance to reflect on their experience and to record that experience.

Learning through reflection

Reflection in relation to learning has been extensively researched by, among others, Boud *et al.* (1985), Kemmis (1985) and Kolb and Fry (1975). The concept of reflection-in-action was further enhanced by work that Schön carried out in conjunction with Argyris (Argyris and Schön 1974). Reflection-in-action is based on the concepts of Model I and Model II behaviour, where Model I is seen as the traditional client–professional relationship and Model II as the foundation of reflective practice (Schön, 1987).

Model I learning produces a view of the professional as the expert, taking unilateral decisions and as giving advice, where problems are seen in clear-cut terms and as amenable to solution by routine methods.

Model II learning, on the other hand, promotes a view of the professional as one with specialized knowledge and experience, who will work with the client/patient towards finding an individual solution or amelioration for their individual problem. The experience of this, as well as continued conventional learning, will help in forming solutions to future problems which have similar features but are equally individual.

A study by Davies *et al.* (1994) showed that there are professionals with many years' experience who are superb practitioners, respected by colleagues and patients alike, and from whom students gain a great deal. This situation is one familiar to most nurses. However, equally familiar is the practitioner with a similar number of years experience who is no more effective now than they were when newly qualified and from whom students learn little. This leads to the question of why there is this difference and what factors promote it. A reading of *Theory in Practice* (Schön, 1983) and *Educating the Reflective Practitioner* (Schön, 1987) highlighted the problem and led to the incorporation of this theoretical framework as part of the study.

The use of learning-reflective journals

Probably all of us reflect but some do so more than others and for those, being reflective can be an orientation to their everyday lives. For others, reflection comes about when the conditions in the learning environment are appropriate – when there is an incentive or some guidance. This section focuses on practical activities that will provide a context in which reflection can be encouraged. The activities are mostly no more than situations in which various conditions which favour reflection are accentuated or harnessed in a formalized manner, for example, as in a learning journal. The activities are grouped for convenience according to these 'accentuated conditions', though there will be much overlap.

The use of journals as a vehicle for reflection in educational situations is becoming common and because the literature on writing journals is relatively abundant, the use of journals to enhance learning and practice warrants attention. There is a form of journal called a 'dialogue' journal which involves written conversation between two or more people, which will be relevant for you and your students.

In terms of journals in formal education, Moon (1999) suggested that the method is more suitable for courses where there are 'smaller numbers of mature students who have a clearer sense of their own goals', as opposed to the higher education situation where traditional patterns of expectations of teaching, learning and assessing may cause difficulties. These are, however, only the same problems that occur for any unusual self-managed form of learning and some of these rigid expectations need to be overcome in any programme of study in the development towards a future functional employee.

There are many purposes for using journals, some of which relate to personally initiated writing and some to formal educational situations. In the latter cases, in particular, a clear statement of purpose can be important for the success of the activity. The following, advised by Moon (1999), is a list of purposes which journal writing could serve.

A means of reflection

There are a number of words used in the literature synonymously with 'journal', such as log, diary, dialectical notebook, workbook or autobiographical and reflective writing, profile or 'progress file'. Precisely defining words seems to be fairly unhelpful here so by 'journal' we refer to predominantly written material that is based on reflection and is relatively free writing, though it may be written within a given structure. A journal is written regularly over a period of time rather than in a single session. Within this generalized form there are many variations and this section is an attempt to capture the essence of the activity in its relation to reflection in order that it can be applied elsewhere.

To record experience

The primary purpose of journal writing may be to record experience, with the emphasis initially being put onto the recording rather than the reflective activity, although this may come later. Recording of experience may entail long-term or short-term input.

To develop learning in ways that enhance other learning methods

This represents a group of purposes generally specified in formal learning situations. Writing a journal can, for example, encourage the valuing of personal observation and knowledge.

To deepen the quality of learning

Moon (1999) quotes Mortimer (1998), who described the use of portfolio development with reflective commentary as a means of increasing critical ability and encouraging the adoption of a deep approach to ... 'learning'. The technique that is crucial for developing critical approaches to learning is the initial noting of detail – the 'look' and the 'look again', returning to the material to reflect on it in a double-entry journal.

To enable the student to understand the process of their own learning

Examples of the use of journals for this purpose tend to be from situations where a group of individuals is being taught to teach or train another group of students. Morrison (1996) suggested that a journal helps students to self-direct and gain control of their own cognitive processes, '... e.g. using preferred learning styles in organising tasks'.

Journals enable students to understand the limitations of their own learning styles. In this way they can be better facilitators of the learning of others, when they themselves become registered practitioners.

To facilitate learning from experience

Journal writing is about learning from experience of events but some writers have been clearer in their specification of this purpose. For example, Boud *et al.* (1985) designed a journal in which the sequence of recording takes account of the cycle of experiential learning, with the initial recording of an event, then reflection, an account of the subjective inner experience and further reflection and generalization. On a broader basis, journals that accompany fieldwork or work experience provide a method of developing the meaning of experiences so that the student can relate their unique experience to established theory or develop their own theory.

As a means of assessment in formal education
Journals may be used as a form of assessment. In terms of learning, this will be enhanced if the appropriate assessment criteria can be identified in advance between the practitioner, the staff and the student. A journal can accompany a submission for the assessment of prior experiential learning which can give returning (to learning) adult students exemption from parts of a programme of learning.

To enhance professional practice or the professional self in practice
A common purpose for journal writing is to encourage the development of what is called reflective practice, which has many identities. This is often in the professional development context but increasingly there is a more generalized application of the term. The central issue in improving practice is the translation of the products of reflection into the real world of action so that they affect practice and something is done differently. Some journal structures seem to follow this objective more clearly than others, in requiring the students to think about what they will do that is actually different. The issue of transfer of ideas into practice is problematic where initial education is concerned. The journal can only facilitate appropriate attitudes towards practice and perhaps encourage the habits of reflection.

In the context of professional development, electronic (email) journal writing has been used as a means of communication by students on clinical practice at a distance from their tutors. An example of this occurs on the Postgraduate Certificate of Education course at the School of Social Sciences, University of Wales, Cardiff.

Reflection in action and knowledge in action

The concept of reflection in action is associated with the acquisition of knowledge in the practice setting (Benner, 1984; Schön, 1983). It arises from an increasing crisis of confidence in professional knowledge which has been detected in modern society (Smyth, 1986). Schön argues that there is a mismatch between forms of professional knowledge and the changing characteristics of practice settings which exist in any practical profession. Practice settings are complex, uncertain, unstable, unique and value ridden. In such a setting, professionals are increasingly asked to perform 'tasks' for which they have not been educated. Even if they have been prepared adequately in their initial professional education, the rate of social and technical change makes this obsolete as the years progress (Knowles, 1975).

Professionals are now confronted with an unprecedented requirement for adaptability. This cannot be achieved where the dominant forms of knowledge are theoretical in nature, which Schön (1983) describes as 'technical-rational'. To counter this domination and achieve practical adaptability, Schön proposed the 'practicum' as the setting in which professionals should acquire those forms of knowledge which are more relevant to problem solving in practice settings. Schön goes on to describe a practicum as simply a setting designed for the task of learning practice.

The primary goal for the student of a practice profession is the acquisition of what has been termed 'tacit knowledge' by Polyani (1958). Tacit knowledge is that knowledge which is not given in the scientific literature but is known by experts in the discipline (Benner, 1984). Carroll (1988) argues that tacit knowledge is inherent in the process of clinical decision making by the nurse practitioner. Wood (1982) stated:

> Tacit information ... is usually not given in texts but is known by the experts in the discipline. However, the experts are usually unaware of that knowledge and cannot easily describe it. Usually we acquire that tacit knowledge by 'experience'; for example, an experienced professional 'just knows' when a decision sounds wrong, yet she/he cannot explain why. Alternatively they might intuitively know what to do in a complex situation yet when asked why, they might answer 'experience'.

Practitioners' behaviour may inhibit or enhance the acquisition of tacit knowledge by influencing student nurses' decision-making habits (French, 1989). It is the acquisition of tacit knowledge in the practicum which enhances professional adaptability. This learning in action can take two forms: knowing-in-action and reflection-in-action.

Knowing-in-action is characterized by knowing how to do things, a lack of conscious awareness of having learned these things and an inability to describe the knowledge which the action reveals. This has been found to be typical of the pre-registration preparation of nurses in England and Wales (French, 1989). A professional education in a practicum, however, requires what Schön (1983) calls reflection-in-action. This involves the development of a consciousness of the action/problem-solving process and its context. In this way a reflective practitioner will be developed as a student progresses through the nurse education course, provided that curricula are planned to develop reflection-in-action in the practice setting and that there is a progression from knowledge-in-action to reflection-in-action as soon as it is possible during the course. The opportunities must be made available for all students and practitioners to reflect on their experiences, which is called reflection-on-action.

Learning from experience

> Reflection is an important human activity in which people recapture their experience, think about it, mull it over and evaluate it. It is this working with experience that is important in learning. The capacity to reflect is developed to different stages in different people and it may be this ability which characterises those who learn effectively from experience. (Boud et al., 1985, p.19)

Learning effectively from experience is a complex process the outcomes of which depend, to a large extent, on the cognitive and affective responses of the individual concerned and the context in which he/she is learning. We will explore this process using a model (see p.17) developed by Boud *et al.*, (1985) analysing the experience(s) that precipitate reflection, the three stages of reflection – returning to experience, attending to feelings, and reevaluating experience and – some of the possible outcomes.

What is experience?

Activity

What does the word 'experience' mean to you? It may have different meanings depending on the context in which it is used. Take a little time now to think about the concept of 'experience' and make a note of your ideas.

Watson (1991) found that the word 'experience' was used in four ways:

- exposure to an event, a situation, an emotion or to information
- an event, a situation or an emotion
- the amount of knowledge gained over a period of time
- time spent in the service (practice).

Watson (1991) proposed that the word 'experience' is often used as though it were synonymous with 'learning', although whether any of the four definitions cited above leads to new understandings and appreciations depends on the nature of the experience and the response of the individual to that experience. It is, however, a common belief that the longer we live, the more experience we have and the wiser we become, but some would argue that the passing of the years does not necessarily bring gifts of understanding within one's own life. Twenty years' experience, it has been said, may be no more than one year's experience repeated 20 times.

An individual's response to a new experience will be significantly determined by past experiences. Not only is the person affected by an event or situation but the event or situation is also affected by the person. Dewey (1938, pp.39–40) states:

> *We live from birth to death in a world of persons and things which in large measure is what it is because of what has been done and transmitted from previous human activities. When this fact is ignored, experience is treated as if it were something which goes on exclusively inside an individual's body and mind. It ought not to be necessary to say that experience does not occur in a vacuum. There are sources outside an individual which give rise to experience. It is constantly fed from these springs.*

Thus, no experience occurs in isolation from what has happened before.

Taking this to a logical conclusion, every experience that a person has is influenced by the cumulative effects of both their own previous experiences and those of their outer world. Viewed over time, Dewey (1938, p.37) suggested that experience can be described as a dynamic continuum, where:

> *every experience affects for better or worse the attitudes which help decide the quality of further experiences.*

Cell (1984) argued that each experience contains something of our past and our future. This is very important since what is learnt from an experience may be dysfunctional and lead us to act in the future in ways which may inhibit or distort our future development and growth.

So it seems fair to suggest that although all learning stems from experience, not all experience results in learning (Boud *et al.*, 1985; Cell, 1984; Dewey, 1938).

Making sense of experience

To learn from our experience we first need to make sense of it. We interpret our experience all the time, subconsciously in routine or familiar situations but more consciously in unexpected or unfamiliar situations. To interpret an experience implies that it has meaning, but do events or situations have any meaning in themselves? Since any event or situation is subject to a variety of interpretations depending on the person experiencing it, it seems fair to say that meaning resides with the person and is not intrinsic to the situation or event.

Cell (1984, p.177) argued:

> *Our experiential learning is often dysfunctional, always incomplete. We need to use present experience to test our beliefs, correcting the misinterpretations we've made, lifting veils we've placed between ourselves and reality. We also need to see and hear and feel where we've been blind and deaf and unfeeling. Yet we often manipulate our experience to fit our beliefs. We see and hear and feel selectively, tending to experience what we expect to experience, wish to experience, or fear to experience. In this way, we simply impose our maps upon our present perceptions, endlessly renewing the mistakes, the distractions, the partialities of our past learnings. If we are not to bind ourselves to portions of our past, we need to break these cycles of reindoctrination, using our experience to test what we have learned rather than merely to re-embody it.*

The process of reflection increases the potential learning from experience. As Boyd and Fales (1983) asserted, it:

> *is the core difference between whether a person repeats the same experience several times, becoming highly proficient at one behaviour, or learns from experience in such a way that he or she is cognitively or effectively changed!*

There are many 'models' which are aimed at helping practitioners to reflect. Heath (1998, p.592) suggested that models are meant to provide guidance, not rules for reflection, and practitioners should be encouraged to develop a flexible approach to their use, giving some thought to which parts of the model are most useful in the situation described. She goes on to advise:

> *Rigid use of a model focuses attention on the model rather than practice and could inhibit depth of exploration thus deflecting the original aim of the model's author.*

Boud *et al.* (1985) identified three elements which they believe to be important in the reflective process: returning to experience, attending to feelings, reevaluating the experience. These three stages provide a useful framework for a 'how to' guide to writing reflective accounts of your own. Johns (1994) added a fourth stage – learning.

Stage 1   Return to experience
- Describe the experience, recollect what happened in chronological order. The description should be fairly detailed but without judgement.
- *Notice* what happened/how you felt/what you did.

Remember that you need to reflect on what actually happened, not on what you *wished* had happened. The purpose of this stage is to help you stand back from the experience, clarify your perceptions and look at it again with the benefit of time and concentration.

Stage 2   Attend to feelings
- Note any positive or negative feelings, e.g. pleasure, annoyance, elation, anxiety, frustration, sense of achievement.
- Acknowledge negative feelings but don't let them form a barrier.
- Work with positive emotions.

Stage 3   Reevaluate the experience
- Connect ideas and feelings of the experience to those you had on reflection.
- Consider options and choices.

Stage 4   Learning
- How do I now feel about this experience?
- Could I have dealt better with this situation?
- What have I learnt from this experience?

The outcomes of reflection on your experience may be that:

- you would do something differently next time
- an issue has been clarified
- you become aware of new ideas
- you consider options and choices.

Comment on whether these outcomes apply to you and in what way.

Remember that change/learning may be small/large, visible/non-visible to others, cognitive/affective.

These activities are designed to help you practise the skills of reflection-on-action.

Activities

1 Drawing on your own recent professional experience, identify an incident/issue/problem. It may have been positive (something you did/ coped with well/something that pleased you/an event which was satisfying) or negative (an unexpected outcome/a situation that made you feel uncomfortable/an event that angered, frustrated or upset you).
   - Write down everything that you can remember about this event. Take your mind back and try to relive and describe events as they unfold. Don't try to analyse or justify yet.
   - Use Boud/John's model of structured reflection to help you focus on your description of the experience and reflect upon it. Write your thoughts down as you reevaluate the experience.
2 Work with a partner and take turns to share your reflective accounts. The person hearing the reflective account should use the 'focus questions' in John's model of structured reflection and the skills of reflective listening to give their partner the opportunity to share his or her experience and reflect more deeply on it.
3 What are the advantages and difficulties of using reflection as a teaching/ learning strategy? Consider this from your own viewpoint as a 'student' as well as in your professional capacity as a mentor/assessor.
4 As a mentor/assessor, what difficulties/dilemmas might you face in facilitating reflection-on-action in your students/trainees/supervisors?
5 How helpful do you find reflection-on-action?

MENTORING

What's in a name?

A review of the literature identifies a lack of consensus regarding a definition of the term 'mentor' (Davies *et al.*, 1994; Hagerty, 1986; Morle, 1990). This lack of consensus and clarity in definition of terms is also a subject for debate in fields outside nursing. Hagerty (1986) highlighted this general difficulty when criticizing the flawed methodology in several research studies on mentoring in business and adult education spheres, as well as in nursing.

In nursing, the roles that mentors may be expected to undertake in practice areas are somewhat disparate. Initially unclear role specification may be further complicated by the use of the terms 'mentor', 'preceptor' and 'supervisor', by some, as synonyms. However, most authors distinguish between 'mentor' and 'preceptor' along the lines reflected by the Welsh National Board (WNB, 1992).

For situations in which a student in a practice area is assigned to a staff nurse for the duration of the allocation, in which the two work parallel shifts, and in which the student is supported as he or she works towards the planned learning outcomes for the placement, we would suggest the term 'preceptor'...

whereas:

...The Board would recommend that the term 'mentor' is reserved for longer term relationships between two people, one of whom is significantly older and/or more experienced than the other. The nature of the relationship is implicit in the term 'protégé' suggesting as it does a recognition of potential and a concern for the individual's well-being, advancement and general progress.

Mentorship is seen as a broader, longer term relationship, aimed at guiding the student towards an established place in the profession (Armitage and Burnard, 1991; Zwolski, 1982). Preceptorship has a narrower emphasis on individualized teaching, learning and support in the clinical environment. With the passage of time and development in the relationship, preceptorships may well become mentorships (Pelosi Beaulieu, 1988).

I would argue that an understanding of the role and functions associated with a particular title has implications for who is best suited to undertake that role. If the role of a mentor is different from the role of a preceptor, then people may be suited to one but not the other. Equally, if there are different expectations of a mentor, then an individual may be capable of meeting some but not all of these.

A good mentoring relationship is a dialogue between two people committed to improvement'. (Neary, 1994)

The upward spiral of the mentor and mentee relationship

Learning is a process that allows us to move on an upward spiral of growth, change and continuous improvement (Figure 2.1). Through learning we increase our mental capacity with the aid of reading, writing, thinking and reflecting. We mature socially and emotionally by making consistent commitments to the mentor/mentee relationship and in helping the mentee to develop, also in an upward spiral.

What is a mentor?

In the Davies *et al.* study (1994), 'mentor' was the term preferred by practitioners in practice placements. For the purpose of this book a mentor is someone who assists and supports an adult student taking a pre-registration nursing course. In this case, it means that you will be guiding students through many hours of clinical or practical work. As a mentor, you will also keep in touch with the course tutor or personal tutor in order to forward the student's progress.

Figure 2.1

Upward spiral of continuous improvement.

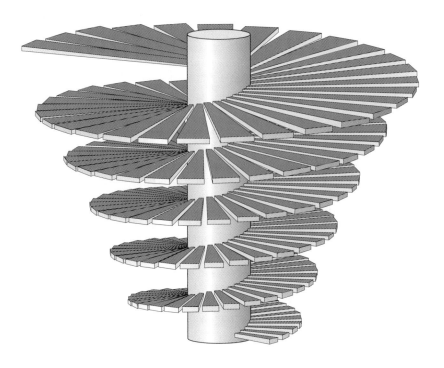

*Progress has not followed a straight, ascending line, but a spiral
with rhythms of progress and retrogression,
of evolution and dissolution.*
Goethe

In *An A–Z of Open Learning*, published by the National Extension College, the mentor is described as:

> *a person who accepts the role of facilitating an individual's learning
> …. the mentor … carried out activities as requested by the learner.
> Many open learning schemes strongly encourage the learner to select
> a mentor. The schemes often provide briefing materials for both
> partners.*

The publication further describes the mentor as using 'a very wide range' of methods to help, depending on the learner's needs. This help may resemble tutoring if it is related closely to the subject matter. It may be similar to coaching if the approach needed is in applying skills. It may have aspects of counselling when problems of learning need to be tackled (Figure 2.2).

The making of a good mentor

People who themselves have been well trained and supported in their professional careers tend to be good mentors in turn. They tend to be people who are:

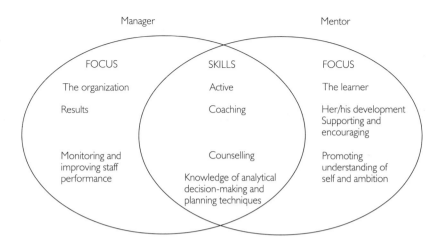

Figure 2.2

Manager–mentor skills overlap
difference in focus.

- prepared to allocate both time and mental energy to the role
- up to date with recent initiatives and are prepared to be flexible and innovative
- competent in the core skills of coaching, counselling, facilitating, giving feedback and networking
- interested and willing to help others
- themselves willing and able to learn and see potential benefits
- able to demonstrate the many characteristics advocated by Lu Ann Darling (1986) (see p.23). Revisit this page now and reflect on these characteristics.

What is Mentoring?

Intimate personal relationships frequently developed between the master and the apprentice. (Clutterbuck, 1985 p.1)

The original Mentor appears in Homer's *The Odyssey*. As an old and trusted friend of Odysseus, he is called to look after Odysseus' son. Athena, goddess of wisdom, speaks through him at critical times through the epic. Thus Mentor is both male and female.

Mentors, it seems, have something to do with growing up; a classic transitional figure, helping the youth achieve their adulthood and confirm their identity in an adult world.

It could be argued that a student (mentee) should be exposed to a wide variety of practice placements and more than one mentor during their clinical experience, as this would ensure broader learning opportunities and exposure to various 'skills'. One skill mentors have to offer is the management of the learning environment, creating learning opportunities for students. This should benefit the organization as a whole as well as the student.

Your role as a mentor

According to Tanner (1989) the exact nature of your role as a mentor will depend on a number of factors. These include:

- the amount of time you can spend with the student you are guiding
- the atmosphere and organization at your place of work
- your own skills and experience
- the needs and interests of the student.

Your role will probably include functions which might be categorized as teacher, advocate, friend and facilitator.

As a **teacher** you might need to:

- answer questions about the course material
- discuss ways of applying what is learned to the work situation
- give feedback on the student's achievements
- assist with planning how objectives and learning outcomes might be achieved
- coach in or demonstrate practical skills
- help the student review performance.

Being an **advocate** means acting on behalf of the student to preserve or increase confidence and self-esteem. In this role you might:

- arrange for practical experience
- manage access to libraries
- delegate functions which give the student extra responsibility.

Finally, in your role as a **friend** you might:

- give the student a lift when morale is low
- make yourself available to listen and advise
- point out where the student is going wrong
- point out ways to improve.

What is your role as a **facilitator**?

The relationship is frequently a new one for both you and the student you are guiding, so you will need to agree the degree and the nature of the involvement that you are willing to undertake. An important part of the mentor's role is to build an effective working relationship and to establish a partnership based on mutual trust, honesty and respect.

Here is what four students have said about the way in which their mentors help them:

I test my ideas out by talking them through with her; it helps to get another person's views and perspectives. They're usually a bit different from mine.

He points out things in the course that I might have skimmed over too quickly.
We discuss the assignments together before I begin work myself.

Our regular meetings help me to keep up my momentum.

Assessing your potential as a mentor

In deciding on how you will act as a mentor, you will want to clarify the kind of support the student you are guiding requires. You will also need to be sure about what you can offer. This will involve assessing your strengths for such a role.

Characteristics of a mentor

In her research into the characteristics that students perceive as valuable and helpful in a mentor, Lu Ann Darling (1986) has identified the following.

- A **model** the student can look up to, value and admire and may wish to emulate.
- An **envisioner** who gives a picture of what teaching management can be, is enthusiastic about opportunities or possibilities and inspires interest.
- An **energizer** who makes the 'profession' or 'job' fascinating and is enthusiastic and dynamic.
- An **investor** who spends a lot of time with the learner, spots potential and capabilities and can hand over responsibility.
- A **supporter** who is willing to listen, is warm and caring and is available in times of need.
- A **standard-prodder** who is very clear about what level of performance is required and pushes and prods the learner to achieve it.
- A **teacher-coach** who can instruct about setting priorities, help to develop interpersonal skills, give guidance on patient problems and encourage the learner to gain from experience.
- A **feedback giver** who can offer both positive and negative feedback and help the student to examine the things that go wrong.
- An **eye opener** who inspires interest in research and is able to facilitate understanding of wider issues, such as hospital politics and the total impact of departmental initiatives on the unit as a whole.
- A **door opener** who includes the student in discussions, asks the student to be a representative on committees and delegates a range of tasks to the student.
- An **idea bouncer** who not only discusses issues, problems and goals, but also allows the learner to present and argue ideas.
- A **problem solver** who helps the student to figure out and try out new ideas and who can analyse strengths and create ways to use them for the benefit of the profession or job.
- A **career counsellor** who gives guidance and support in career planning.
- A **challenger** who questions opinions and beliefs and forces the student to examine decisions.

Activity

Use the chart below to assess yourself in terms of the characteristics just described. Be honest, acknowledge your strengths, but own up to your weaknesses even in a characteristic you wish you had.

- *This is a particular strength of mine* means that you have a natural ability to behave in this way, without thinking about it.
- *I can offer* this means that you can easily adopt the characteristic, but must do so consciously.
- *This is not a particular strength* means that you do not count this attribute as one of your own.
- *I don't want this role* means that this is not a characteristic that you would like to develop.

Characteristic	This is a particular strength of mine	I can offer this	This is not a particular strength	I don't want this role
Model	☐	☐	☐	☐
Envisioner	☐	☐	☐	☐
Energizer	☐	☐	☐	☐
Investor	☐	☐	☐	☐
Supporter	☐	☐	☐	☐
Standard-prodder	☐	☐	☐	☐
Teacher-coach	☐	☐	☐	☐
Feedback giver	☐	☐	☐	☐
Eye opener	☐	☐	☐	☐
Door opener	☐	☐	☐	☐
Idea bouncer	☐	☐	☐	☐
Problem solver	☐	☐	☐	☐
Career cousellor	☐	☐	☐	☐
Challenger	☐	☐	☐	☐

Ways of helping the mentee

Here, in an overview, are a number of areas in which you might be able to help the mentee.

- *Record progress.* You could play a very important part in helping the mentee to complete their record of progress which details their learning. A substantial part of the evidence of learning will be developed 'on the job' and you can help identify suitable areas and encourage their development. Again, this will be one of the significant mechanisms by which the mentee's work is kept in line with the needs of the employer.

- *Mentee project development.* You could also have an important role to play in helping the mentee to negotiate, complete and evaluate the self-development project that is required as part of the ongoing progress.
- *Feedback.* If possible, you should become familiar with your mentee's progress, based on observation as well as discussion. You could also encourage the mentee to involve her/his own subordinates and to work fully with other staff, where this is possible, in the planning process.
- *Planning.* You can also help the mentee with the planning of their own learning. This might often involve discussion, setting realistic objectives and identifying learning opportunities at the start of each practice placement.
- *Evaluation.* You can help the mentee to understand the importance of evaluation – of the learning process as well as their own progress.
- *Problems.* You may well be the experienced person to whom the mentee can turn when professional problems arise. Your relationship with your mentee should be such that problems can be aired *in confidence* and progressed without the mentee feeling that they have been judged negatively. The emphasis should not be on success or failure; indeed, it would be best if it were non-judgemental throughout. In this way the mentee can be encouraged to share existing problems and weaknesses and take some risks in trying to develop new skills and approaches.
- *Difficulties arising.* The student may want to talk to you about problems which may arise. You can arrange to meet the mentee's personal tutor/supervisor.
- *The future.* The mentee may want to talk about future staff development opportunities. You may be able to help!
- *Personal development.* Mentees and mentors need to develop an appropriate, professional, supportive and confidential relationship. Thus the mentor role is to provide support to the mentee and feedback as well as comment on their achievements, in addition to the supervisory role.

You may also find you need to offer more general support to the mentee, such as the following:

- acting as a sounding board when the mentee has a decision to make and needs to talk it through
- helping the mentee to evaluate their own progress in relation to increasing their insight into the wider role of their job
- challenging the mentee to face up to opportunities and problems and to recognize personal strengths and weaknesses
- acting as a gateway to other people and sources of knowledge in the system so that they might be used to their best effect in the job

- helping the mentee to identify and explore what might be appropriate tasks, assignments and studies to undertake for the mutual benefit of the establishment
- passing on 'know-how' and essential thinking patterns and attitudes
- discussing with the mentee strategies and issues appropriate to maintaining and managing an effective working environment relevant to his/her particular job
- providing opportunities for the mentee to learn more about the setting, organization and service in which they work
- enabling the mentee, when appropriate opportunities arise, to broaden their outlook and experience, e.g. attend certain meetings, observe more experienced colleagues, become involved in projects and other developments
- encouraging the mentee and helping them to develop the skills necessary to evaluate their own performance and to explore the resultant issues
- providing the challenge for the mentee to take the next step in their professional development and growth.

Ways of helping significant others

As a mentor, you could help the mentee's personal tutor and assessor in evaluating:

- the quality of the mentee's work experience
- all aspects of the job in relation to the present and future needs of the mentee and the institution in which she/he works.

There should be periodic meetings of mentors, assessors and personal tutors which could give you an opportunity to:

- discuss issues with other mentors
- discuss issues with members of the nursing management team
- develop your competence in, and explore issues arising from, your role as mentor
- set up a support group, e.g. a mentor support action group.

The need for a mentor

There is a strong workplace tradition of mentorship in many industries and professions, whereby new recruits are assigned to a more experienced worker who initiates them into the workings of the organization and helps them to develop their skills, understanding and attitudes.

Gains for the employing institution
- Improved communication between individuals at different levels.
- Increased motivation of staff as interest is shown in their professional input.
- Skills of staff are recognized more quickly.
- Higher calibre staff are attracted.
- A contribution to staff development across the whole institution.

- Another mechanism by which the aims of staff appraisal and individual performance review (IPR) can be achieved.
- The establishment of a body of mentors for general use with new students.

Gains for the mentee
- Improved self-confidence and motivation.
- Fuller understanding of the mission and purpose of the institution.
- Becoming more familiar with the ways of working of the establishment in areas such as health and safety, staff development and equal opportunities.
- Fuller and better use of existing resources; development of new resources.
- More creative response to environmental and administration pressures.
- Personal and career development.
- Specific help with meeting the outcomes of the institution.
- Help in ensuring that the support of education is relevant to their work.

Gains for the mentor
- Improved job satisfaction – the role of mentor boosts your self-esteem.
- Increased recognition within the establishment.
- New perspectives are gained as you look at procedures in a fresh light.
- Improved communications between you and other staff.
- Opportunity for accredited training.
- Membership of a new and wider network of other mentors and trainers.
- Introduction to lifelong learning.

Ground rules in mentorship

Ground rules that govern the mentor and mentee meetings will vary according to the needs of the parties concerned, but the following might form a basis for developing your own ground rules.

- *Time.* Neither party should make excessive demands on the other's time. The mentor and mentee should negotiate a system for the best use of each other's time.
- *Authority.* The mentee should only use the mentor's authority with the mentor's consent.
- *Autonomy.* The mentor should assist the mentee in achieving his/her objectives and learning outcomes but allow the mentee to run his/her own show as much as possible.
- *Privacy I.* The mentor should only enquire or intrude into the mentee's personal life by invitation.
- *Privacy II.* The mentor should not discuss his/her knowledge of the mentee with other people without the consent of the mentee.

- *Personal development*. The mentor should encourage the mentee to undertake work which will assist his/her personal and professional development.
- *Ground rules*. The mentor and mentee should agree any additional ground rules they need to govern their relationship.

The selection of a mentor

In order to make the most of the benefits of mentorship, it is important that careful consideration is given to the selection of mentors. It is important for the mentee to consider:

- his/her needs and wants
- the need to match the mentor and the mentee in terms of subject interest/practice placement
- the level of support the mentee is likely to need.

It is also essential that the mentor is a person who can build an effective, trusting and confidential relationship. It is important to take account of the mentor's:

- professional competence
- recent experience in comparable jobs or subject areas
- interpersonal support and counselling skills
- commitment and sensitivity to the role
- availability to fulfil the role effectively
- willingness to support, teach and assess students' progress.

Skills and strategies of mentoring

As a mentor you may find yourself using and developing the skills of coaching, counselling, facilitating and giving feedback in order to support your mentee. However, a mentor is not a professional therapist or personal counsellor (see Figure 2.3). You should feel in charge of the amount of time and degree of commitment you are able to give to your mentees. The following section should help you to consider some of the skills and strategies you might find yourself employing during your time as a mentor.

Coaching

Coaching is a process of helping another person to a better under-standing of work issues and helping them improve their capabilities.
   The core skills of coaching include:

- suspending immediate judgement and listening with an open mind
- seeing the issue from the other's perspective
- identifying behaviour that needs to change
- helping the individual understand, and come to terms with, strengths and weaknesses
- giving constructive feedback
- setting practical exercises that stretch the mentees without going beyond their capabilities

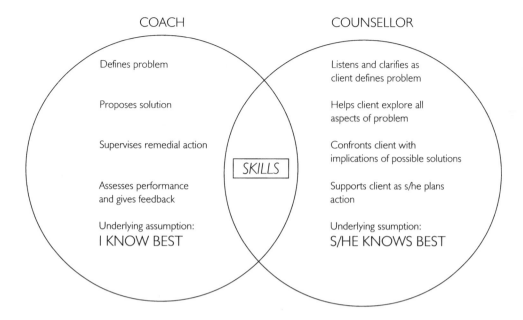

COACH

- Defines problem
- Proposes solution
- Supervises remedial action
- Assesses performance and gives feedback
- Underlying assumption: I KNOW BEST

SKILLS

COUNSELLOR

- Listens and clarifies as client defines problem
- Helps client explore all aspects of problem
- Confronts client with implications of possible solutions
- Supports client as s/he plans action
- Underlying ssumption: S/HE KNOWS BEST

Figure 2.3

Coach–counsellor skills overlap and difference in focus.

- clarifying – making sure you have reached a shared understanding
- 'working through' – patiently taking the mentee step by step through actions and behaviours, to identify what could have been done better
- putting goals, objectives and outcomes in sufficiently clear terms
- ensuring that the meaning of terms is understood and agreed
- setting a realistic time scale
- working out what sort of resources will be needed
- thinking about how you can support and encourage
- being aware of what is appropriate for the mentee to do on his/her own account
- ensuring that a supportive, friendly environment helps the coaching process
- giving positive reinforcement to encourage responses
- using honesty and eye contact to gain trust.

Effective coaching strikes a balance between seeking and telling. Seeking information, ideas, solutions, etc. is a more effective technique than telling, because it builds the mentee's commitment. There is a role, however, for telling in terms of providing additional information or insights to help the mentee achieve the goals/objectives/outcomes which have been agreed.

Counselling

Counselling is a process of helping another person work through his/her own motivations and intentions with a view to resolving a problem or making important choices. *It is not an opportunity for the counsellor to convert the client to his/her own way of thinking.*

The core skills of counselling include:

- listening – withholding comment unless it helps to bring out the other person's thoughts
- focusing on observable behaviours rather than on personality traits
- relinquishing control of the interview, so that the other person does not feel threatened
- being adept at handling negative information without driving the other person into an emotional corner
- avoiding unconstructive arguments
- being able to move rapidly into a constructive problem-solving mode
- knowing when to call in specialist advice.

Counselling can be a highly skilled role and to do it professionally requires intensive training, but the following tips might help you when you act as a mentor.

- Put the other person at ease from the start.
- Ask open-ended questions – take care not to ask questions that make your own views and opinions transparent.
- Show that you are listening.
- Ensure that there is agreement on both sides.
- Explore alternatives.
- Don't impose solutions.

The stages of counselling include:

- setting the scene/gaining empathy
- establishing the issues
- generating options and approaches
- agreeing action.

Facilitating

Facilitating is the process of helping things to happen. The approach here is very much in the hands of the mentor to facilitate according to his/her own particular style. Most of us facilitate colleagues to carry out tasks, work with peers as members of a team and negotiate with superiors and external agencies. We often use informal contact to influence official decision making, although this is something that must be used with discretion if it is to be of benefit to the mentee.

The core skills of facilitating include:

- being very clear about what needs to be done and why
- recognizing potential barriers and what causes them
- providing advice and guidance on how to overcome barriers
- undertaking a force-field analysis where appropriate
- smoothing the way by calling upon experience, contacts and extra resources
- sharing an understanding of the 'politics' of the organization and how it works

- helping the student to diagnose, plan, implement and evaluate systematically.

  Before becoming a mentor one needs to be able to:

- manage the education environment for the mentee
- manage resources for self and mentee
- manage people
- manage change
- write standards and methods of evaluation.

Setting standards

The resulting standards and criteria should maintain a mentee focus. Within each topic a number of subtopics can be identified. Throughout the formulation of standards the mentor and mentee must attempt to ensure that all outcome criteria are measurable and/or observable. Precise mechanisms for assessment should be included and the practising mentor should be able to design measurement tools which meet the mentee's needs. Inherent in setting standards is the fact that they require continued evaluation and refinement to meet the needs of a constantly developing professional/manager.

The standards

Are you a competent mentor? How do you know? The *standards* provide the answer. They indicate a range of **activities** (the elements of competence) a competent mentor should be capable of performing. They also provide the **indicators** (the performance criteria) by which you can tell whether you are performing competently or not.

So are you a competent mentor? Look carefully at the standards below and assess your performance against them. The possible answers are as follows.

- Yes, I am now competent (*halo supplied*). I do all the activities and I meet all the performance criteria.
- No, I am not yet fully competent. But I know what I need to work on and I will be competent by................. (*target date*).

Checklist of standards

Role definition
A mentor's role is to contribute to the learning, development and integration of the student into the profession to the mutual benefit of all involved in health care.

Elements of competence
The overall function of the mentor is achieved by carrying out the elements of competence listed below.

The mentor is able to:

- contribute to the initial development of the student's learning and development programme
- establish contact/relationship with the student
- create (as far as practical) a physical environment appropriate to meetings/contact with the student
- provide support for the student's progress on the learning and development programme
- contribute to modifications to the student's learning and development programme
- review and report progress to motivate and encourage the student
- provide guidance on possible future career development to the student (when required)
- assist in the assessment of student performance
- assist in minimizing/avoiding conflict in the student's learning and development programme
- liaise with other members of teaching staff and significant others on the student's progress
- terminate the formal mentor relationship with the student.

The performance criteria

These indicate whether or not the elements of competence are being met properly. Some examples are given below, attached to their respective elements of competence.

ELEMENT 1 CONTRIBUTE TO THE INITIAL DEVELOPMENT OF THE STUDENT'S LEARNING AND DEVELOPMENT PROGRAMME

Performance criteria

- Makes constructive suggestions to university staff about the learning experiences appropriate to the student's workplace learning and development programme.
- Gives advice on practicable time scale for the agreed learning and development programme.
- Assists in identifying learning experiences appropriate to the student's learning and development programme.
- Identifies possible problem areas and makes suggestions for overcoming them.
- Obtains copies of the student's learning outcomes and development programme.

ELEMENT 2 ESTABLISH CONTACT/RELATIONSHIP WITH STUDENT

Performance criteria

- The student is formally greeted on arrival to the practice placement.
- Date and venue for the first meeting are agreed.

- Roles within the relationship are discussed.
- The appropriate outlines of the relationship are identified and mutual expectations are agreed.
- A timetable and venue(s) for future meetings are established and agreed.
- A brief report/summary of the meeting is produced and a set of guidelines is agreed upon.
- The student is treated in a manner which is supportive but not imposing.

ELEMENT 3   PROVIDE SUPPORT FOR THE STUDENT'S PROGRESS ON THE LEARNING AND DEVELOPMENT PROGRAMME

Performance criteria

- Affords opportunities for the student to reflect on and evaluate learning experiences.
- Elicits the student's perception of his/her own strengths and weaknesses.
- Examines the relationship between the student's approach and the design of the learning and development programme.
- Ensures that any additional work is agreed with the student.
- The student is treated in a manner which is supportive.
- Constructively offers guidance and support between formal meetings.

Activity

Using the Donabedian (1966, 1982) model of structure, process and outcome in Figure 2.4, formalize a working document that each nurse practitioner and student can complete together. See Example 2.1.

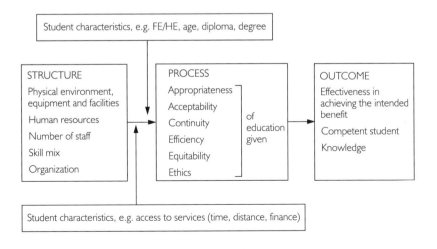

Figure 2.4

Flow chart to create standard setting statement (based on Donabedian, 1966).

Example 2.1   Standard setting statement.

The student will receive support and guidance from a named mentor, in order to facilitate their development as a practitioner.

Structure	Process	Outcome	Monitor/evaluate	Comments
Mentor must be willing to undertake this role and have a minimum of one year's experience since qualifying as a nurse	The mentor should be identified prior to the student starting work in the practice placement	The mentor is able to identify areas in which his/her professional development is occurring		
A mentor is defined as an experienced nurse who demonstrates interpersonal and negotiation skills in an advisory capacity	A contract will be negotiated within one week of commencement	Both parties are able to express that the relationship is mutually beneficial		
The senior manager will arrange for a mentor to work with the student	The mentor and mentee will have regular meetings at intervals acceptable to both parties	The relationship will be terminated at a mutually agreeable time		
The relationship will be agreed by the mentor and mentee	Areas of non-development will be identified and appropriate action taken			

NB: 'Mentor' can be exchanged for 'practitioner'

Activity——————————————————————————

Read the following scenarios and participate in the activities that follow.

Scenario 1: a mentoring pair

The mentor

M had been a senior lecturer in the university's nursing and health studies department for the last four years and was an active and highly regarded academic in her field. While her teaching load was rather heavy by university standards, leaving her little time to devote to research, she loved teaching.

However, she was becoming increasingly aware that her career was not advancing steadily, in marked contrast to some of her male colleagues, no more qualified than she. At the same time, as the most senior woman in the department, she felt increasingly isolated and frustrated.

One day, she received a letter from the university equal opportunities office, asking for women to volunteer as mentors in a pilot mentor scheme for women from the university and from the newly merged teacher training Institute. 'Why not?' M decided after reflection. 'I would love to meet women from other areas. I'm not sure that I have a great deal to offer though, except perhaps research and survival skills.' She sent back her reply, agreeing to attend the training session where she would meet her mentee. As she looked forward to the training session, she was really beginning to wonder how one went about mentoring.

The mentee

L had been a nurse lecturer for many years and she was a highly skilled and popular teacher. Her heavy teaching load, being a link tutor to clinical areas, and her administrative duties, plus her availability to students in the clinical areas, left her little time for further study in her chosen area. However, she derived great pleasure from seeing her students develop.

The merger with the university left her feeling very unsettled. She felt a little helpless and inadequate as a university academic and realized that she was rather ignorant about research grants, promotion procedures and what she imagined was 'formal' academic writing.

One day she received a letter from the university equal opportunities office, offering her the chance to volunteer as a mentee in a pilot mentor scheme for women. She noticed that M (whom she had long admired) was a mentor offering research skills. It seemed almost too good to be true to L as she sent back her acceptance – fast. She hoped M would not consider her too inadequate and that her questions would not seem too dumb. She looked forward to the training session with pleasure and a little trepidation.

Scenario 2: an experiential educator

P had been working experientially with groups of new teachers for many years, learning gradually from participant feedback which activities led to positive outcomes and which were too threatening or time consuming for the benefits derived. However, the all-male groups in one particular course were known to be highly resistant to the learning offered. They took an anti-intellectual stance to whatever threatened their identities as tough, aggressive, 'no-nonsense' men and were unreflective, apparently arrogant and interested only in 'tried and true' procedures, rather than an exploration of new and more productive possibilities.

When P began to 'lecture' to them, many were angry and negative about their situation. Attempts to discuss new practices and discourses more appropriate to their current profession were strongly resisted. They were sexist and racist in their humour and, in spite of exhibiting signs of considerable stress, were quite hostile when encouraged to share these feelings of anxiety, even within small groups. Indeed, it seemed to P that many were deeply afraid of contravening the cultural code of toughness established among group members.

Group problem solving regarding the course often led to stalemate; they wanted to discuss among themselves their experiences in school classrooms, but without exploring any new ideas or critically reflecting on the potential impact of their practices. While group discussion was an important part of the course, under these circumstances it often led to conclusions which P thought could ultimately be damaging, both to them and to their students. Exploration of their concerns elicited, for the most part, the blaming of others, including P, rather than attempts to analyse how they might act or think differently.

Challenging their views resulted in much defensiveness. However, a few would express agreement with P, privately after class, and occasionally would risk telling stories in the group in support of the ideas she introduced. Yet this failed for a long time to change the general culture of negativism established.

P felt frustrated, helpless and very disappointed and, in spite of continuing success with other groups, began to question her identity as a competent teacher educator. Nothing in the literature seemed to afford assistance. She also felt dismayed by the thought that she was betraying the students in the schools where these particular course participants were teaching.

1 Choose one of the scenarios to work on and consider the following questions.
   - With what aspects of your chosen scenario do you identify most strongly?
   - What are your own concerns as a facilitator of experiential learning or as a mentor/mentee?
   - What for you is the strongest message conveyed by your chosen scenario? How do the language used, the attitudes and feelings expressed and the concepts most frequently used create this message?
2 Form pairs and share your answers so far.
3 Construct your own story, based on a critical incident which epitomizes one or more of your concerns. Actively listen to the other person's story and note down the main elements.
4 Analyse each other's stories with respect to the language used, the attitudes and feelings expressed and the concepts employed most frequently. What is the most powerful element of the story?
5 What are the most important issues that have emerged for you? Prepare to reflect on these issues and if you are keeping a learning or reflective journal, write your reflections.
6 How has this activity helped you to become a more effective mentor?

The need for support from mentors will naturally vary from mentee to mentee. Some mentees will be more self-sufficient than others. Some will be reluctant to enlist the help of a mentor and others will call for a good deal of guidance and support. However, the combination of manager and mentor guidance, working together in harmony, will provide the help and information that is needed at the time and in the form that is most likely to be accepted and to be effective. However, both the mentor and mentee should be aware of the skills overlap of manager and mentor (see Figure 2.2).

Psychosocial functions

Psychosocial functions are those aspects of a relationship that enhance an individual's sense of competence, identity and effectiveness in a professional role. These functions include role modelling, acceptance and confirmation, counselling and friendship. The student (mentee) finds support for who they are becoming in a new work role that increases a sense of competence, effectiveness and self-worth. The nurse practitioner (mentor) can satisfy important needs by enacting the role of mentor. While career and professional functions depend on the nurse practitioner position and influence in the organization, psychosocial functions depend more on the quality of the interpersonal relationship. The role relationship is not as crucial as the emotional bond that underlies the relationship.

Role modelling is a most frequently reported psychosocial function. A mentor's attitude, values and behaviour provide a model for mentees to emulate (Davies *et al.*, 1994). Role modelling involves the practitioner (mentor) setting a desirable example and the student (mentee) identifying with it. It is both a conscious and an unconscious process. A practitioner may be unaware of the examples they are providing for a less experienced individual such as a student who may be unaware of the strength of identification. At the same time, interaction around nursing practice, organizational concerns and larger professional issues is a conscious modelling process.

Assessing and giving feedback

Assessing and giving feedback is a skill that you will use in many roles, in both your working and social life. Your mentoring will give you the opportunity to practise and develop this skill.

The way you assess and give feedback to your mentee is a vital component in the success of the mentoring and development process. Above all, always be constructive!

If your feedback is overjudgemental, the mentee may not hear it. The mentee who lacks confidence may only hear the things they have done wrong. The mentee who is overconfident will only hear the things they have done right. In both cases opportunities for further development may be lost.

The purpose of constructive feedback from mentor to mentee is to open the way for dialogue about the mentee's strengths and how to build on them and about the mentee's weakness and how to work on their improvement.

Constructive feedback: 10 key points

1 *Let your mentee have the first say.* Give them the chance to express what they have experienced and what issues have been identified and analysed. By doing this, you give the mentee the control and the opportunity to identify development needs on problem areas for themselves. This will help in 'owning' the changes required. Your

role then consists of agreeing or modifying where necessary and suggesting possible ways in which progress might be achieved.

2 *Give praise before criticism.* Most people will find it difficult to try to improve if they feel they are a 'lost cause'. By focusing first on strengths and then helping to recognize weaker areas you will give your mentee enough confidence to deal with the more negative aspects of their performance.

3 *Limit what you cover.* Don't try to cover everything in one feedback session; focus on only two or three key areas for development.

4 *Be specific, not vague.* Try and avoid general comments which don't help your mentee to identify the problem. It's not very useful to say to someone "You didn't use the whiteboard very well". It's much more useful to say, "It was difficult to read what you had written, because your writing was rather small and that green marker pen you used didn't show up very well under the lights".

5 *Concentrate on things that can be changed.* Feedback must allow for the possibility of improvement. If there are things which you know can't be changed then feedback relating to them is a waste of time and can cause frustration. It is far more useful to concentrate on what can be changed.

6 *Give the mentee time to think and respond.* A good mentoring relationship is a dialogue between two people committed to improvement. If you've given the mentee a new perspective on something they've been doing, then it will take some time for it to be absorbed. Only then might a response be made and planning for improvement begin.

7 *Explore possible alternatives.* There will be many situations where there is no real 'right' or 'wrong' way of doing something. Sometimes you will have to distinguish between situations where a mentee really is wrong and those where they are only doing something that you think is wrong (it's not something that you would do!). Either way, get the mentee to check it out, get them to look at the implications of what they are proposing or what they are doing. Get them to look at alternatives and develop a wider range of values.

8 *Listen to how the feedback is received.* Be aware of how your mentee is reacting. Make sure they understand the points you are making and agree with what you are saying. If you sense disagreement, draw out the reasons behind it.

9 *Think of the language you are using.* Try not to use 'disciplinary' language – 'You shouldn't do that', 'You handled that the wrong way'. Remember you are only feeding back your impression of what you have observed. Instead, try and use questions to draw out from your mentee what problems they experienced, where they felt that things had gone wrong and help them to identify why.

10 *End on a positive note.* End the feedback session having agreed some positive action that can be taken to address any areas for development that have been identified. End with some encouragement as well!

ADULTS AS LEARNERS

Student nurses come from a wide variety of social backgrounds and many already have years of work experience under their belt. As facilitators and assessors of learning, nurse practitioners need to be aware of the experiences these adult and mature students bring with them into nursing. An understanding of the concept of andragogy (adult learning) may help.

The andragogical model of learning is based on six main assumptions (Knowles, 1990).

1 The need to know – adults need to know *why* they need to learn something.
2 Self-concept – adults hold a concept of being responsible for their decisions and their own lives and have a need to be seen and treated by others in a way that acknowledges this 'self-direction'.
3 Role of the learner's experience – adult learners bring a wealth of experience which can be different in both quantity and quality from that of younger learners.
4 Readiness to learn – an adult needs to know something for their everyday life; they become ready to learn that which is relevant.
5 Orientation to learning – adults tend to be problem centred in learning and wish to apply this to life.
6 Motivation – this mostly comes from 'internal pressures', e.g. increased job satisfaction, self-esteem, quality of life.

Taking these points into account is essential when considering how best to approach education for adult learners. As pointed out by Lindeman (1956; cited in Knowles, 1990), the learning process needs to be a:

> *... co-operative venture in non-authoritarian, informal learning, the chief purpose of which is to discover the meaning of experience; a quest of the mind which digs down to the roots of the preconceptions which formulate our conduct.*

For each of the assumptions, there are potential problems and issues to consider, e.g. one of the first tasks for a practitioner is to help each student become aware of the 'need to know'. This can be aided by helping the student discover knowledge gaps and 'appropriate starting points' (Lindeman, 1956; cited in Knowles, 1990). Many students enter the world of nursing believing they already possess the required skills and qualities, e.g. listening and empathy. Although this is often true to some degree, it is necessary to develop these a good deal more. One of the initial tasks of a practitioner would be to help the student realize the depth of skill required, e.g. by presenting relevant scenarios.

In relation to self-concept, it is essential to facilitate a learning experience which offers support during the transition from 'dependent to self-directed learners' (Knowles, 1990), e.g. exploring why some students enter nursing (to find direction, make decisions and explore).

It is essential to acknowledge the richness and value of the experience brought by each student. This could be related to the nurse/patient/client situation in 'prizing' the uniqueness of each client (Rogers, 1969). However, the self-awareness element of nurse education also requires recognition of concepts having potentially negative effects, e.g. bias and prejudice.

Developmental strategies are part of the learning process and this in itself induces some amount of readiness as the exercises relate to the student's life experiences. The material on nurse education courses is life/problem centred due to its very nature, e.g. how to support someone in crisis or making decisions. The experiential exercises, such as practicums, give context to the skills being learned. The nature of the material and participatory exercises also assists in gaining an understanding of internal pressures which affect motivation.

Burnard (1996, p.107) stated that 'the fundamental principles of andragogy echo the basic principles of experiential learning. Experiential learning has been suggested by Knowles as one of the components of andragogy'.

Students need to develop reflective and evaluative skills but this is only possible once an individual has experience of a situation. The practitioner needs to make experiences available and teach the students to use reflective and evaluative skills. The central nervous system responds to active stimulation to a greater extent than to passive stimulation. The following example illustrates this: when teaching a client to move following a stroke they respond far better when actively facilitated to move than by being told how the movement happens. This active learning will therefore impact positively on the student's skill acquisition.

Practitioners need to be aware that students bring with them a wealth of information, knowledge and experience to the practice placement and this needs to be recognized and used in order to motivate and encourage the students. Practitioners also need to encourage the students to play an active role in the learning process, through discussion, brainstorming, etc. Students playing a central role in their own education is a good example of andragogy.

Encouraging students to question involves them in active learning and also assists in dissolving some of the power division between student and practitioner. Practitioners need to relinquish some of their control over the individual's learning. This is becoming more apparent in educational establishments where students and educators develop learning contracts. This is a negotiated contract where the student and educator each suggest the learning needs and a compromise is reached whereby a set of objectives, tasks and outcomes is agreed upon. Learning in this way gives the student greater ownership and therefore there is likely to be greater motivation to learn. It also fulfils one of the principles of adult learning (andragogy).

Using the principles of andragogy helps to ensure that the student will not become dependent upon the practitioner. If the student takes an active role in their education, they merely require facilitation at set points rather than continuous supervision. This encourages the student to become an independent learner. Practitioners only have a set amount of skills and knowledge that they can convey to the student but if the practitioner teaches the student where to look for information and how to research topics, they are able to access a limitless amount of information.

Pedagogy has traditionally been associated with oppressive educational methods e.g. Victorian-style teaching. Andragogy may therefore be better accepted in relation to the modern ideas of caring for and supporting students. Rather than drawing the dichotomy of andragogy/pedagogy, andragogy could be seen as a distinct field within the broad concept of pedagogy (Savicevic, cited in Milligan, 1995).

Practitioners need to help students to become aware of and evaluate their experience by utilizing a wide range of teaching and learning strategies which would encourage students to examine and assess their existing level of knowledge and experience. This may include everything from problem-solving techniques to open class debate where students apply their experience in a working situation to which they could easily relate.

The practice of reflection on, and in action, encourages the student to evaluate their experience and to apply that experience to resolve issues or analyse situations. As Lindeman (1956; cited in Knowles, 1990) stated:

> *Our academic system has grown in reverse order. Subjects and teachers constitute the starting point, [learners] are secondary. In conventional education the [learner] is required to adjust himself to an established curriculum ... Too much of learning consists of vicarious substitution of someone else's experience and knowledge. Psychology teaches us that we learn what we do ... Experience is the adult learner's living textbook.*

Clearly Lindeman saw 'experience' as an ongoing and lifelong textbook which could only grow in quality and status and should be used as the basis for evaluation of all further learning experience. In the learning situation adults can draw on a wealth of life experience which is not yet available to the child learner. It is the process of evaluation of that experience which enables the adult learner to contextualize the situation.

Dr Wayne Clugston (cited in http://www.net.edu.au/volv/resource/archgen#Discussion) offered the following advice:

> *They (adult learners) usually are goal oriented and are interested in learning through problem-solving activities. Since adult learners are willing to assume responsibility for acquiring content on their own, the primary responsibility of the instructor is to facilitate the learning process by selecting appropriate learning activities and encouraging application of the content.*

The primary task of the practitioner is to create an educational setting in which adult students can develop their latent self-directed learning skills. Key points to include would be:

- establishing an environment which is physically and psychologically conducive to learning and with mutual respect among all participants
- emphasizing collaborative modes of learning and that learning is pleasant
- establishing an atmosphere of mutual trust and support.

To summarize, practical considerations for adult educators should include the following points.

- Practitioners need to be facilitators or resources to learners.
- Content should be based on real-life scenarios, telling it like it is, not how it should be.
- Whenever possible, representatives from the target audience should be included in planning learning experiences.
- Self-evaluation components need to be incorporated into the experience rather than teacher-directed evaluation.
- New information must be connected to what is already "known" if learning is to truly take place.

Development of andragogy

The concept of andragogy has been increasingly accepted by many in adult education (Davenport and Davenport, 1985) since the publication of Malcolm Knowles' work *The Modern Practice of Adult Education: Andragogy Versus Pedagogy* (1970). This relatively new concept, described by Brookfield (1984) as 'the single most important contribution to a uniquely adult theory of teaching and learning', is still developing and is not without its opponents.

Davenport and Davenport (1985) described the early criticism of Knowles' work by citing Houle (1972) and London (1973), whose view of education as a single process (i.e. a unity of education) is in opposition to the dichotomy between adult and child education. McKenzie (1977), also cited in Davenport and Davenport (1985), suggested that the authors' different philosophical bases might have influenced this debate. He describes the metaphysical origins of the 'unity of education' approach whilst classifying the andragogical approach as having phenomenological origins. The opposition to the dichotomy continues. Darbyshire (1993) in expressing his own opposition, cites the work of Hartree (1984) and Thompson (1989). These more recent criticisms occur in the light of Knowles' (1984) acceptance that the contrast between andragogy and pedagogy was an error. He now describes andragogy as a "system of concepts that, in fact, incorporate pedagogy rather than opposing it".

Development in educational theories and concepts suggest an overlap and possible confusion in the exact nature of andragogy. The Nottingham Andragogy Group (1983) describe a model and theory of andragogy based on their own research and reflection. They acknowledge that the work was supported by the pedagogy of Paulo

Friere, although Davenport and Davenport (1985) suggest other recent andragogical research was not referred to. Jarvis (1985) clearly identifies andragogy with his 'education of equals' and describes its position in the 'romantic form of curriculum'. Darbyshire (1993) discusses a change in nurse education towards a caring pedagogy. Cohen (1993) suggests a phenomenological approach to this caring pedagogy. The 'care' theme is also described in andragogical terms. Milligan (1995) suggests the salient features of the Nottingham Andragogy Group's (1983) model can be identified in the description of care. Burnard (1990) linked his work on experiential learning in nursing with that of Knowles. Cohen (1993), who does not mention Knowles although her work included a 'thorough review of the literature in education...', provides evidence to support the caring pedagogy. Milligan (1995) however, described her findings as being consistent with andragogy. The classification of andragogy has also led to confusion. Knowles (1975) initially described his work as 'exploring a comprehensive theory ... to educational practice'. Knowles (1984) acknowledges the argument by Cross (1981) and now describes his work as 'a systematic framework of assumptions, principles and strategies'. Others, however, continue to describe it as a theory (Brookfield, 1984; Milligan, 1995). The Nottingham Andragogy Group describe their work as a 'concrete model and theory of andragogy'. Davenport and Davenport (1985) suggested that although both opponents and proponents have very different ideas, neither 'side' has established definitions that could be used to resolve the conflict.

Although andragogy has been gaining prominence for almost 20 years there is still opposition amongst educators to the concept. Davenport and Davenport (1985) suggested that the opponents and proponents argue their positions from personal perspectives, ignoring the body of evidence. They call for more research-based data to enable definitions, measurement and evaluation of andragogy to take place. However, it remains to be seen whether those who have previously argued their opposition from a personal perspective and have, to date, ignored the available evidence, will embrace any new evidence and change from opponents to proponents.

Why are some educators opposed to the concept of andragogy?

The purpose of this section is to get you to reflect on a concept that is readily accepted by the nursing profession without first critically examining its assumptions.

Education can be defined as a lifelong process of discovering what is not known. Many researchers have suggested that adults and children learn in different ways (Knowles, 1990) and consequently different educational theories, philosophies and teaching approaches have been developed. These include *pedagogy* – 'the Art and Science of teaching children' – and *andragogy* – 'the Art and Science of helping adults learn' (Edwards *et al.*, 1995, p.82).

Adults always learn voluntarily and they simply walk away from learning experiences that don't satisfy them. Knowles (1975) defined andragogy as a process in which individuals take the initiative, with or without the help of others, in diagnosing their learning needs, formulating learning goals, identifying human and material resources for learning, choosing and implementing appropriate learning strategies and evaluating learning outcomes.

This model of adult learning encourages personal autonomy, facilitates self-actualization and avoids dependency. It assumes that the individuals are self-motivated, have a readiness to learn, have some life experience and can engage in self-directed, problem-based learning. Due to these foundational assumptions of andragogy, some educators are opposed to this concept of teaching and feel that a caring pedagogical approach offers a more radical alternative for 20th-century adult education.

The authors claim that andragogy's vision seems divisive and fragmentary. They criticize the developmental differences between adults and children described by Knowles (1975) and suggest that andragogy seeks to elevate the status of adult education by demeaning the education of children (Darbyshire, 1993).

Further criticism has been made on the issue of self-motivation that adults possess in contrast to children. This is connected to an adult's willingness to learn, where Knowles (1975) assumed that adult learning is seen to be directed towards more worthy goals than the thinking of a child. This is deemed untenable by most 'anti-andragogy' educators who claim that an adult's readiness to learn could be linked to their career prospects or social roles and it is unfair to state that readiness is not an equally marked feature of children's learning (Darbyshire, 1993).

Another assumption which has been opposed by educators is that of a child's life experiences being qualitatively of lesser value than those of an adult. This suggestion is a developmental progression whereby the adult is now mature enough to define their self in terms of personal experiences, while the child's understanding of self is seen as being external (Knowles, 1990). This view of an insular self and person is prominent in Western society where autonomy and individualism are applauded. However, Milligan (1995) rephrased this assumption and stated that it is the quantity of experience that is seen as significantly different and not the quality.

Due to flaws in his theory, Knowles did attempt to revise his andragogical model and it may be better to conceptualize andragogy as a field within the broad concept of pedagogy (Milligan, 1995). Many theorists believe that separating andragogy and pedagogy was a deceiving attempt to enhance the field of adult education. Darbyshire (1993) concluded that in patriarchal society, caring professions such as teaching and nursing have been given a lesser status. If the teaching and nursing professions were given a higher profile and value in our society, then the construction of andragogy may never have happened!

Jarvis (1995) suggested that every adult is a learner but that there are definite characteristics of and types of person who attend the variety of educational provisions that exist. The adult learners are located within

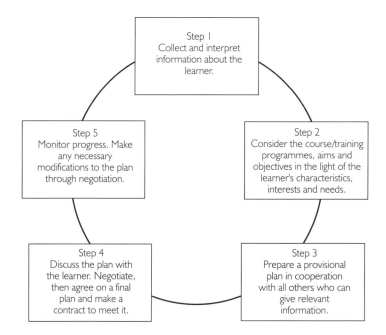

Figure 2.5

Steps in designing an individual programme. (These steps form a cycle which will need to be repeated throughout the course training programme.)

their sociocultural framework and both milieux have to be taken into consideration when endeavouring to construct a theory of adult learning. Interested readers will find the further reading useful if they wish to pursue this area of study. For the purpose of the book I offer a model (Figure 2.5) which you may find helpful when preparing to meet your student during their allocation to your clinical area. Part of your planning will be to consider the student as an adult, as an individual who needs a well-structured learning programme which will enable them to achieve the agreed learning outcomes.

As a mentor and assessor you will need to have clear leadership and functional roles which will ensure that students are exposed to high standards of nursing and health care (Figure 2.6). You will also need to be aware of the differences when enacting the role of 'teacher' and 'facilitator' as you will be placed in these functional positions by your adult student (Figure 2.7).

UNDERSTANDING COMPETENCIES

There has been much debate over the last 20 years on issues relating to objectives, competencies and competence. Whilst much is written to help clarify meaning, at the same time much confusion still exists, so let's start with understanding.

Runciman (1990) described 'competence' as over- rather than ill-defined. The growing concern to find ways of assessing it seems to have heightened such confusion. The critics of the competence-based movement (Ashworth and Saxton, 1990; Fagan, 1984; Hyland, 1992, 1993; Jessup, 1989, 1990, 1994; Marshall, 1991; McAleavey and

Figure 2.6

The wheel of challenge.

Key players must have clear leadership and functional roles:
- identify education and training needs
- set realistic action plans
- ensure mechanisms are in place for high quality health-care and education, and training outcomes.

Figure 2.7

Characteristics of a teacher and facilitator.

Teacher	Facilitator
Focuses on teaching	Focuses on learning
Teacher centred	Student centred
Control	Sharing
Superior–subordinate relationships	Partnership
Director	Participant
Knowledge given	Knowledge available
Treats all the same	Perceives individual learning needs
Focus on groups	Focus on individual
Closed learning environment	Open learning
Controls parameters of learning	Lets learner set parameters
Narrow horizon	Wider horizon

Skills required of a facilitator

1   Identifying learning needs and styles of students.
2   Devising coping strategies for dealing with mixed-ability classes.
3   Devising methods of assessing how much learning has taken place.
4   Devising remedial methods for lack of learning and extra learning for those who want more.
5   Techniques for teaching in small groups or one to one.
6   Role change from paternalistic to partnership.

McAlleer 1991) have claimed that competence-based education is essentially concerned with performance in employment. They castigate the attempt to specify what is to be achieved and measured as nothing more than reconstituted behaviourism, in which traditionalist origins are clearly to be found. While constructed out of a fusion of behavioural objectives and accountability (Fagan, 1984, p.5), specific accounts of competence seek to remain true to the behaviourist enterprise by insisting that the assessment of competence is independent of any learning process and should ideally "be undertaken in the workplace" (NCVQ, 1988, p.5). This specific conception of competence, founded squarely on behaviourist learning principles, suffers from all the weakness traditionally identified with such programmes (Redford and Govier, 1980). Nevertheless, it is our contention that comprehensive assessment only occurs when natural interactions are guided and not bound to behavioural objectives.

Competence-based education and assessing competency have been the foci in the American nursing literature for the past 10 years (Benedum *et al.*, 1990). In the UK, since the introduction of statutory competencies in 1983, education programmes and their assessment schemes have been developed around these competencies. It would have been better had we concentrated on learning outcomes to be achieved, which lead to becoming a competent practitioner. There still remains, however, the potential conflict noted by Benner (1982) between the responsibility for producing a safe practitioner and the elusive nature of what competence means in relation to these very broad statutory competency statements.

The UKCC formally introduced the Nurses Rules in 1983, reviewed them in 1989 (see p.141), and created new competencies in 1999 (see Appendix 5). All courses throughout the UK leading to registration have begun to prepare students formally to work toward the achievement of the competencies which they identified. A competent practitioner has become the focus of assessment in nurse education. However, the question remains of what is meant by the term 'competence' and how it can be assessed, especially at different levels of development. The recent UKCC report *Fitness for Practice* defines competence thus.

> *…describe the skills and ability to practice safely and effectively without the need for direct supervision. This concept of competence is fundamental to the autonomy and accountability of the individual practitioner and therefore to the Code of Professional Conduct (UKCC, 1992). (UKCC, 1999, 4.8, p.35)*

The standard Training Agency (1989, p.1) accounts of the meaning of competence is:

> *… (Standards) will form the prime focus of training and the basis of vocational qualifications. Standards development should be based on the notion of competence which is defined as the ability to perform the activities within an occupation. Competence is a wide concept which embodies the ability to transfer skills and knowledge to new situations within the occupational area. It encompasses organisation and planning of work, innovation and coping with non-routine activities. It includes those qualities of personal effectiveness that are required in the workplace to deal with co-workers, managers and customers.*

Brown and Knight (1995, p.27) argued that:

> *Competence probably replaces, albeit at a more sophisticated level, the concept of skills. That doesn't necessarily make it easier to understand what competencies are, let alone how they are to be recognised.*

Miller *et al.* (1988) suggested two senses in which competence can be defined. First, competence may be equated with performance, the ability to perform nursing tasks and, second, competence may be viewed as a 'psychological construct', requiring evaluation of students' abilities to integrate cognitive, affective and psychomotor skills when delivering nursing care. While Runciman (1990) recognized the difficulty in observing this psychological construct, she suggested that it can be 'seen' through the individual's competent performance. It can be argued, therefore, that the two senses are not mutually exclusive. Miller *et al.* (1988) suggested that the level of the students' performance is dependent on the development of their psychological constructs.

Ashworth and Morrison (1991, p.257) argued that the notion of competence cannot be the only basis of nurse training and suggest that there are theoretical and practical problems associated with a competence-based system. They asked:

> *Are competencies personal mental capacities or bit of behaviour actions, or a particular outcome of behaviour irrespective of how it was arrived at?*

Such ambiguity about the meaning of the term 'competence' has, they argued, important implications for nurse education. Wolf (1989) argued that 'competence' was about the ability to perform at agreed standards and incorporated in statement of competence which specified the nature of the particular, performable occupational role. Competence is a construct and not something that we can observe directly.

However, we may be able to find good, observable, measurable proxies. Messick (1975, 1982) agrees that the available definitions were not in fact very specific, but did tend to indicate what sort of measures definers accepted as a source of evidence. Most of the situations in which people were serious about measuring competence tended to be vocational, such as nursing, social work and teaching. 'Definers' usually meant the people who controlled licensing and qualifications. In nursing, competencies to be achieved were identified by the professional body. In developing competence-based vocational training and qualifications, most emphasis has been on 'output', on encouraging the direct assessment of 'performance', preferably in the workplace, as the preferred measure of competence. Contemporary psychological theory sees human beings as creators of mental models, general 'schemata' which they apply to particular circumstances and modify with experience (Jeeves and Greer, 1983; Race, 1992; Snow *et al.*, 1980; Sternberg, 1986). This approach emphasizes that 'knowing' something involves knowing when to access it and being able to do so when appropriate. Messick argued:

> *At issue is not merely the amount of knowledge accumulated, but its organisation or structure as a functional system for productive thinking, problem solving, and creative invention. The individual's structure of knowledge is a critical aspect of ... achievement... A person's structure of knowledge in a subject area includes not only declarative knowledge about substances (or information about what), but also procedural knowledge about methods (or information about how), and strategic knowledge about alternatives for goal setting and planning (or information about which, when and possibly why) ... Knowledge structure basically refers to the structure of relationships among concepts. But as knowledge develops, these structures quickly go beyond classifications of concepts as well as first-order relations among concepts and classes to include organised systems of relationships or schemes. (Messick, 1982, pp.1–3)*

Another way of putting this is to say that whenever we learn something specific, we also learn something general.

Whatever the knowledge is which goes to make up an occupational or professional competence, it is unlikely to be just factual. All the research on clinical reasoning (Forsythe *et al.*, 1986) found information to be a necessary condition of competence. However, Eraut (1985) argued that tests which measure only factual recall are inadequate measures of knowledge and unlikely to provide much evidence of professional competence. Neary's (1996) study also supported this view.

An overall competence is made up of a number of 'elements', but the way in which complex activities are 'made up' of elements of competence is unspecified. In fact, the individual elements of a complex skill cannot even be defined independently of the rest. Consider the following competence: "to advise on the promotion of health and the prevention of illness" (UKCC, 1989, Rule 18). What are the specific elements which comprise this particular competence? Do these elements add up to the competence and this alone? Surely they are intermeshed aspects of a very broad and complex intention. Take the further example of 'asepsis'. A student may learn what to do and what not to do by assimilating a long list of rules such as hand washing, disposal of soiled dressings, bed spacing and so on. But this does not ensure that the student knows the principles of asepsis. All of the elements need to be seen as together constituting a common whole if competent care is to be achieved. Some tutors may overcome this problem by emphasizing the rationale for teaching the principles of asepsis, rather than demonstrating the step-by-step approach favoured by others.

According to Ashworth and Morrison (1991) the model of competence being advocated in the UK (Training Agency, 1989; Whittington and Boore, 1988) contrasts sharply with that advocated in the US by Benner (1984). On the issue of 'elements of competence', she argued:

This approach differs from the elemental or enabling skills that educators teach students in their early educational experience. In contrast, the exemplars [provided in her book] will illustrate nursing performance that represents a complex of enabling skills. Only as we see the whole can we adequately appreciate the significance of the nurse's contribution to patient welfare. (Benner, 1984, p.41)

McGagaghie *et al.* (1978) argued that the desirable attributes of a health professional, whether physician or nurse or basic medical scientist, are determined by many influences. Expert opinion, the practice setting, the types of clients and patients or the health-care problems to be encountered, the nature of a discipline or a specialism, the stage of socioeconomic development of a community or nation (present as well as future) all need to be considered. In reaching a decision about the competence goals for a specific curriculum, planners may either examine all or select only a few of these essential determinants, depending upon the type of health professional being trained, the curriculum level or simply the time and resources available. Whatever sources are employed, the primary consideration in planning must always be the nature of the professional role a student must play, not merely the information that college staff or experts are most comfortable in teaching.

The critics of this model rarely get beyond the question: 'What is competent practice?' It would be pointless to suggest that there is a single definition. Competence includes a broad range of knowledge, attitudes, and observable patterns of behaviour which together account for the ability to deliver a specified professional service. The competent nurse can correctly perform numerous (but not necessarily all) clinical tasks, many of which require knowledge of the physical and biological sciences or comprehension of the social and cultural factors that influence patient care and well-being. Competence in this sense also involves adoption of a professional role that values human life, improvement of the public health and leadership in settings of health care and health education. The competencies to be achieved are many and multifaceted. They may also be ambiguous and tied to local custom and constraints of time, finance and human resources. Nevertheless, a competence-based curriculum in any setting assumes that the many roles and functions involved in the nurse's work can be defined and clearly expressed. It does not imply that what are defined are the only elements of competence but rather that that which can be defined represents the critical point of departure in curriculum development. Careful delineation of these components of nursing practice can be regarded as the first and most critical step in designing a competence-based curriculum.

When students master the functions that comprise an acceptable repertoire of professional practices, they are judged to be ready to work as competent nurses. But what does mastery learning require and how can a student's mastery of the necessary competencies be assured?

Block (1971) suggested that, technically, mastery learning means that given adequate preparation, unambiguous learning goals, sufficient learning resources and a flexible time schedule, students can, with rare exceptions, achieve the defined competence at high levels of proficiency. The technology of mastery learning requires:

- knowledge of what a student brings to a learning task, not merely what is to be taken from it
- that broadly defined competencies be dismantled into smaller, cumulative steps, through which students may work at individual rates using many learning resources (books, laboratory experience, teachers, etc.) according to their own needs and rates of progress
- that student achievement be thoroughly assessed at each learning stage in order to document the growth of 'professional competence' and to provide valuable feedback on the quality of instruction, teaching and assessing.

The principles of learning for mastery, including entry-level testing, stepwise instruction, flexible time scheduling and frequent assessment, describe the possible operational characteristics of a competence-based curriculum model, which leads to cumulative learning along a continuum of increasing sophistication. Nevertheless, assessment of students' performance remains a complex issue. The literature highlighted that in the past, the assessment of practice was offered little priority by those assessing and could be irrelevant to and estranged from it (Darbyshire *et al.*, 1990). With the move towards preparing all first-level nurses for either diploma or graduate status, entailing acquisition of higher education validation, clear criteria and standards for clinical assessment needed to be set by academic validating bodies in collaboration with the service side – a true partnership model.

Teaching for competence

According to Boss (1985), teaching for clinical competence is the most challenging aspect of a nurse tutor and practitioner's role. With the vast increase in knowledge, technology and complexity in health care, staff must respond to constant demands for educated competent nurses who not only need knowledge and skill but must also be able to make critical clinical judgements and life-saving decisions, solve highly complex problems, think critically and be reflective practitioners. In the complicated world of health care, the need for nurses who can form productive relationships with clients, families, other health-care professionals and organizations in which they function makes the development of sound professional behaviours mandatory.

During the past 20 years, various instructional strategies have been proposed and described in the literature. Each method was claimed to increase the effectiveness of student learning. While evidence showed that organization and presentation could induce a difference in students' learning, each method also needs to be seen in relation to a greater goal: that of teaching for clinical competence. The challenge for the lecturer and practitioner is to select appropriate learning outcomes which will lead to achieving the competencies, specify evaluation indicators and develop a functional instructional delivery system.

Practitioners argued that competence is more than knowledge and skill. Values, critical thinking, clinical judgement, formulation of attitudes, the integration of theory from the humanities and the sciences into the nursing role are also competencies. These are major attributes of professional nurses (Neary, 1996).

According to Boss (1985, pp.8–12), competence-based education should aspire to include the following characteristics.

1   Competencies should guide educational planning, where each describes the desired behavioural outcome and this guides the planning, implementation of learning experiences and the prescription of methods of evaluation.

2   Competencies should derive from roles and emphasize performance rather than knowledge, describing how the student will use their acquired knowledge in the client care setting, accepting that application of knowledge does not end with simple recall. The competency should always be stated in such a way as to answer the question: 'What will the student be doing with the client?' or 'the research?' or 'the nursing team?'.

3   Competencies should emphasize clinical judgement, not just psychomotor skill, for clinical competence is not simply performing a skill. It includes making some judgement about the accuracy and appropriateness of the skill and it implies a standard of excellence. The competency should be oriented to directing and ensuring learning in the higher levels of cognitive, affective and psychomotor domains.

4   Competencies should state the conditions under which a student performs actions or behaviours and the standard of such performance. Examples of a competency statement might be:
    (a) Given a client experiencing psychological stress (*condition*), the student will be able to assess and intervene (*action*) so that the client can more effectively cope with the stress (*standard of performance*).
    (b) Given a postoperative client (*condition*), the student will assess (*action*) fluid and electrolyte status and implement (action) nursing interventions that will assist the client to maintain fluid and electrolyte balance (*standard of performance*).
    (c) Based on the principles of design and analysis (*condition*), the student will be able to analyse (*action*) critically (*standard of performance*) a research study and determine the applicability of the findings to nursing practice.

Such a competence-based model clearly called for new skills on the part of teaching staff – practitioners who enact the roles of mentor and assessor and evaluator of students' learning. Moreover, its existence presupposes the identification of 'experts' from whom judgements are sought. An example of the machinery that might be used in such an

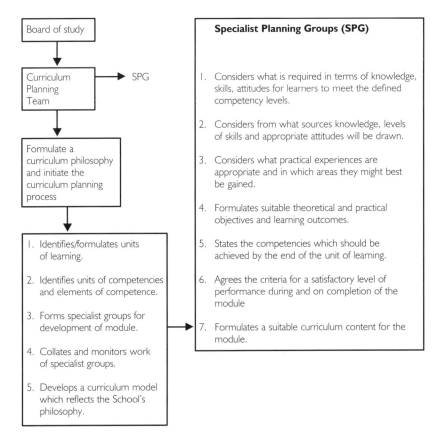

Figure2.8

Using experts in specialist groups to define competencies.

exercise was undertaken by Neary (1992a) in the specialist field of accident and emergency nursing where the Curriculum Planning Team (CPT) brought together a number of nurse practitioners and other health professionals with proven expertise in their specialist area of practice. These professionals became the Specialist Planning Group (SPG). Their remit was to respond to the seven activities shown in Figure 2.8.

A conceptual framework of professional competency

Instead of attempting to utilize every element in the professional role, Jarvis (1983, p.35) has suggested that it is necessary to analyse the concept of competency and this might help provide a basis upon which a curriculum could be constructed. It was suggested that this could be built upon the triple foundations of the practitioner's knowledge, skill and attitude.

- *Knowledge and understanding of*: relevant academic discipline(s), psychomotor elements, interpersonal relations, moral values.
- *Skills to*: perform the psychomotor techniques, interact with members of the role set.
- *Attitudes that result in*: a knowledge and commitment to

professionalism, a willingness to play the role in a professional manner.

From such a basis it should be possible to devise the content of any training curriculum but, at the same time, it allows for negotiation between all interested parties as to what is actually included. However, it might be objected that attitudes should not constitute part of the training but, since adult education is a humanistic enterprise, it is maintained here that attitude education is an important element in the preparation of educators of adult students.

The idea that nursing competence must be measured is not universally shared. Over 20 years ago Sheehan wrote of his concerns about a lack of valid measurement in nursing education but concluded:

Those concerned with nursing education should measure but should not confine themselves to measurement. (Sheehan, 1979, p.56)

Benner also warned that it is premature to place too much faith in assessment of certain competencies. She feels there is a danger that we may be: 'carried along by a technological, measurement-orientated age...' (Benner, 1982, p.303). Similarly Andrusyszyn (1989, p.77) addressed the problems in trying to assess competencies in the affective domain and noted:

... the subjectivity associated with clinical evaluation of the affective domain renders it difficult to measure and grade. Although the mechanisms discussed are useful tools with which to provide insight into students' attitudes and values, they may not provide hard data that can be measured for the purpose of assigning a grade.

Since the 1960s there have been many attempts to reach the goal of a more objective clinical assessment. A number of techniques have been tested including simulation exercises and group video testing, critical incident technique and the use of the computer for clinical assessment (Matthews and Viens, 1988; Miller *et al.*, 1988; Ross *et al.*, 1988). Boreham (1978), however, pointed out the validity problems of not assessing the 'real-life' situation, which presents its own problems according to the study by Long (1976). He identified that ward sisters carrying out assessments found little time to complete the assessment forms and final interviews. They were open to influence by factors other than the student's ability. They spent little time with the students in practice and the statements were difficult to understand. Much of this has been supported more recently by Darbyshire *et al.* (1990).

The literature identified many who recognize the need to continue the development of assessment schemes in nursing. Ross *et al.* (1988) and Benner (1982) emphasized the need for this to be based in the context of the 'real world'. Benner (1982) recognized that as the student gains expertise, their actions become much more situationally determined and therefore much less formalized.

While I have focused on the need for measurement of nursing skills and stressed the need for a scientific basis for the assessment instruments used, I also acknowledge that there are some areas of nursing care for which no currently acceptable assessment method has yet been devised. However, the UKCC report *Fitness for Practice* suggests that:

> *practice placements should be designed to achieve agreed outcomes which benefit students' learning and provide experiences of the full 24 hours per day and 7 days per week nature of health care. (UKCC, 1999, Recommendation 18, 4.47, p.41)*

I suggest that this can be achieved if the nurse academics and the practitioners work together in identifying 'core' learning outcomes and specific learning outcomes for each practice placement (Neary, 1996). Examples of ward/department learning opportunities can be found in Appendix 4.

LEARNING OUTCOMES

There is much activity in this area of teaching and assessing of learning. The recent document *Fitness for Practice* (UKCC, 1999) highlighted the need for clarity in this area. Nurse education has for many years found the assessment of clinical competence and learning outcomes in practice placement problematic (Neary, 1996; UKCC, 1999).

According to UDACE (1991):

> *Aims and objectives are primarily the language of course designers. They describe what the course sets out to do and can tend to preserve traditional course structures by discouraging comments and input from other professionals, employers, government, students and significant others, e.g. WNB, ENB, UKCC.*

Definition

A learning outcome is a statement of what a student is expected to know, understand or be able to do at the end of a period of learning. It will include an indication of the evidence required to show that the learning has been achieved. This may be contained in a separate assessment criterion statement or within the learning outcome statement.

Writing learning outcome statements

Differences in style

There are several styles of writing learning outcomes (see below). Figures 2.9 and 2.10 give examples. It may be seen as appropriate to specify one style for adoption but since some suggest that style may vary with subject matter, a broad policy that emphasizes clarity may be preferable. It is possible to tighten up the regulations at a later date. Some styles for writing learning outcomes are as follows.

- *Learning outcome incorporates assessment criteria*, providing an indication of what the learner will be expected to do in order to demonstrate that the learning has been achieved.
- *Learning outcome used with separate assessment criteria – more learning outcomes than assessment criteria*. The assessment criteria indicate what must be done to demonstrate achievement of the learning. Having fewer assessment criteria than learning outcomes means that assessment criteria are written in a more general manner and are less prescriptive of the form of assessment to be used (or are easier to apply when a single assessment, e.g. essay, is used).
- *Learning outcome used with separate assessment criteria – fewer learning outcomes than assessment criteria*. This is similar to the point above, but the assessment criteria will tend to be more detailed.

Figure 2.9

Learning outcome statement: communications.

Elements of competence	Performance criteria/learning outcomes
The use of appropriate communication skills to enable the development of helpful, caring relationships with patients/clients, their families and friends.	Discusses the rights of the individual to be involved in all aspects of his/her care.
	Discusses the different methods of communications observed and experienced.
The use of appropriate communication skills to initiate and conduct therapeutic relationships with patients/clients.	Communicates the observations made during patient/client interactions.
	Identifies the patient's/client's usual forms of communication and social interaction.
	Communicates effectively by talking and listening to the individual and his/her family or friends.
	Identifies the patient's/client's communication difficulties.

At the end of the period of allocation, for every performance criterion, student and assessor must enter their signature and the date (in ink) in the appropriate box.

Figure 2.10

Learning outcome statement: individualize patient/client study.

Elements of competence	Performance criteria/learning outcomes
The recognition of common factors which affect physical, mental and social well-being of patients/clients and take appropriate action.	Identifies the documents used to record the psychosocial and/or nursing/medical history of an individual.
The use of appropriate communication skills to enable the development of helpful, caring relationships with patients/clients, their families and friends.	Recognizes factors which contribute to the physical, mental and social well-being of a patient/client.
	Identifies those factors which adversely affect the individual's health and well-being.
	Discusses the effects of an altered level of functioning on an individual's role in the family unit.
	Discusses the strategies used to assist the individual to cope with his/her altered level of functioning.

At the end of the period of allocation, for every performance criterion, student and assessor must enter their signature and the date (in ink) in the appropriate box.

There are other types of learning outcome statements that, for example, use performance criteria instead of or in addition to assessment criteria, or include range statements to define the scope of learning.

Specifications

Learning outcomes do not specify content for learning, though they may give an indication of it; nor do they specify what is taught or the strategy by which it is learned. They are written in language that is simple, non-technical and takes account of its audience. Since learning outcomes may be introducing the module to potential students, they may be regarded as having a motivational role.

Most learning outcomes (with or without assessment criteria included, see above) are written in a format that follows from 'At the end of the period of learning, the learner will be able to...'

The explicit and entailed nature of the learning outcomes makes it easier for nurse educators to understand the nature of the nurse education curriculum and to make realistic inputs to its development. Learning outcomes also make it easier for students to understand what is expected of them and to take greater responsibility for their own learning. Learning outcomes can also help practitioners in the assessment of students' clinical competence once they know what students are expected to achieve. This can be a means of developing alternative approaches to teaching and learning, resulting in greater flexibility and wider participation in nursing practice. However, if learning outcomes are too specific they can restrict student learning. If too much emphasis is placed on a predetermined outcome it can result in a dangerously narrow approach to learning. However, all practitioners do need to have a sense of what it is they want their students to achieve by the end of a particular practice placement. The learning outcomes, when achieved, lead the student towards becoming a competent practitioner.

General considerations

There are some issues of learning outcomes and assessment that may need to be considered on an institutional policy basis. For example, the failure to achieve one learning outcome should not mean that the whole module has not been achieved but only that the non-achieved learning outcome needs to be reassessed. Following on from this, compensation is difficult to justify in a fully learning outcome-based system. On a more positive note, learning outcomes in some modules may match those already achieved elsewhere and will not need to be assessed a second time.

Learning outcomes need to be understood by everyone, not just subject experts. Every practitioner and student should be able to understand any of the outcomes developed and comment in terms of clarity (see below). Issues on the perception of the task can usefully be raised in a mixed group. One of the ideas behind the institution of learning outcomes is, after all, the generation of consistency and clarity across all subject areas.

Distinction from teaching intentions

Used in their more casual manner, aims and objectives have not always been required to distinguish between teaching intentions ('to review methods of maintaining a safe environment, etc.') or those focused on learning ('learners will be able to discuss simple methods of maintaining a safe environment, etc.'). A useful 'warming up' exercise is to present a list of aims and objectives written in both modes, requesting that they are separated.

Learning outcomes written by several people are usually of a better quality

It is useful if outcomes are reviewed by others. Apart from the quality issue, this can ensure that improvement in technique continues.

Specificity

While learning outcomes should be clear and precise, too much specificity or too clear an identification of the performance required restricts flexibility in learning and assessment strategies that will fulfil the outcome. Provision of exemplars will help to clarify this issue.

The number of learning outcomes

Opportunistic learning in practice placements (see Appendix 4, Opportunistic learning) can be described in less than 10 learning outcomes. The existence of more will probably mean that they are too specific.

Words used in learning outcomes

Learning outcomes should employ terms that indicate a recognizable standard. For example, a word such as 'good' tends to be personally referenced and a word such as 'understand' raises the question of 'when do you know a thing is understood?' Qualifying words or the inclusion of range statements can help.

Learning which is difficult to describe in terms of learning outcomes

In such cases a change of frame of reference usually helps. For example, negotiated learning can be written in terms of the activities of negotiation and implied self-management (or why else use this strategy?) in the form of learning contracts.

The structure of learning outcomes

A learning outcome is likely to contain the following components:

- a verb that indicates what the learner will be able to do. This will indicate a means of demonstrating that the learning has been acquired
- word(s) that indicate what the learner is acting on/with or word(s)

that describe the verb (i.e. how the activity is done) when the outcome is a skill

- word(s) that indicate the nature (in context or standard expected) of the performance required as evidence that the learning has been achieved.

The components of the assessment criteria will be much the same, but emphasizing the demonstration of learning to a defined standard.

Vocabulary for writing learning outcomes (modified from Moon, 1998)
Finding the right words when writing learning outcomes can be difficult, particularly when the learning outcome and/or assessment criterion must mesh with the generic level descriptors (see Figure 2.11). The following list is provided as an aid in this process. The words are organized for convenience under headings that might be seen to accord with those from Bloom's taxonomy. However, no hierarchy is intended. Some words would fit several headings and a child of eight years can synthesize a word from a series of letters. The words are simply a vocabulary list gleaned from a variety of sources.

Activities giving evidence of knowing
Define, describe, identify, label, list, name, outline, reproduce, recall, select, state, present, be aware of, extract, organize, recount, write, recognize, measure, underline, repeat, relate, know, match.

Activities giving evidence of comprehension
Interpret, translate, estimate, justify, comprehend, convert, clarify, defend, distinguish, estimate, explain, extend, generalize, exemplify, give examples of, infer, paraphrase, predict, rewrite, summarize, discuss, perform, report, present, restate, identify, illustrate, indicate, find, select, understand, represent, name, formulate, judge, contrast, translate, classify, express, compare.

Activities giving evidence of application of knowledge/understanding
Apply, solve, construct, demonstrate, change, compute, discover, manipulate, modify, operate, predict, prepare, produce, relate, show, use, give examples, exemplify, draw (up), select, explain how, find, choose, assess, practice, operate, illustrate, verify.

Activities giving evidence of analysis
Recognize, distinguish between, evaluate, analyse, break down, differentiate, identify, illustrate how, infer, outline, point out, relate, select, separate, divide/subdivide, compare, contrast, justify, resolve, devote, examine, conclude, criticize, question, diagnose, identify, categorize, point out, elucidate.

Activities giving evidence of synthesis
Propose, present, structure, integrate, formulate, teach, develop, combine, compile, compose, create, devise, design, explain, generate,

modify, organize, plan, rearrange, reconstruct, relate, reorganize, revise, write, summarize, tell, account for, restate, report, alter, argue, order, select, manage, generalize, précis, derive, conclude, build up, engender, synthesize, put together, suggest, enlarge.

Activities giving evidence of evaluation
Judge, appraise, assess, conclude, compare, contrast, describe how, criticize, discriminate, justify, defend, evaluate, rate, determine, criticize, choose, value, question.

Format for writing course aims/objectives as learning outcomes
The following format may be useful in writing learning outcomes for courses which are currently described in terms of teaching intentions (in the form of aims or objectives). It is based on the notion that many teaching intentions (box a) can be translated fairly easily into learning outcomes (box b).

There may, however, be some learning outcomes that are not expressed in teaching intentions. For example, teaching intentions may not specify expected learning or attainment resulting from private study time, while learning outcomes should express this. Provision is made for these extra learning outcomes in box c.

Box d, Assessment details, will contain a brief description of assessment tasks in order to demonstrate how the tasks are related to the assessment criteria within (or alongside) the outcome statements.

Teaching intentions (aims/objectives) (a)	Learning outcomes (b)
	Extra learning outcomes (c)
Assessment details (d)	

Within the higher education institution the learning outcomes will be written to reflect the different levels required by courses at certificate, degree and Master's level, for the purpose of academic accreditation. In practice placements learning outcomes will also be written at different levels to reflect the competencies to be achieved at the various stages of the learning programme.

Descriptors (Figures 2.11 and 2.12)
Four higher-education levels are described (1, 2 and 3 at undergraduate stages and M for Master's stage). They are arranged under subheadings in three categories – operational context, cognitive descriptors and other transferable skills. These subheadings describe vocational, academic and, in some cases, social learning. The descriptors are classified in two formats: one in which the different descriptors are grouped under one level (e.g. all level 1 descriptors on the same page, etc.; Figure 2.11) and one in which all of the levels are described under each of the categories (Figure 2.12, adapted from WAV and SEEC, 1995). It is thought that the former arrangement will be more convenient for practitioners.

Most descriptors will be relevant for most disciplines/study but some will not be relevant to some disciplines/study. For example, it is unlikely that psychomotor skills will have much relevance to study of the social health policies.

Characteristics of the descriptors
The generic level descriptors are generalized learning outcomes for learning at four stages in higher education. These stages do not necessarily accord with year of study (but may do; for example, in the traditional three-year undergraduate degree). This means that a degree of four or five years can still fit the structure of level descriptors.

The descriptors can be seen as a set of templates which can, among their range of uses, guide the writing of learning outcomes for modules or be used to identify the level of work presented for accreditation of prior learning. In order to use the generic level descriptors as templates, it is helpful to read the descriptors both in their vertical and horizontal contexts.

The writing of learning outcomes for a module will be guided by the level descriptors. This means that a module with its learning outcomes will only be relevant to one level. It is primarily the assessment criteria part of a learning outcome that will characterize the level.

The writing of learning outcomes with reference to explicit level descriptors can help to ensure consistency of outcome statements across subject/discipline areas. Learning outcomes facilitate consistency in providing a common format for the description of disparate forms of learning. Academic, vocational, experiential learning, on or off campus, work-based or community-based learning can all be described in learning outcomes and thus more easily compared.

Modules described in a similar style using learning outcomes are more comprehensible. Beneficiaries of this clarity are learners and those who guide learners in their choices of learning course, and staff from the same and different subject areas. For example, the planning of

Figure 2.11   Generic level descriptors (arranged by stage of study) (Wales Access Unit and SEEC, 1995).

LEVEL M

	CHARACTERISTICS OF CONTEXT	RESPONSIBILITY	ETHICAL UNDERSTANDING
	Characteristics of context are:	**Requirements of responsibility are:**	**Requirements of ethical understanding are:**
1. Operational contexts	Complex, unpredictable and normally specialized contexts demanding innovative work which may involve exploring the current limits of knowledge.	Autonomy within bounds of professional practice. High level of responsibility for self, possibly others.	Awareness of ethical dilemmas likely to arise in research and professional practice. An ability to formulate solutions in dialogue with peers, clients, mentors and others.

	KNOWLEDGE AND UNDERSTANDING	ANALYSIS	SYNTHESIS/ CREATIVITY	EVALUATION
	The learner:			
2. Cognitive descriptors	Has great depth of knowledge in a complex and specialized area and/or across specialized or applied areas. S/he may be working at the current limits of theoretical and/or research understanding.	Can deal with complexity, lacunae and/or contradictions in the knowledge base and make confident selection of tools for the job.	Can autonomously synthesize information/ideas and create responses to problems that expand or redefine existing knowledge and/or develop new approaches in new situations.	Can independently evaluate/argue alternative approaches and accurately assess/report on own/ others' work with justification.

	PSYCHOMOTOR	SELF-APPRAISAL, REFLECTION ON PRACTICE	PLANNING AND MANAGEMENT OF LEARNING	PROBLEM SOLVING	COMMUNICATION AND PRESENTATION	INTERACTIVE AND GROUP SKILLS
3. Other transferable skills descriptors	Has technical mastery of a skill, performing smoothly, precisely and efficiently. Able to plan strategies and tactics and adapt effectively to unusual and unexpected situations.	Engages with a critical community; reflecting habitually on own and others' practice in order to improve own/others' action.	Is autonomous in study/ use of resources; makes professional use of others in support of self-directed learning.	Can isolate, assess and resolve problems of all degrees of predictability in an autonomous manner.	Can engage in a full professional and academic communication with others in their field.	Can work with and within a group towards defined outcomes and can take role as recognized leader or consultant. Has ability to negotiate and handle conflict. Can effectively motivate others.

Figure 2.11 Continued

LEVEL 1

	CHARACTERISTICS OF CONTEXT	RESPONSIBILITY	ETHICAL UNDERSTANDING
	Characteristics of context are:	**Requirements of responsibility are:**	**Requirements of ethical understanding are:**
1. Operational contexts	Defined contexts demanding use of a specified range of standard techniques.	Work is directed, with limited autonomy within defined guidelines.	Awareness of ethical issues in current area(s) of study. Ability to discuss these in relation to personal beliefs and values.

	KNOWLEDGE AND UNDERSTANDING	ANALYSIS	SYNTHESIS/CREATIVITY	EVALUATION
	The learner:			
2. Cognitive descriptors	Has a given factual and/or conceptual knowledge base with emphasis on the nature of the field of study and appropriate terminology.	Can analyse with guidance using given classifications/principles.	Can collect/collate and categorize ideas and information in a predictable and standard format.	Can evaluate the reliability of data using defined techniques and/or tutor guidance.

	PSYCHOMOTOR	SELF-APPRAISAL, REFLECTION ON PRACTICE	PLANNING AND MANAGEMENT OF LEARNING	PROBLEM SOLVING	COMMUNICATION AND PRESENTATION	INTERACTIVE AND GROUP SKILLS
3. Other transferable skills descriptors	Able to perform basic skills with awareness of the necessary tools and materials and their potential uses and hazards. Needs external evaluation.	Is largely dependent on criteria set by others but begins to recognize own strengths and weaknesses.	Can work within a relevant ethos and can access and use a range of learning resources.	Can apply given tools/methods accurately and carefully to a well-defined problem and begins to appreciate the complexity of the issues.	Can communicate effectively in a format appropriate to the discipline and report practical procedures in a clear and concise manner with all relevant information.	Meets obligations to others (tutors and/or peers); can offer and/or support initiatives; can recognize and assess alternative options.

Figure 2.11   Continued

LEVEL 2

	CHARACTERISTICS OF CONTEXT	RESPONSIBILITY	ETHICAL UNDERSTANDING
	Characteristics of context are:	**Requirements of responsibility are:**	**Requirements of ethical understanding are:**
1. Operational contexts	Simple but unpredictable or complex but predictable contexts demanding application of a wide range of techniques.	Management of processes within broad guidelines for defined activities.	Awareness of the wider social and environmental implications of area(s) of study. Ability to debate issues in relation to more general ethical perspectives.

	KNOWLEDGE AND UNDERSTANDING	ANALYSIS	SYNTHESIS/CREATIVITY	EVALUATION
	The learner:			
2. Cognitive descriptors	Has a detailed knowledge of (a) major discipline(s) and an awareness of a variety of ideas/contexts/frameworks which may be applied to this.	Can analyse a range of information within minimum guidance, can apply major theories of discipline and can compare alternative methods/techniques for obtaining data.	Can reformat a range of ideas/information towards a given purpose.	Can select appropriate techniques of evaluation and can evaluate the relevance and significance of data collected.

	PSYCHOMOTOR	SELF-APPRAISAL, REFLECTION ON PRACTICE	PLANNING AND MANAGEMENT OF LEARNING	PROBLEM SOLVING	COMMUNICATION AND PRESENTATION	INTERACTIVE AND GROUP SKILLS
3. Other transferable skills descriptors	When given a complex task, can choose and perform an appropriate set of actions in sequence to complete it adequately. Can evaluate own performance.	Is able to evaluate own strengths and weaknesses; can challenge received opinion and begins to develop own criteria and judgement.	Adopts a broad-ranging and flexible approach to study; identifies strengths of learning needs and follows activities to improve performance; is autonomous in straight-forward study tasks.	Can identify key elements of problems and choose appropriate methods for their resolution in a considered manner.	Can communicate effectively in a format appropriate to the discipline and report practical procedures in a clear and concise manner with all relevant information in a variety of formats.	Can interact effectively within a learning group, giving and receiving information and ideas and modifying response where appropriate. Is ready to develop professional working relationships within discipline.

Figure 2.11 Continued

LEVEL 3

	CHARACTERISTICS OF CONTEXT	RESPONSIBILITY	ETHICAL UNDERSTANDING
	Characteristics of context are:	Requirements of responsibility are:	Requirements of ethical understanding are:
1. Operational contexts	Complex and unpredictable contexts demanding selection and application from a wide range of innovative or standard techniques.	Autonomy in planning and managing resources and processes within broad guidelines.	Awareness of personal responsibility and professional codes of conduct. Ability to incorporate a critical ethical dimension into a major piece of work.

	KNOWLEDGE AND UNDERSTANDING	ANALYSIS	SYNTHESIS/CREATIVITY	EVALUATION
	The learner:			
2. Cognitive descriptors	Has comprehensive/detailed knowledge of (a) major discipline(s) with areas of specialization in depth and an awareness of the provisional nature of the state of knowledge.	Can analyse new and/or abstract data and situations without guidance, using a wide range of techniques appropriate to the subject.	With minimum guidance can transform abstract data and concepts towards a given purpose and can design novel solutions.	Can critically review evidence-supporting conclusions/recommendations including their reliability, validity and significance and can investigate contradictory information/identify reasons for contradictions.

	PSYCHOMOTOR	SELF-APPRAISAL, REFLECTION ON PRACTICE	PLANNING AND MANAGEMENT OF LEARNING	PROBLEM SOLVING	COMMUNICATION AND PRESENTATION	INTERACTIVE AND GROUP SKILLS
3. Other transferable skills descriptors	Can perform complex skills consistently, with confidence and a degree of coordination and fluidity. Able to choose an appropriate response from a repertoire of actions, and can evaluate own and others' performance.	Is confident in application of own criteria of judgement and in challenging received opinion in action and can reflect on action.	With minimum guidance, can manage own learning using full range of resources for discipline; can seek and make use of feedback.	Is confident and flexible in identifying and defining complex problems and the application of appropriate knowledge and skills to their solution.	Can engage effectively in debate in a professional manner and produce detailed and coherent project reports.	Can interact effectively within a learning or professional group. Can recognize or support leadership or be proactive in leadership. Can negotiate in a learning/professional context and manage conflict.

Figure 2.12 Individual descriptors.

Cognitive descriptors

LEVEL	KNOWLEDGE & UNDERSTANDING The learner:	ANALYSIS	SYNTHESIS/CREATIVITY	EVALUATION
M	Has great depth of knowledge in a complex and specialized area and/or across specialized or applied areas. S/he may be working at the current limits of theoretical and/or research understanding.	Can deal with complexity, lacunae and/or contradictions in the knowledge base and make confident selection of tools for the job.	Can autonomously synthesize information/ideas and create responses to problems that expand or redefine existing knowledge and/or develop new approaches in new situations.	Can independently evaluate/argue alternative approaches and accurately assess/report on own/others' work with justification.
3	Has a comprehensive/detailed knowledge of (a) major discipline(s) with areas of specialization in depth and an awareness of the provisional nature of the state of knowledge.	Can analyse new and/or abstract data and situations without guidance, using a wide range of techniques appropriate to the subject.	With minimum guidance can transform abstract data and concepts towards a given purpose and can design novel solutions.	Can critically review evidence supporting conclusions/recommendations including their reliability, validity and significance and can investigate contradictory information/identify reasons for contradictions.
2	Has a detailed knowledge of (a) major discipline(s) and an awareness of a variety of ideas/contexts/frameworks which may be applied to this.	Can analyse a range of information within minimum guidance, can apply major theories of discipline and can compare alternative methods/techniques for obtaining data.	Can reformat a range of ideas/information towards a given purpose.	Can select appropriate techniques of evaluation and can evaluate the relevance and significance of data collected.
1	Has a given factual and/or conceptual knowledge base with emphasis on the nature of the field of study and appropriate terminology.	Can analyse with guidance using given classifications/principles.	Can collect/collate and categorize ideas and information in a predictable standard format.	Can evaluate the reliability of data using defined techniques and/or tutor guidance.

Figure 2.12 Continued

Other transferable skills descriptors

LEVEL	PSYCHOMOTOR The learner:	SELF-APPRAISAL, REFLECTION ON PRACTICE	PLANNING AND MANAGEMENT OF LEARNING	PROBLEM SOLVING	COMMUNICATION AND PRESENTATION	INTERACTIVE GROUP SKILLS
M	Has technical mastery of a skill, performing smoothly, precisely and efficiently. Able to plan strategies and tactics and adapt effectively to unusual and unexpected situations.	Engages with a critical community reflecting habitually on own and others' practice in order to improve own/others' action.	Is autonomous in study/ use of resources; makes professional use of others in support of self-directed learning.	Can isolate, assess and resolve problems of all degrees of predictability in an autonomous manner.	Can engage in full professional and academic communication with others in their field.	Can work with and within a group towards defined outcomes and can take role as recognized leader or consultant. Has ability to negotiate and handle conflict. Can effectively motivate others.
3	Can perform complex skills consistently, with confidence and a degree of coordination and fluidity. Able to choose an appropriate response of actions and can evaluate own and others' performance.	Is confident in application of own criteria of judgement and in challenging of received opinion in action and can reflect on action.	With minimum guidance, can manage own learning using full range of resources for discipline; can seek and make use of feedback.	Is confident and flexible in identifying and defining complex problems and the application of appropriate knowledge and skills to their solution.	Can engage effectively in debate in a professional manner and produce detailed and coherent project reports.	Can interact effectively within a learning or professional group. Can recognize or support leadership or be proactive in leadership. Can negotiate in a learning/professional context and manage conflict.
2	When given a complex task, can choose and perform an appropriate set of actions in sequence to complete it adequately. Can evaluate own performance.	Is able to evaluate own strengths and weaknesses; can challenge received opinion and begins to develop own criteria and judgement.	Adopts a broad-ranging and flexible approach to study; identifies strengths of learning needs and follows activities to improve performance; is autonomous in straight-forward study tasks.	Can identify key elements of problems and choose appropriate methods for their resolution in a considered manner.	Can communicate effectively in a format appropriate to the discipline and report practical procedures in a clear and concise manner with all relevant information in a variety of formats.	Can interact effectively within a learning group, giving and receiving information and ideas and modifying response where appropriate. Is ready to develop professional working relationships within discipline.
1	Able to perform basic skills with awareness of the necessary tools and materials and their potential uses and hazards. Needs external evaluation.	Is largely dependent on criteria set by others but begins to recognize own strengths and weaknesses.	Can work within a relevant ethos and can access and use a range of learning resources.	Can apply given tools/ methods accurately and carefully to a well-defined problem and begins to appreciate the complexity of the issues.	Can communicate effectively in a format appropriate to the discipline and report practical procedures in a clear and concise manner with all relevant information.	Meets obligations to others (tutors and/or peers); can offer and/or support initiatives; can recognize and assess alternative options.

Figure 2.12   Continued

Operational contexts

LEVEL	CHARACTERISTICS OF CONTEXT — Characteristics of context are:	RESPONSIBILITY — Requirements of responsibility are:	ETHICAL UNDERSTANDING — Requirements of ethical understanding are:
M	Complex, unpredictable and normally specialized contexts demanding innovative work which may involve exploring the current limits of knowledge.	Autonomy within bounds of professional practice. High level of responsibility for self, possibly others.	Awareness of ethical dilemmas likely to arise in research and professional practice. An ability to formulate solutions in dialogue with peers, clients, mentors and others.
3	Complex and unpredictable contexts demanding selection and application from a wide range of innovative or standard techniques.	Autonomy in planning and managing resources and processes within broad guidelines.	Awareness of personal responsibility and professional codes of conduct. Ability to incorporate a critical ethical dimension into a major piece of work.
2	Simple but unpredictable or complex but predictable contexts demanding application of a wide range of techniques.	Management of processes within broad guidelines for defined activities.	Awareness of the wider social and environmental implications of area(s) of study. Ability to debate issues in relation to more general ethical perspectives.
1	Defined contexts demanding use of a specified range of standard techniques.	Work is directed, with limited autonomy within defined guidelines.	Awareness of ethical issues in current area(s) of study. Ability to discuss these in relation to personal beliefs and values.

related and possibly overlapping modules is facilitated by clear statements of learning outcomes for each. Similarly the presence of learning outcomes that are related to level descriptors can facilitate discussions between course leaders and external examiners.

Centralized or departmental record keeping is aided by clarity and consistency in description of modules. This can be related to the development of student transcripts and there are similar advantages where students transfer from one institution to another or where they apply for accreditation of their prior learning.

There are educational implications for staff in the act of explicitly anticipating the learning that can result from their professional activities. The design of teaching activities can be more focused and with learners able to be clearer about what is expected of them, the teaching/ learning processes can be made mutually more effective. Because it is desirable to write learning outcomes in collaboration with others (Neary, 1996), there is an opportunity to develop more coherence within and between modules.

The transparency created by the writing of learning outcomes in relation to generic level descriptors can be a threat in demonstrating various inconsistencies across an institution or institutions. However, in the solution of these inconsistencies lies one means of upholding standards in nurse and higher education.

More recently, much has been written about learning outcomes and competencies. Interested readers should study Barton (1999), Bradshaw (1998), Chapman (1999), Day (1997), Le Var (1996), Luker *et al.* (1996), McAteer and Hamilly (1997) and Moon (1999).

Activity

Study the generic level descriptors (Figure 2.11) and structure your own learning outcomes to reflect the learning opportunities you have to offer to a:

- year 1/CFP student
- branch-specific student.

You should include both theory and practice learning outcomes.

LEARNING CONTRACTS AND CONTRACT ASSIGNMENTS

The UKCC *Fitness for Practice* (1999) recommendation 13 (p.38) states:

> *Students, assessors and mentors should know what is expected of them through specified practice outcomes which form part of a formal learning contract.*

Learning contracts and contract assignments can, if carefully negotiated between student, mentor and personal tutor, fulfil this recommendation.

A learning contract can be described as an individualized learning plan that has been negotiated between the practitioner and/or personal tutor and the student. Although not a legally binding document, it is a written, signed agreement that specifies aims, learning objectives and outcomes to be accomplished, resources which can be used, criteria and methods for evaluation and final assessment, and the responsibilities of the student and the nurse practitioner/personal tutor.

The term 'contract' is a familiar one, in our adult lives we frequently enter into a 'contract'. A contract binds two (or more) people in an agreement to carry out specific behaviours, usually within a certain period of time. It is essential before signing a contract that all parties are in agreement about goals and have a clear understanding of responsibilities of each participant. Contracts can often be renegotiated when the situation of either party alters the ability to meet commitments. These facets of a contract apply equally to learning contracts.

Neary (1998) suggested that the contract should be a document drawn up by the nurse practitioner and the student in which they specify what the student will learn, how this will be achieved, within what timespan and the criteria for measuring the success of the venture. Contract assignments are an integral part of a learning contract, continuous assessment and adult learning and should be made explicit (Neary, 1992a).

Nurse education is concerned with the education and training of adults so the processes used should be based on andragogical principles (i.e. should be student centred and self-directed) rather than pedagogical principles (i.e. teacher centred, as in the teaching of children). There is evidence that if adults learn on their own initiative they learn more permanently than if they learn by being taught (Rogers, 1983). Psychological research shows that a characteristic of adults is the need and capacity to be self-directed. The use of contract assignments could be a means of reconciling the requirements imposed by the present structure of nurse education and the students' need to be self-directing. Having stated this assumption that our (adult) students will be mainly self-directing learners, it must of course be remembered that there will still be some variation in their learning styles.

The use of contract assignments provides an individually negotiated degree of support and freedom and thus caters for these variations, without losing the obvious benefit to the students of developing the ability to direct their own learning. This flexibility was discussed by Boud (1981), in relation to learning contracts, who found that some adult students will be happier with informal discussion whilst others may prefer a more structured approach and that 'the learning contract may therefore be used to create a climate of informality and ease, or to support a framework of proceedings with firm definitions of roles and responsibilities'. Recent studies (Davies *et al.*, 1994; Jowett *et al.*, 1994; Neary, 1996, 1998; O'Neill *et al.*, 1993) show that the assessment and evaluation of this form of learning must therefore be through contract assignments.

I YEAR		2 YEARS		TRANSITION PERIOD
Foundation Programme		**Branches**		**Staff Nurse Designate**

Foundation of nursing theory and practice
 	
Basic concept of theory and practice of nursing care
	Summative assessment	Specialist subject applied to branch specific
		
		Advanced nursing product and skills
			Summative assessment / Last 3 months	Professional development
				
				Professional development in the workplace,
				e.g. preceptorship
				     mentorship
				     teaching and assessing
				
				Application of management theory

Formative ▸▸ ▸▸ ▸▸ ▸▸   ▸▸ ▸▸ ▸▸ ▸▸ ▸▸ ▸▸   FORMATIVE   ▸▸ ▸▸ ▸▸ ▸▸ ▸▸ ▸▸

APPLICATION OF THEORY TO PRACTICE
CONTINUOUS ASSESSMENT VIA

LEARNING CONTRACT _____   CONTRACT ASSIGNMENTS _____

OPPORTUNISTIC LEARNING _____ _____

Figure 2.13

Course structure for pre-registration nurse education.

COLLEGE **Theory**	CONTRACT ASSIGNMENTS + OPPORTUNISTIC LEARNING	**PRACTICE SETTING** **Nursing Practice**

STUDENT CONTRACTS WITH <u>BOTH</u> PRACTICE MENTOR AND PERSONAL TUTOR

The end product is an integrated project which is continually assessed at various stages
Therefore FORMATIVE ASSESSMENT
The completed assignment = summative

Figure 2.14

Curriculum design.

There is much concern about the theory–practice gap in professional education and many attempts are being made to bridge this gap (joint appointments; mentor/clinical facilitator roles). Contract assignments are used as a bridge between the college academic input and clinical practice (Figures 2.13 and 2.14), particularly in the use of projects related to client/patient groups (such as nursing care studies and scenario-based critical incident analysis or activities), as the shared 'plan of learning' (learning contract + opportunistic learning), and the shared accountability for learning between mentor, student and nurse practitioner would enhance communication and give written clarity to the 'practice based on theory' concept.

Handing over the control

The use of learning contracts and contract assignments requires the handing over of the control of learning to the student. This challenges the basic assumption underlying the traditional approach to health professional education and thus some antagonism, and resistance to the idea, has to be expected.

Neary (1992a) argued that contract assignments, when an integral part of learning contracts and continuous assessment, shift power and control over to the student, helping them towards independence, while Keyzer (1986, p.104) argued that:

> *... learning contracts are explicit of the social distribution of power and the principles of social control in the educational establishment and, therefore, in the relationships held by students and teachers in the learning programme.*

Clearly, any assessment programme is based on an unequal distribution of power which is initially accepted by both parties as a matter of necessity. In order to modify these power relationships in a changing assessment strategy, the first task is to identify the nature of this uneven relationship and the changes which are likely to occur as the student is, for example, gradually directed to independence. The rate of such change might be slow at first, quickening later as confidence, experience and autonomy increase, although it need not be consistent and there are times when students might need to be 'reeled in'. Such contingencies need to be incorporated into the design of any scheme.

Many mentors or assessors take for granted their position of power in the assessment relationship. A particularly interesting finding of Neary's (1996) study was the extent to which the 'taken for granted' has become explicit at early stages of the process, as the assessor sought to confirm their expertise and establish the subordination of the student in power terms. Changes in power dynamics occur as students move from novice to expert and to varying degrees of autonomy. Appreciating such changing power relations is the key to the design and development of contract assignments.

This kind of relationship can be problematic, especially in nurse education institutions where, according to Crout (1980), students have been actively discouraged from questioning 'the facts' and are not taught to argue logically or to substantiate argument. These may be seen as attempts by teachers and assessors to retain power and have been a source of much criticism in nurse education for many years. However, with the introduction of the nurse education reforms this is becoming a thing of the past.

In the context of contract assignments, the intentions and interpretations of the mentor/assessor should be made explicit. The criteria for contract assignments have to be balanced explicitly, taking into account

Figure 2.15

Unit of competence. Standard of performance statement: under the supervision of a skilled practitioner.

Nature: Continuous assessment and responsive assessment

Demonstrate their ability to apply theory to practice, the student will produce an assignment on patient/client profile.

Elements of competence	Related performance criteria	Date	Signature of student	Self-assess comments	Signature of assessor	Comments
a) The recognition of common factors which affect physical, mental and social well-being of patients/clients.	1. Identifies the documents used to record the psychosocial and/or nursing/medical history of an individual.					
b) The use of appropriate communication skills to develop relationships with patients/clients, their families and friends.	2. Recognizes factors which contribute to the physical, mental and social well-being of a patient/client.					
	3. Identifies those factors which adversely affect the individual's health and well-being.					
	4. Discusses the effects of an altered level of functioning on an individual's role in the family unit.					
	5. Discusses the strategies used to assist the individual to cope with his/her altered level of functioning.					
Responsive assessment						
a) Practitioners observation of student standards of care		Comments				
b) Student's perceptions of own performance		Comments				
c) Action plan agreed		Signed		Practitioner		
		Dated		Student		

factors which include getting to know students better in order to diagnose their strengths and weaknesses (formative assessment), helping to recognize learning needs and activities which help others to be better informed about the student at the end of a set period of learning and achievement (summative assessment). Contract assignments are advocated by Neary (1992a) as an integral part of continuous assessment, as depicted in Figure 2.15. Continuous assessment can help to provide the mentor and assessor with the basis for adjusting their teaching and assessing tactics according to how a student is developing, via a process within which contract assignments can, at best, provide students with immediate feedback on their strengths and weaknesses in relation to specific requirements, and fit comfortably within the principles of responsive assessments (pp.134–138).

Portfolios and projects

With a devolved examination system and a move towards continuous assessment, the use of portfolios and projects is likely to increase even further so it is time to look at more effective applications of these in nurse education. A familiar type of project work currently utilized in nurse education is the 'nursing care study'.

Nursing care studies have been a part of student assessment for some years at many colleges of nursing and midwifery. There has been frequent, informal discussion regarding the actual learning which takes place during the production and on completion of these studies. There can be a lack of creativity in the finished products and much of the information gathered and presented is not highly relevant to the development of the student's understanding of nursing theory and practice. The care study format is fairly prescriptive in its requirements and many students put a lot of effort into producing what they perceive the teacher wants, with relatively minimal educational gain for themselves (Neary, 1996).

There are benefits inherent in the student studying the care of a chosen patient which could be enhanced by the use of a contract assignment which enables flexibility, encourages critical analysis of care given and allows the learner to offer intelligent (research-based) alternatives to care and can be extended to become part of a practice portfolio to demonstrate a student's 'fitness for practice' (UKCC, 1999, p.38).

Students undertaking the care study appear to experience confusion and ambiguity related to what is expected from them and what they can gain from the study. The use of a contract assignment would ensure that both the student and their personal tutor or practitioner (mentor) agree the aims of the study, the learning outcomes and the assessment criteria; thus there would be clarity of expectations and the freedom for the student to direct their own learning within their own contracted framework. The personal tutor is there to help the student achieve the aims and learning outcomes of a satisfactory project and to learn in the process, not to provide another difficulty for the student to overcome.

Definition of terms

Learning contracts and contract assignments are:

- drawn up by the students and their personal tutor or mentor, specifying what the students will learn, how this will be accomplished, within what period of time and what the criteria of the evaluation will be
- a written agreement between the concerned parties, which identifies the nature of the relationship held, the expectations each individual can have of the other, the time period covered by the contract, the means whereby success can be identified and the way in which the contract is to be terminated
- explicit statements of the social distribution of power and the principles of social control in the educational establishment and, therefore, in the relationships held by student, teacher and mentor in the learning programme.

These contracts are not a means of negating our accountability and responsibility as a teacher or mentor, nor are they a means of keeping students dependent on our knowledge and expertise.

Learning contracts lie along a continuum, with teacher/mentor controlled and initiated at one end and student initiated and controlled at the other end. In between these two extremes lie a host of contracts which represent the degrees of power sharing negotiated by the teacher and the student.

(**Note:** A written agreement can be used to formalize the contract and become part of a student's portfolio and profile and a record of student progress.)

Guidelines on developing a learning contract and contract assignment

Emphasis must be placed on student choice and participation so that the learning is largely student directed.

The negotiated outcome of *all* the following points must be put in writing and the contract signed by both parties.

1 Clarify, in writing, any fundamental learning outcomes, e.g. what the nursing care study must include:
   - an assessment of the chosen patient's social, psychological, physical and spiritual status
   - a problem-solving care plan or identification of needs
   - a critical evaluation.
2 Negotiate the aims, broader objectives and learning outcomes of the learning contract (these will differ according to the specific learning situation and the individuals). Examples of learning outcomes for the nursing care study could be:
   - acquired skills of finding, interpreting and presenting material (in written form)

- developed the ability to assess, plan and implement care using a problem-solving approach or identification-of-needs process
- developed the ability to analyse critically the care planned and/ or given to a chosen patient
- developed the ability to question care and to find and offer alternative care strategies.

3 Negotiate percentage marks to be aimed at and how these marks will be divided between the aim of the project and the finished product (the student may feel more able in some areas of the study than in others). The marks can be renegotiated during the course of the project if either party feels it necessary.

4 Agree on resources which can be utilized and help the student to make the best use of them.

5 Agree guidelines for the process of learning and criteria for assessment. Agree how the work will be planned and collated and strategies to be used.

6 Agree guidelines for the endproduct. Negotiate the learning outcome and expectations, including length of study, material to be covered. Agree on what is relevant or irrelevant.

7 Negotiate a timetable of events:
- mutually satisfactory meeting times for discussion, support, feedback, guidance
- importance of all parties keeping to contracted times
- completion date and pre-completion date (to allow for discussion, renegotiation and alterations)
- if considered by all parties to be helpful, set time limits for sections of the project (this may be useful for those students who have not yet mastered self-directed learning).

8 Clarify the student and teacher/mentor roles in the learning contract and contract assignment.
- Role of teacher, personal tutor/skilled practitioner/mentor. The personal tutor is there to help the student achieve the goal of a satisfactory project and to learn in the process, not to provide another difficulty for the student to overcome. 'Personal role' – giving the student emotional support and encouragement. 'Task role' – helping the student to 'get the job done' with guidance, information and resources.
- Role of student. To acquire skills and knowledge *through completion* of the contract.

9 Contract assignments can also be used to help link theory to practice (see Figure 2.15).

Activity

Take time out and try to relate the process of a learning contract and contract assignments to your own profession.

Before going on to the next page, write down what you think learning contracts and contract assignments provide.

Learning contracts and contract assignments provide the following.

1   The safety for students to make decisions about their learning within the boundaries set by the curriculum framework and objectives.
2   The opportunity for teachers and students to utilize the individual's internal motivation to learn and/or change.
3   A framework for supporting students who may fail to do well because of their unstructured approach to learning.
4   A vehicle by which the external needs of the organization and the internal needs of the individual can be met.
5   A means for identifying the individual's preferred learning styles.
6   A means whereby the pace of learning can be adjusted to the needs of the individual.
7   A vehicle for integrating theory and practice – this is extremely important for practice-based professions.
8   The basic unit for auditing the learning programme and the identification of performance indicators:
    - students
    - teachers
    - programme.

Contract assignments can also be used as a vehicle to identify:

- gaps in learning with reference to learning opportunities available in practice settings
- new learning that students want to achieve
- learning needs to make links with previous experience and learning.

Contract assignment steps and progression

A contract assignment is a criteria-based assessment, therefore the fact that it is critical for a pass or fail must be clearly stated.

Figure 2.16 demonstrates the process of contract assignment and helps to give structure and guidance for planning.

Figures 2.17 and 2.18 help to show the status of contract assignments and give an example of assessment criteria and the strategy for competence to be achieved.

Guidelines for the review of learning contracts and contract assignments

1   Are the learning outcomes clear, understandable and realistic? Do they describe what the student proposes to learn?
2   Are there any other outcomes which should be considered?
3   Do the learning strategies seem reasonable, appropriate and efficient?
4   Are there other strategies or resources which could be utilized?
5   Does the evidence of accomplishment seem relevant to the various outcomes and is it convincing?
6   Is there other evidence that could be sought?
7   Are the criteria and means for validating the evidence clear, relevant and convincing?

Figure 2.16

The process of contract assignment.

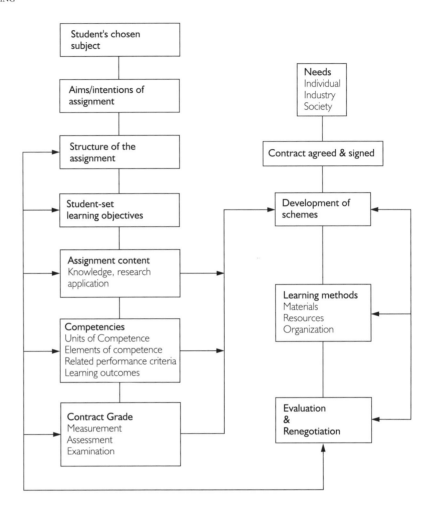

8 Are there other ways of validating the evidence that should be considered?

9 Are the key factors and 'dynamics' explicit in the nurse education curriculum (Figure 2.19)?

Activity

Before turning to the next page:

1 write down what you consider to be the role of the student and teacher/mentor in a contract assignment process.

2 what are the advantages of contract assignments and learning contracts?

Role of student and teacher in a contract assignment process

- The process stresses understanding and procedures.
- All is negotiated during the contract.

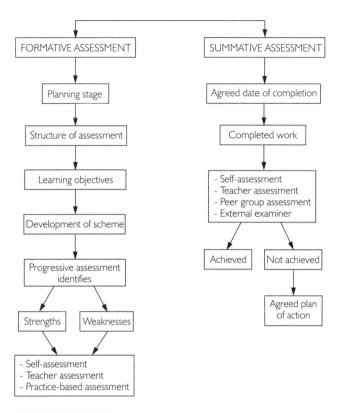

Figure 2.17

Contract assignments, an integral part of continuous assessment.

ASSESSMENT STATUS

Formative assessment: During the planning and progressive stages, student will be assessed by clinical mentor and personal tutor

Summative assessment: Student-completed project is assessed and agreed status given, i.e. pass/fail

- Student activities involve experiencing and reflecting.
- Student is an investigator and explorer.
- Motivation is via involvement.
- Encourages creative thinking.
- Mentor/teacher sees student as individual.
- Learning is student centred.
- Student sees teacher as learner, explorer, critic, developer, resource finder.
- Mentor/teacher encourages student autonomy.
- Mentor/teacher sees teaching as artistic activity, tentative, open to challenge and change.
- Student sees mentor/teacher as pursuing understanding.
- Both see assessment as ongoing part of learning.
- Encourages reflection-in-action plus reflection-on-action.
- Both develop relationship of theory and practice as problematic and complex.

Figure 2.18 Assessment criteria – an example (Neary, 1994).

COMPETENCIES	COMPETENCE ACHIEVEMENT STRATEGY	RESOURCES	CRITERIA FOR ASSESSMENT AND EVALUATION
Ability to find, interpret and present material (in writing). Ability to assess, goal-set and plan care using a problem solving approach.	Patient/client interview (with consent or parental consent). Interviews of relatives/friends (with patient's/client's consent)	Chosen patient/client and relatives/friends and significant others.	The completed study will contain an assessment, a plan of care (including goals) an in-depth evaluation of care, and a critical appraisal. Possible alternative care strategies must be included when relevant (preferably research based).
Ability to analyse critically the care planned and/or implemented.	Study of Nursing (or other professions) with consent of Primary Nurse (if applicable) and/or significant other.	For example: College Staff Learning Resources Centre, Hospital Libraries, Journals etc., Personal Tutor and Clinical Mentor.	The data gathered will identify the patient's/client's strengths and weaknesses, his/her priorities for care (or parents') and his/her contributions to the care (or parental contributions).
Ability to question care and to find and offer alternative care strategies based on research when possible.	Discussion with Primary Nurse and/or significant other.		The model on which the care was based should be defined and critically evaluated.
Has in depth knowledge of chosen client's/patient's social, psychological, physical spiritual status and ability to relate these to his/her identified needs/care.	Taught theory and taught practice. Discussions with other health professionals involved. Discussion with personal tutor.		Record of:- Negotiated work Negotiated dates Negotiated marks Tutor and student meeting times agreed. Application of taught theory to taught practice.

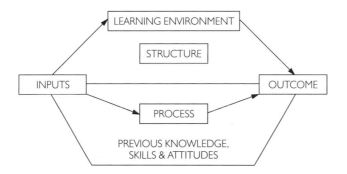

Figure 2.19

Educational courses – key factors and dynamics.

Inputs
Subject content
Skills (from human and inanimate sources)
Meaningful experiences
Cultural issues
Opportunistic learning

Processes
Perceptions
Conceptualizations
Cognitive strategies
Emotional experiences
Motivation
Attitude and value
'Formative skill learning

Outcomes
Personal growth
  • increased knowledge
  • enhanced skills
Change in behaviour
Change in values
Maintenance of motivation
Academic credibility
Competent professional
  practitioners

- Both can specify aims, but refer them to principles of practice.
- The process needs flexibility of time.
- The process covers less ground but enables better assimilation, greater motivation.

Advantages of contract assignments and learning contracts

Readiness to learn
- Students demonstrate curiosity, leading to self motivation and self-direction.
- Students develop qualities of the reflective practitioner leading on to critical appraisal

Assessment criteria
- Assessment is made against agreed criteria and agreed standards.

Learning needs/opportunity
- Learning experience of student, teacher and mentor.
- Identify resources for learning and evaluate outcomes.
- The experience itself provides learning opportunities.

Partnership
- Partnership is based on a collaborative process.
- Contracts are based on dialogue.
- Partnership offers a two-way process.
- Partnership is liaison between clinical mentor, student and personal tutor.

Personal and professional development
- This is a lifelong process resulting in an increase in perception and change in behaviour.

Challenge the separation of assessment and curriculum
- Ensure the curriculum content is being assessed.

Narrow the theory–practice gap
- Broaden the student's learning ability.
- Integrate theory and practice.
- Apply theory to practice.
- Transfer learning to other sites and situations.

Relationship and development
- Development occurs through the social interaction between tutor, mentor, student and significant others.
- Help student to put views in a non-threatening and non-defensive way.

Activity

In order to give structure to contract assignments, it is helpful to have a 'contract form' on which you and your students can agree the following:

- aims of assignment
- rationale for study
- learning outcomes/learning objectives
- resources to be used
- dates agreed to meet student, etc.
- criteria for success.

Have a go! Choose your own specialist area of practice, design your own and then compare it with the two example contract forms on pp.83–87.

CONTRACT

This is a contract signed between:

. . . . Student

. . . . Tutor/Named Practitioner

It is agreed that . . . . Student

will undertake the professional educational study on: . . . .

STAGE 1   The aim of the project is:

. . . .

. . . .

. . . .

STAGE 2   The detailed objectives are:

. . . .

. . . .

. . . .

. . . .

STAGE 3   In order to achieve the above aims and objectives, the student
undertakes to do the following:
(a) Identify the rationale for the above study
(b) Identify the resources needed to complete the study
(c) Show how this study has helped him/her to integrate theory
    and practice.

STAGE 4   The following resources, people and organizations will be
involved:

. . . .

. . . .

. . . .

STAGE 5   It is agreed that the study will be assessed and evaluated by self/
the tutor/mentor/peer group in the following manner:

. . . .

Figure 2.20

An example of a contract.

STAGE 6   It is considered that the work involved is suitable to be accomplished in the term period

CFP	Branch

✓ tick the appropriate box

or

Year 1	Year 2	Year 3

STAGE 7   The end product will be delivered to the personal tutor or mentor by the following date: . . . .
Exact dates to be negotiated with your tutors.

Signed this . . . . Day of 2000

By: . . . . (Student)

By: . . . . (Tutor/Named Practitioner/Mentor)

THIS CONTRACT SHOULD BE RETAINED AND RETURNED WITH YOUR COMPLETED PROJECT.

Figure 2.20

Continued

EDUCATIONAL PROPOSAL

First Meeting: Stage 1

This is an educational proposal signed between:

. . . . (Student)

. . . . (Tutor)

It is agreed that . . . . (Student)
will undertake the professional educational project outlined below.

Working title:
- The aim for the project is: . . . .

  . . . .

  . . . .

- Rationale for the project is: . . . .

  . . . .

  . . . .

  . . . .

- The objectives are: . . . .

  . . . .

  . . . .

  . . . .

Second Meeting: Stage 2

NB: Responsibility for contacting/meeting personal tutors is that of the student. In order to achieve the above aims and objectives, the student undertakes to do the following:

. . . .

. . . .

. . . .

Agreed by student and tutor on the following date . . . .

Figure 2.21

An example of an educational proposal.

• The following resources, people and organizations will be involved:

. . . .

. . . .

. . . .

• The endproduct of the project will be a 4000-word essay. To be included:
  – all changes to aims and objectives identified as agreed by personal tutor
  – self-assessment, e.g. what did you learn from the project?
  – plan of action for further development

• It is agreed that the study will be assessed and evaluated by the tutor in the following manner:

. . . .

. . . .

<u>Stage 3</u>
• The first draft will be delivered to the personal tutor for marking on (date) after which students will present their final work in (date).

<u>Third Meeting: Stage 4</u>

• To agree the content for presentation at the students mini conference. The agreed date for submission is (date).

THIS CONTRACT SHOULD BE RETAINED AND RETURNED WITH YOUR COMPLETED PROJECT. YOUR CONTRACT ASSIGNMENT *CANNOT* BE MARKED *WITHOUT THIS DOCUMENT*.

Signed: . . . . Student . . . . Tutor

Date: . . . .

<u>NB:</u> Failure to submit on time = <u>fail</u>

Figure 2.21

Continued

CONTRACT ASSIGNMENT

Criteria checklist

Within the scope of the assignment, the student has/has not demonstrated:

1. an understanding of the chosen area
2. evidence of familiarity with relevant literature
3. ability to use resources
4. an ability to present an argument, supported with wider reading
5. skills of analysis, synthesis and evaluation
6. good writing skills, consistent referencing and an accurate bibliography
7. academically sound arguments
8. that he/she has met his/her own stated and agreed objectives.

(**Tutors:** Tick words or phrases above to show which criteria have been met satisfactorily and circle words or phrases to show those criteria which have not been met satisfactorily. Use the space below to expand on these.

Taking into account the criteria, and in relation to comments made, this assignment is judged to be SATISFACTORY/UNSATISFACTORY.

Signed . . . . (Tutor) . . . . (Date)

Figure 2.21

Continued

Further reading

Mentoring and reflective practice

Andrews M (1996) Using reflection to develop clinical expertise. *British Journal of Nursing* 8(8): 508–513.

Boud D, Keogh R, Walker D (eds) (1985) *Reflection: turning experience into learning*. London: Kogan Page.

Clarke A (1995) Professional development in practicum settings: reflective practice under scrutiny. *Teacher and Teacher Education* 11(3): 243–262.

Clutterbuck D (1985) *Everyone needs a mentor: how to foster talent within the organisation*. London: Institute of Personnel Management.

Copeland W, Birmingham C, Cruz E (1993) The reflective practitioner in teaching: toward a research agenda. *Teaching and Teacher Education* 9(4): 347–359.

Coutts-Jarman J (1993) Using reflection and experience in nurse education. *British Journal of Nursing* 2(1): 77–80.

Donovan J (1990) The concept and role of mentor. *Nurse Education Today* 10(4): 294–298.

Francis D (1995) The reflective journal: a window to pre-service teachers' practical knowledge. *Teacher and Teacher Education* 11(3): 229–242.

Hatton N, Smith D (1995) Reflection in teacher education: towards definition and implementation. *Teacher and Teacher Education* 11(1): 33–50.

Heath H (1998) Keeping a reflective practice diary: a practical guide. *Nurse Education Today* 18: 592–598.

Hoover L (1994) Reflective writing as a window on pre-service teachers' thought processes. *Teacher and Teacher Education* 10(1): 83–93.

Hovey SR, Vanderhorst R, Yurkovich EB (1990) Elective preceptorship: a co-operative opportunity for baccaulaureate nursing education and nursing service. *Journal of Nursing Education* 29(6): 285–287.

Hsieh NL, Knowles DW (1990) Instructor facilitation of the preceptorship relationship in nursing education. *Journal of Nursing Education* 29(6): 262–268.

Hunt D, Michael C (1983) Mentorship: a career training in development tool. *Academy of Management Review* 3: 475–485.

Jackson B (1991) Mentorship in nurse management. *Nursing Standard* 5(39): 36–39.

Johns C (1994) Nuances of reflection. *Journal of Clinical Nursing* 3(2): 71–75.

Lilley A, Newton S (1990) Mentorship: supporting the adult learner. An investigation of the working of a mentorship scheme. *Journal of Further and Higher Education* 14(3): 71–82.

Lutz WJ, Chickerella BG (1981) Professional nurturance preceptorships for undergraduate nursing. *American Journal of Nursing* 81(1): 107–109.

Morle KMF (1990) Mentorship – is it a case of the emperor's new clothes or a rose by any other name? *Nurse Education Today* 10: 66–69.

Neary M (1997) Defining the role of assessors, mentors and supervisors. *Nursing Standard*. Part 1: 11(42): 34–39. Part 2: 11(43): 34–38.

Schön D (1991) *The reflective practitioner*, 2nd edn. San Francisco: Jossey Bass.

Smith A, Russell J (1991) Using critical learning incidents in nurse education. *Nurse Education Today* 11: 284–291.

Tanner L (1998) *Nurse mentor guide*. London: Health and Care Section, Open College.

Adults as learners

Caffarella R, O'Donnell JM (1989) *Self-directed learning*. Nottingham: Department of Adult Education, University of Nottingham.

Davenport J, Davenport JA (1985) A chronology and analysis of the andragogy debate. *Adult Education Quarterly* **35**: 152–159.

Elias JL (1979) Andragogy revisited. *Adult Education* **29**(4): 252–256.

Jarvis P (1995) *Adult and continuing education: theory and practice*. London: Routledge.

Knowles M (1990) *The adult learner* (4th edn). Houston: Gulf.

London J (1973) Adult education for the 1970s: promise or illusion. *Adult Education* **24**(1): 60–70.

Merttens R (1998) Pedagogy and intimacy. *Prospero – A Journal of New Thinking in Philosophy for Education* **4**(1): 10–14.

Milligan F (1995) In defence of andragogy. *Nurse Education Today* **15**: 22–27.

Mocker DW, Noble E (1981) Training part-time instructional staff. In: Gnabowski S *et al.* (eds). *Preparing educators of adults*. San Francisco: Jossey Bass.

Rogers A (1992) *Adults learning for development*. London: Cassell.

Rogers CR (1964) *On becoming a person. A therapist's view on psychotherapy*. London: Constable.

Understanding competencies

Andrusyszyn MA (1989) Clinical evaluation of the affective domain. *Nurse Education Today* **9**: 75–81.

Ashworth P, Morrison P (1991) Problems of competence-based nurse education. *Nurse Education Today* **11**: 256–260.

Ashworth P, Saxton J (1990) On competence. *Journal of Further and Higher Education* **14**(2): 3–25.

Benedum E, Kalup A, Freed D (1990) A competency achievement program for direct caregivers. *Nursing Management* **21**(5): 32–46.

Benner P (1982) Issues in competency-based testing. *Nursing Outlook* **30**(5): 303–309.

Block JH (ed.) (1971) *Mastery learning: theory and practice*. New York: Holt, Rinehart and Winston.

Bloom BS (1965) *Taxonomy of educational objectives*. London: Longman.

Boreham NC (1978) Test–skill interaction errors in the assessment of nurses' clinical proficiency. *Journal of Occupational Psychology* **51**: 249–258.

Boss LA (1985) Teaching for clinical competence. *Nurse Educator* **10**(4): 8–12.

Brown S, Knight P (1995) *Assessing business in higher education*. London: Kogan Page.

Darbyshire P, Stewart B, Jamieson L, Tongue C (1990) New domains in nursing. *Nursing Times* **86**(27): 73–75.

Jeeves M, Greer B (1983) *The analysis of structural learning*. London: Academic Press.

Jessup G (1989) Foreword. In Burke JW (ed.). *Competence based education and training*. Lewes: Falmer Press.

Long P (1976) Judging and reporting on student nurse clinical performance – some problems for the ward sister. *International Journal of Nursing Studies* **13**: 115–121.

Marshall K (1991) NVQs: an assessment of the outcomes approach in education and training. *Journal of Further and Higher Education* **15**(3): 56–64.

McAleavey M, McAleer J (1991) Competence-based training. *British Journal of In-service Education* **17**(1): 19–23.

McGagaghie WC, Miller GE, Sajid AW, Telder TV (1978) *Competency-based curriculum development in medical education: an introduction*. Geneva: WHO.

Messick S (1975) The standard problem: meaning and values in measurement and evaluation. *American Psychologist* **October**: 955–966.

Messick S (1982) *Abilities and knowledge in educational achievement testing: the assessment of dynamic cognitive structure*. Princeton, New Jersey: Educational Testing Service.

Ross M, Carrol G, Knight J *et al*. (1988) Using the OSCE to measure clinical skills performance in nursing. *Journal of Advanced Nursing* **13**: 45–56.

Runciman P (1990) *Competency-based education and the assessment and accreditation of work-based learning in the context of Project 2000 programmes of nurse education: a literature review*. Edinburgh: National Board for Nursing, Midwifery and Health Visiting for Scotland.

Sheehan J (1979) Measurement in nursing education. *Journal of Advanced Nursing* **4**(1): 47–56.

UDACE (1991) *What can graduates do?* Consultant document. Leicester: UDACE.

Whittington D, Boore J (1988) Competence in nursing. In: Ellis R (ed.). *Professional competence and quality assurance in the caring profession*. London: Chapman and Hall.

Wolf A (1989) Can competence and knowledge mix? In: Burke JW (ed.). *Professional education and training*. Lewes: Falmer Press.

Wood V (1982) Evaluation of student nurse clinical performance – a continuing performance. *International Nursing Review* **29**(1): 11–18.

Learning contracts and contract assignments

Aavedal M, Coombe E, Fisher C, Jones M, Staneven M (1975) Developing student–professor contracts in the clinical area. *International Nursing Review* **22**: 105–108.

Akinsanya J (1987) Teaching by contract. *Senior Nurse* **7**(6): 26–27.

Boud D (1981) *Developing student autonomy in learning*. London: Kogan Page.

Burnard P (1987) Teaching the teachers. *Nursing Times* **83**(49): 64–65.

Crancer J, Maury-Hess S, Dun J (1987) Contract systems and grading policies. *Journal of Nursing Education* **16**(1): 29–35.

English National Board (1987) *Managing change in nursing education. Section 2, unit 6: learning contracts*. London: ENB.

Jones WJ (1981) Self-directed learning contracts to support change in courses and nursing organisations. *Nurse Education Today* **6**(3): 103–108.

Keyzer DM (1986) Using learning contracts. *Nursing Education Today* **6**: 103–106.

Knowles M (1975) *Self-directed learning. A guide for learners and teachers*. Chicago: Follett Publishing Company.

Knowles M (1984) *The adult learner: a neglected species*. Houston: Gulf.

Langford T (1978) Establishing a nursing contract. *Nursing Outlook* **26**: 396–398.

Layton Jones E (1972) Students select their own grades. *Nursing Outlook* **20**(5): 236–329.

Neary M (1992) Contract assignments. An integral part of adult and continuous assessment. *Senior Nurse* **12**(45): 14–17.

Neary M (1992) Planning, designing and developing an assessment tool. *Nurse Education Today* **12**: 357–367.

Neary M (1998) Contract assignments: change in teaching, learning and assessment strategies. *Educational Practice and Theory* **20**(1): 43–58.

Norton A (1989) Contract learning in nurse education: bridging the theory/practice gap. *Senior Nurse* **9**(8): 26–28.

Rauen K, Waring B (1972) The teaching contract. *Nursing Outlook* **20**(9): 594–596.

Richardson S (1987) Implementing contract learning in a senior nursing practicum. *Journal of Advanced Nursing* **12**: 201–206.

Searight MW (1976) *Preceptorship study: contracting for learning*. Philadelphia: FA Davies.

Waltho BT (1987) Contract learning – a student's perspective. *Senior Nurse* **7**(6): 28–29.

Whittaker AF (1984) Use of contract learning. *Nurse Education Today* **4**(2): 36–40.

Teaching and facilitation of learning

3

Introduction

Chapters 3–5 move towards the application of teaching, learning, assessing and evaluating to your own practice placement. There are a number of exercises throughout which encourage you to become engaged with the material in this book, which should help you to become a confident and competent facilitator, assessor and evaluator of learning.

Practitioners as teachers

The Royal College of Nursing (RCN) survey (Birch, 1975) on clinical teachers (CT) showed that on completion of a formal course, CTs were discontented with the extent to which they were able to use their hard-earned knowledge for the benefit of the students. Many CTs felt that they were thought of a 'failed tutor'. This is a situation we want to avoid with the introduction of mentors and/or assessors. We do not wish mentors and/or assessors to feel that they too have little opportunity to use the knowledge and expertise which they have gained during their years of practice. The role of a mentor is mainly to help students achieve and maintain high standards of nursing care. At present, however, most practitioners feel that the responsibility of teaching, supporting and assessing students is just another extra job added to their already overburdened workload (Davies *et al.*, 1994).

Fitness for Practice (UKCC, 1999, p.49 Sec. 5.23, Recommendation 26) suggests that service providers should support dedicated time in education for practice staff to ensure that practice staff are competent and confident in teaching and monitoring roles. Neary (1997) suggested the development of a partnership model whereby a named practitioner, supernumerary to the nursing team, has responsibility for organizing the learning environment in practice areas.

Nurse education is at present undergoing great changes but whatever happens, the practice placements within hospitals and communities will remain important. For more detailed information, read *Fitness for Practice* (UKCC, 1999).

Effective teaching in the practice placement

According to Kyriacou (1991, p.33):

> *The essence of effective teaching lies in the ability of the teacher to set up a learning experience which brings about the desired educational outcome.*

To achieve the desired learning outcome, students must be engaged in the activity of learning. It is important when thinking about effective teaching to take account of the particular characteristics of the context of the learning activity and the particular learning outcome desired. In our case, the context is patient/client nursing care and the outcome is to help students to develop into skilled, competent practitioners who can demonstrate 'fitness for practice'. The question of effective teaching comprises two main elements: first, what aspects of the learning experience contribute to effectiveness? Second, how do these aspects have the effect they do? The answers may be found in the following.

1   The quality of the teaching itself and the quality of the teacher.
2   The quality of the students and their willingness and motivation to learn.
3   The construct of active learning time, i.e. how much time is spent on outcome-related activities.

To these qualities of effective teaching we need to add the use of reinforcement, directing attention and promoting transfer of learning and skills. The characteristics of a 'good' teacher will include clarity, cognitive matching and pacing. Figure 3.1 helps to illustrate these elements.

Mocker and Noble (1981, pp.45–46) constructed a fairly full list of competencies for an adult educator, but even they warn their readers that it is neither exhaustive nor is it a blueprint for training. According to these authors, an adult educator should be able to:

Figure 3.1

Characteristics of a good teacher–student relationship.

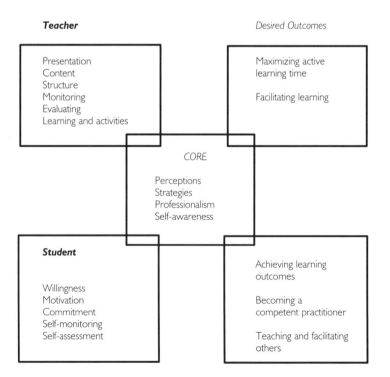

92

1 communicate effectively with learners
2 develop effective working relationships with learners
3 reinforce positive attitudes towards learners
4 develop a climate that will encourage learners to participate
5 establish a basis for mutual respect with learners
6 adjust rate of instruction to the learner's rate of progress
7 adjust teaching to accommodate individual and group characteristics
8 differentiate between teaching children and teaching adults
9 devise instructional categories that will develop the learner's confidence
10 maintain the learner's interest in classroom activities*
11 adjust a programme to respond to the changing needs of learners
12 use classrooms and other settings that provide a comfortable learning environment*
13 recognize learners' potentiality for growth
14 place learners at their instructional level
15 summarize and review the main points of a lesson or demonstration
16 participate in a self-evaluation of teaching effectiveness
17 provide continuous feedback to the learners on their educational progress
18 select those components of a subject area that are essential to learners
19 coordinate and supervise classroom activities*
20 determine those principles of learning that apply to adults
21 demonstrate belief in innovation and experimentation by willingness to try new approaches in the classroom
22 plan independent study with learners (in our case, action plans)
23 apply knowledge of material and procedures gained from other teachers
24 relate classroom activities to the experience of learners.

* In our case, in clinical practice placements.

TEACHING AND LEARNING

Let us start with three reflective statements.

> *If you give a man a fish, he will have a single meal. If you teach him how to fish, he will eat all his life. (Kwan Tzu, Chinese poet)*

> *What I hear, I forget.*
> *What I see, I remember.*
> *What I do, I understand. (Anonymous)*

> *You can't teach a man anything, you can only help him to find it within himself. (Galileo)*

Nurses and the other health-care professionals in the ward situation are frequently heard to say, 'I haven't the time to teach - I'm here to care for the patient!' When evaluating a clinical placement, students have frequently said that they learned nothing because there were no lectures or teaching sessions.

It is a sad reflection that these perceptions of learning fail to acknowledge that teaching does not have to provide all the material for the student but a stimulating environment for active learning to take place.

Almost everything we do in our daily lives is directly or indirectly the result of learning. Learning as a human ability has been extensively studied and many complex explanations exist. That learning takes place can only be assumed from observable changes. However, the observations we might make do not reflect 'silent' changes that may be taking place within that individual.

Nursing, midwifery and health visiting and other health professions require practitioners to be both credible and competent and up to date in both theory and practice. We should also assist our equals and our subordinates to develop competence in accordance with their needs. For example, the Code of Professional Conduct for Nursing, Midwifery and Health Visiting states (UKCC, 1992):

> *As a registered nurse, midwife and health visitor you are personally accountable for your practice and in the exercise of your professional accountability must: ... assist professional colleagues in the context of your own knowledge, experience and sphere of responsibility, to develop their professional competence and assist others in the care team including informal carers, to contribute safely and to a degree appropriate to their roles...*

Society's needs and expectations of health care are ever changing with the result that nursing is in a reciprocal state of change. Change influences the working notion of competence and being up to date, with the effect that the notion of being competent today may be redefined tomorrow.

> *Whatever competence means today we can be sure its meaning will have changed by tomorrow. The foundation for future professional competence seems to be the capacity to learn how to learn. (Ogier, 1986, pp.52–57)*

The capacity to learn is the raw material that enables health professionals to be accountable for their practice and the exercise of professional accountability.

Activity

1 Examine and reflect on the above statement relating to competence.
2 Examine your own understanding of 'a competent student', 'a competent nurse' and/or 'a competent professional'.

Learning by doing

The widely held belief that people learn best by doing is considered in the following questions.

- What ideas or theories are there to help us to explain and justify the belief that we learn best by doing?
- Does everyone learn by doing in the same way or to the same extent?
- What teaching and learning methods can we use which involve learning by doing?
- How can we change our teaching to involve learning by doing when we are surrounded by constraints?
- What can go wrong?
- How can we encourage our colleagues to change their teaching to involve more learning by doing?

What is learning?

According to Ryle (1983), learning is what occurs when a person makes sense out of what he encounters or experiences in interacting with self, others and the environment. Huddleston and Unwin (1997) also support this view of learning and Child (1981) suggests that learning occurs whenever one adopts new behaviour patterns or modifies existing ones in a way which has some influence on future performance or attitudes.

Teaching in small steps contrasts well with learning in large chunks. *Gestalt* theory sees things as a whole (the whole being greater than the sum of the parts). *Gestalt* theory relies heavily on the use of the student's past experience, the student's correct perception of the present situation and moving from the 'known' to the 'unknown'. As nurse practitioners, you will need to consider the process of learning, which will enable you to create the best possible learning environment, for example:

1   assess the student's learning needs
2   plan the learning
3   implement the learning plan
4   evaluate the learning.

We have already agreed that a large percentage of nursing consists of actions which, when analysed, can be described as psychomotor skills. Psychomotor skills have three characteristics:

1   a chain of muscular movements called motor responses
2   skills involve the coordination of hand and eye movement
3   skills require the organization of chains into a complex response pattern.

A chain is a sequence of actions. These actions involve hand–eye coordination and also information received by the senses. For this reason, skills are also called perceptual-motor skills. According to Fitts and Posner (1969), skills learning falls into three phases – cognitive, fixation and autonomous.

Cognitive

During this phase the student attempts to intellectualize the skill and form a verbal plan which guides execution.

Fixation

Students practise the correct sequences until the chances of making errors are reduced and the behaviour becomes fixed. This will take time and it must be remembered that each student will learn at a different pace and time must be given to allow practice.

Autonomous

These students no longer go through the verbal plan and they increase the speed and accuracy with which they perform the skill. The skill becomes increasingly resistant to stress influences and can be continued despite outside influence as no conscious effort is needed.

What is important when facilitating skills learning is to give positive feedback on the success of each stage of the student's learning. Knowledge of results is important, especially when teaching the intricate skills of nursing care.

Activity

Think of your most vivid learning experience as a practitioner in your practice area. Making some notes about it, answer the following questions.

- Why was it the most memorable?
- How did you feel?
- What happened and what did you learn?

Now reflect on the responses to the above exercise and ask yourself, were the three phases of Fitts and Posner's acquisition of skills evident as part of my learning?

Reflection on teaching and learning

Reactive learning occurs via reflection-in-action. Reflective knowledge is gained and generated from practice. Schön (1994) suggests that reflection on activity helps professionals to understand the complex and highly contextual situations they may encounter in practice.

The use of reflective practice allows deeper analysis to occur and encourages internalization, a proficient mode of learning. With continued use of reflective practice, however, the teacher and student may utilize synthesis skills more readily and quickly bring into the situation dissemination, expertise and evaluative skills. These will be valued particularly highly when completing learning contracts and assignments in practice placements.

THE LEARNING CONTRACT: PROFESSIONAL DEVELOPMENT

As part of self-development, the practitioner will be encouraged to be innovative and creative in the achievement of their own learning outcomes. They must be able to demonstrate how the integration of theory and practice has been successfully achieved. This facilitation will generate a dialogue with the assessor and/or mentor and will also strengthen reflection-in-action for the practitioner. This clarifies what the practitioner is expected to achieve as a minimum. Within the learning contract, it permits practitioners to identify precisely how they intend to achieve those learning outcomes and, indeed, how each of them has integrated the learning outcomes into practice when enacting the role of mentor and/or assessor.

The learning contract does not have columns/boxes which require 'ticks' to be made, as this does not demonstrate that the practitioner has (a) integrated theory to practice or (b) is working at the particular level expected of them. Therefore, the practitioner is required to write in some detail, together with an experienced assessor or mentor, exactly how they have achieved the learning outcomes with some degree of evidence that the learning outcomes have been successfully mastered.

The experiential taxonomy model below (Steinaker and Bell, 1979) illustrates the levels at which practitioners should be focusing within each stage of the teaching and learning process as a facilitator, assessor and evaluator of their own as well as students' learning.

Activity

Read and reflect on the taxonomy and try to identify where you are with:

- your own learning
- your students' learning.

Experiential taxonomy model

1   *Exposure*. Consciousness of an experience. This involves two kinds of exposure and a readiness for further experience.

   1.1   **Sensory**. Through various sensory stimuli one becomes exposed to the possibility of an experience.

   1.2   **Response**. Peripheral mental reaction to sensory stimuli. At this point one rejects or accepts further interaction with the experience.

   1.3   **Readiness**. At this level one accepts the experience and anticipates participation.

2.   *Participation*. The decision to become physically a part of an experience. There are two levels of interaction within this category.

   2.1   **Representation**. Reproducing an existing mental image of the experience, mentally or physically or both, i.e. visualizing, verbalizing, role playing, dramatic play. This can be done in two ways.

2.1.1 *Covertly*: as a private, personal 'walk-through' rehearsal.

2.1.2 *Overtly*: in a small/large group interaction, i.e. the classroom or playground.

2.2 **Modification**. The experience develops with the input of past personal activities and the experience grows. As there is a personal input into the participation, one moves from role player to active participant.

3. *Identification*. As the participant modifies the experience, the process of identification with the experience begins. There are four levels of activity within this category.

3.1 **Reinforcement**. As the experience is modified and repeated there is a reinforcement of the experience involving a decision to identify with the experience.

3.2 **Emotional**. The participant becomes emotionally identified with the experience. It becomes 'my experience'.

3.3 **Personal**. The participant moves from an emotional identification to an intellectual commitment which involves a rational decision of identification.

3.4 **Sharing**. Once the process of identification is accomplished the participant begins to share the experience with others as a positive factor in his life. This kind of positive sharing continues through category 4 (internalization).

4. *Internalization*. The participant moves from identification to internalization when the experience begins to affect the lifestyle of the participant. There are two levels in this category.

4.1 **Expansion**. The experience enlarges into many aspects of the participant's life, changes attitudes and activities as a result of the experience. When these become more than temporary the participant moves to the next category.

4.2 **Intrinsic**. The participant's lifestyle becomes characterized by the experience and that character remains more constant than at the expansion level.

5. *Dissemination*. The experience moves beyond internalization to the dissemination of the experience. It goes beyond positive sharing which began at level 3 and involves two levels of activity.

5.1 **Informational**. The participant seeks to stimulate others to have an equivalent experience through descriptive and personalized sharing (advertising).

5.2 **Homiletic**. The participant sees the experience as an imperative for others to have.

It should be noted that the categories of this taxonomy are stated in positive terms, while an experience can bring forth either positive or negative reactions. For the purpose of teaching and learning, a positive statement of categories is essential. A teacher seldom, if ever, purposefully plans experiences in which learners are expected to react negatively.

This taxonomy of experience relates closely to existing taxonomies of educational objectives. It is perhaps most closely related to the affective taxonomy, particularly at the identification (3) and internalization (4) categories. Yet it augments the affective domain by specifying the exposure and motivational aspects of experience in its exposure (1) category. Additionally, it adds a further dimension of human activity beyond category 3 of the affective taxonomy (characterization of a value complex) by including the process of disseminating an experience. This is not touched upon by the affective taxonomy. This experiential taxonomy provides, therefore, a more complete classification of human activity than does the affective taxonomy.

Activity

1 Examine the taxonomy carefully and place your students at the level you perceive they are at.
2 Having done this, now take the opportunity to work with your students and ask them to place themselves at the level they perceive themselves to be at.
3 On completion, compare the outcomes. If they differ, you will both need to discuss the reasons and a plan of action may need to be agreed upon to help bring the positions closer to each other.
4 You may need to create and agree a new learning contract to enhance further developments.

LEARNING FROM DOING

It is common for courses to be described as either practical or theoretical: as either involving doing or involving thinking. Learning is seen to take place either 'on the job' or in the classroom. Even in courses which contain both elements, they tend to be sharply divided, i.e. an academic or clinical practitioner, a lecture in the classroom whilst a practical assessor/mentor is in charge of the follow-up practical experience in a clinical setting. It is also common for both types of course to have limited success. The UKCC *Fitness for Practice* (1999, Recommendation 19, 4.53, p.42) states 'To make the best use of practice placements, interpersonal and practice skills should be fostered by the use of experiential and problem-based learning, increased use of skills laboratories and access to information technology, particularly in clinical practice'.

Nurse education has a long history of providing practical experience for students, which is not always directly related to the theoretical components of the course (Neary, 1997).

It is not sufficient simply to have an experience in order to learn. Without reflecting upon this experience it may quickly be forgotten or its learning potential lost. It is from the feelings and thoughts emerging from this reflection that generalizations or concepts can be generated and it is generalizations which enable new situations to be tackled effectively.

Similarly, if it is intended that behaviour should be changed by learning, it is not sufficient simply to learn new concepts and develop new generalizations. This learning must be tested out in new situations. The student must make the link between theory and action by planning for that action, carrying it out and then reflecting upon it, relating what happens back to the theory.

It is not enough just to do and neither is it enough just to think. Nor is it enough simply to do and think. Learning from experience must involve links between the doing and the thinking. The four-stage model of learning by doing, which is elaborated in Figure 3.2, is that of Kolb (1978, 1984).

Learning from experience involves four stages which follow each other in a cycle, as shown in Figure 3.2.

The terms used here as labels for the four stages come from Kolb's (1984) experiential learning theory and, placed in this sequence, they form the experiential learning cycle. The cycle can be entered by the health-care student at any point, but its stages must be followed in sequence.

Example 1

A student might start learning how to lift and handle a patient safely by taking part in supervised practice with another student, which would give experience of (a simulation of) what it is like (Stage 1 in Figure 3.2).

The skilled practitioner might then ask: 'How did that feel? What might you have done differently?' to encourage the student to be reflective about the experience (Stage 2).

Figure 3.2

Kolb's four-stage experiential learning theory.

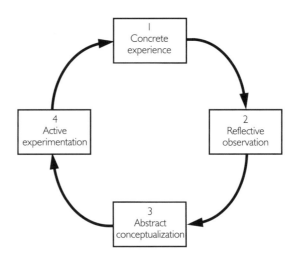

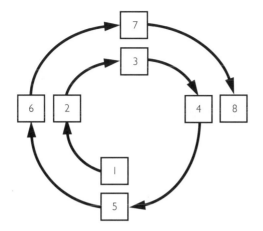

Figure 3.3

Taking and recording blood pressure.

That night the student could look up, in a textbook, how to lift patients and read about the theoretical and practical reasons for doing it in particular ways (Stage 3).

Next day, confronted with a real patient to lift, the student could reflect: 'As a result of what happened yesterday, and because of what I read last night, this is why I ought to do it like this' (Stage 4). This would provide a new experience and develop understanding of the principle of moving, handling and lifting of patients and start the health-care student on the next learning cycle.

Example 2

This learning cycle is exactly the same as that involved in learning to take and record blood pressure. The sequence might involve learning activities illustrated in Figure 3.3.

1   Taking notes in a lecture about the contributory factors that control blood pressure and how blood pressure can be measured and recorded.
2   Taking a sphygmomanometer and a stethoscope and experimenting with the equipment on a colleague.
3   Gaining the experience of identifying the sounds heard in the stethoscope measured against the mercury column and recording them on a chart.
4   Looking at the results and comparing these with others.
5   Discussing possible explanations of these results.
6   Designing and running a trial to test whether exercise or heavy smoking plays a role in blood pressure.
7   Taking and recording the blood pressure of participants in the trial.
8   Looking at the results and comparing them to see whether there are any variations.

Activity

Using example 2, devise an appropriate learning cycle to facilitate students' learning of:

1   knowledge of the pathophysiology of shock
2   the difficulty of assessing blood pressure in a shocked patient
3   the application of knowledge to practice.

OVERVIEW OF EXPERIENTIAL LEARNING

The following list of points may help to clarify what experiential learning is and what it is not.

1   Students are involved in an active exploration of experience. Experience is used to test out ideas and assumptions rather than to obtain practice passively. Practice can be very important but it is greatly enhanced by reflection.
2   Students must selectively reflect on their experience in a critical way, rather than take experience for granted and assume that the experience on its own is sufficient.
3   The experience must matter to the student. Students must be committed to the process of exploring and learning.
4   There must be scope for the student to exercise some independence from the teacher/skilled practitioner. Teachers/skilled practitioners have an important role in devising appropriate experiences and facilitating reflection. However, the transmission of information is but a minor element and the teacher/skilled practitioner cannot experience what the student experiences or reflect for the student.
5   Experiential learning is not the same as 'discovery' learning. Learning by doing is not simply a matter of letting students loose and hoping that they discover things for themselves in a haphazard way through sudden bursts of inspiration. The nature of the activity may be carefully designed by the teacher/skilled practitioner and the experience may need to be carefully reviewed and analysed afterwards for learning to take place. A crucial feature of experiential learning is the structure devised by the teacher/skilled practitioner within which learning takes place.
6   Openness to experience is necessary for students to have evidence upon which to reflect. It is therefore crucial to establish an appropriate emotional tone for students, one which is safe and supportive and which encourages students to value their own experience and to trust themselves to draw conclusions from it. This openness may not exist at the outset but may be fostered through successive experiential learning cycles.
7   Experiential learning involves a cyclical sequence of learning activities. Teaching methods can be selected to provide a structure to

each stage of the cycle and to take students through the appropriate sequence.

Activity

Using example 2.

- Select a particular competency from Appendix 5 and/or from Rule 18 (p.141).
- Devise the appropriate learning cycle.
- Think how you would facilitate the student's learning and assess the student's performance and learning outcomes.

Activity

1 Reconsider your answers to the previous two exercises against Kolb's experiential learning cycle.
2 Reflect on any differences identified.

Learning styles

Just as courses may be seen to be either mainly practical or mainly theoretical, so individuals may have particular preferences to their learning. While one person might prefer to formulate plans and define potential problems, another might prefer to get on and carry out the plans. There are distinct learning styles associated with each of the stages of the experiential learning cycle.

In order to learn effectively from experience it is necessary to utilize the abilities associated with each of the four learning styles in turn.

Rather than have extreme styles, it is preferable to be adaptable and to operate in the style appropriate to each successive stage of the experiential learning cycle at different stages in a learning task. It can be valuable for students to recognize their own habitual learning style and the characteristics of learning tasks as this may help them to become more flexible in meeting the varied demands of learning situations. Practitioners need to become aware that because of their professional and personal experiences, their style of learning and the strategies they use for their own learning can often differ from those of students. Remember, students are individuals with individual learning habits. These abilities are illustrated in Figure 3.4.

Activity

- Take some time out from this session and reflect on your own learning style.
- Write these reflections down.
- At the end of the session write down what you have gained from this exercise.

Figure 3.4

Abilities associated with each stage of the learning cycle.

Concrete experience	
Can carry out plans	Imaginative, good at generating ideas
Interested in action and results	Can view situation from different angles
Adapts to immediate circumstances	Open to experience
Trial and error style	Recognizes problems
Sets objectives	Investigates
Sets schedules	Senses opportunities
Experimentation	*Reflection*
Good at practical applications	Ability to create theoretical models
Makes decisions	Compares alternatives
Focuses efforts	Defines problems
Does well when there is one answer	Establishes criteria
Evaluates plans	Formulates hypotheses
Selects from alternatives	
Conceptualization	

Practical methods to implement the experiential learning cycle

The practical teaching and learning methods identified in this section are categorized according to the phase of the experiential learning cycle with which they are concerned.

1. Planning for experience

This section offers methods for preparing students prior to experiences: for example, through action planning and the negotiation of learning contracts and contract assignments (Keyzer, 1986; Neary, 1992a).

Figure 3.5

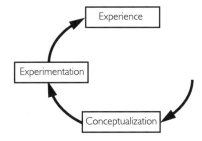

2. Increasing awareness of experience

This section is concerned with methods for heightening students' awareness of their experiences so that they notice more and have more

Figure 3.6

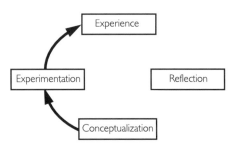

material upon which to reflect afterwards: for example, through the use of log books, reflective journals, learning journals.

3. Reviewing and reflecting upon experience

This section is concerned with what happens after learning experiences and how learning points can be drawn out through structure-led reflection: for example, through the use of video recordings and self-assessment.

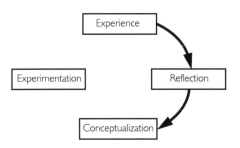

Figure 3.7

4. Providing substitute experience

This section is concerned with ways of providing classroom-based experiences as substitutes for work or other experience: for example, through the use of role plays.

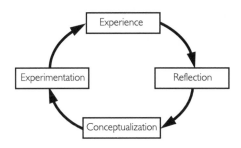

Figure 3.8

(a) *Planning for experience*
- action plans
- setting objectives and learning outcomes
- designing experiments
- observation checklists
- devising criteria
- learning contracts and contract assignments
- action research

Figure 3.9

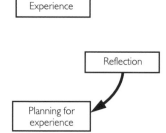

(b)   *Increasing awareness of experience*
- log books and learning journals
- listening exercises
- questions
- increasing awareness of feelings
- silent demonstrations

Figure 3.10

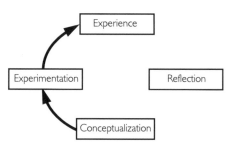

(c)   *Reviewing and reflecting upon experience*
- diaries and reflective journals
- using video and audio recordings
- peer appraisal
- structured discussions
- structured debriefing
- self-assessment
- reflection checklists and questionnaires
- 'shared time' and 'mutual interviewing'
- modelling reflection

Figure 3.11

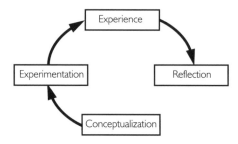

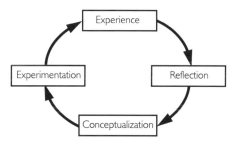

Figure 3.12

(d) Providing substitute experiences
- case studies/learning contracts
- games
- role play
- assessing through substitute experiences

OPPORTUNISTIC LEARNING

As part of the teaching, learning and assessment process, students must be given the opportunity to learn and practise complex nursing skills. Opportunistic learning which will enable students to develop their professional competencies should be identified by both mentors and assessors (Neary, 1992a, 1996).

Opportunistic learning can also form part of a learning contract and contract assignment which will enhance the application of theory to practice, discussed in Chapter 2.

For examples of opportunistic learning, see Appendices 3 and 4 (pp. 193–199).

Activity

1 Think about your own speciality in your profession and try to create learning opportunities for your student.
2 Identify the learning outcomes the students are expected to achieve (revisit Chapter 2 on learning outcomes).
3 Design an action plan which will help you and the student to achieve and reflect on the learning outcomes.

Activity

As the conclusion to this section, now REFLECT, assess and evaluate your own teaching and learning competencies on the next two pages.

COMPETENCY UNIT: PRINCIPLES OF LEARNING

Learning Outcomes: The participant is able to use appropriate and effective teaching and learning strategies. This achievement signifies that the participant has:

STATEMENT OF COMPETENCE	SELF-ASSESSMENT	REFLECTIVE COMMENTS
Identified examples of teaching and learning strategies being applied during given teaching and learning situations.		
Derived a range of key conditions/principles and strategies of learning from the broad theoretical perspectives which are applicable to given teaching learning situations.		
Designed a unit of learning experiences which contains these conditions/strategies and application of related key principles in order to promote effective learning.		
Indicated a range of conditions and situations likely to support the learning required (concepts, skills, attitudes, etc.)		

COMPETENCY UNIT: MANAGEMENT OF LEARNING

Learning Outcomes: The participant is able to create and maintain an effective learning environment and use the appropriate methodologies for teaching and learning. This achievement signifies that the participant has:

STATEMENT OF COMPETENCE	SELF-ASSESSMENT	REFLECTIVE COMMENTS
Stated and explained the main factors affecting the creation and maintenance of an effective teaching and learning environment.		
Applied at least three basic strategies of teaching and learning, i.e. negotiation/facilitation, demonstration, discussion.		
Applied a set of principles of learning to the creation and maintenance of an appropriate environment for learners and/or groups of learners.		
Managed learning in a range of learning encounters using a variety of management strategies.		
Established and applied criteria for an evaluation of his/her management of learning and the learning environment.		

FURTHER READING

Bachman C (1990) Cited in Farley A, Hedry C (1997) Teaching practical skills: a guide for preceptors. *Nursing Standard* **11**(29): 46–48.

Birch J (1975) *To nurse or not to nurse*. London: RCN.

Burnard P (1986) *Learning human skills: a guide for nurses*. London: Heinemann Nursing.

English National Board for Nursing, Midwifery and Health Visiting (1987) *Managing change in nursing education, section 2.4 The nurse teacher's role*. London: ENB.

Entwistle N, Ramsden P (1983) *Understanding student learning*. Beckenham, Kent: Croom Helm.

Farley A, Hedry C (1997) Teaching practical skills: a guide for preceptors. *Nursing Standard* **11**(29): 46–48.

Gagne RM (1970) *The conditions of learning*. New York: Holt, Rinehart and Winston.

Gomez F, Gomez F (1987) Cited in Studdy S, Nicol M, Fox Hiley A (1994) Teaching and learning clinical skills, part 1 – development of a multidisciplinary skills centre. *Nurse Education Today* **14**(2): 177–185.

Hegstad L, Zsohar H (1986) A study of the cost effectiveness of providing psychomotor practice in teaching intravenous infusion techniques. *Journal of Nursing Education* **25**(1): 10–14.

Jones S, Rafferty M (1996) Practical matters. *Nursing Times* **92**(35): 47–52.

Kolb DA (1978) *Learning style inventory. Technical manual*. Boston: McBeri.

Kolb DA (1984) *Experiential learning: experience as the source of learning and development*. Englewood Cliffs, NJ: Prentice-Hall.

Lewis T (1990) The hospital ward sister: professional gatekeeper. *Journal of Advanced Nursing* **15**(7): 808–815.

Minton D (1991) *Teaching skills in further and adult education*. London: Macmillan.

Neary M (1997) Project 2000 students' survival kit: a return to the practical room/ nursing skills laboratory. *Nurse Education Today* **17**: 46–52

O'Donnell J (1995) Learning power. *Nursing Times* **91**(14): 45.

Quinn FM (2000) *The principles and practice of nurse education*. Cheltenham: Stanley Thornes.

Sachdeva A (1996) Preceptorship, mentorship and the adult learner in medical and health sciences education. *Journal of Cancer Education* **1**(3): 131–136.

Studdy S, Nichol M, Fox Hiley A (1994) Teaching and learning clinical skills, part 1 – development of a multidisciplinary skills centre. *Nurse Education Today* **14**(2): 177–185.

Studdy S, Nichol M, Fox Hiley A (1994) Teaching and learning clinical skills, part 2 – development of a teaching model and schedule of skills development. *Nurse Education Today* **14**(3): 186–193.

Weil SW and McGill J (eds) (1990) *Making sense of experiential learning, diversity in theory and practice*. Society for Research into Higher Education. Buckingham: Open University Press.

Assessment of students' clinical competence

4

Introduction

Assessment is a contentious issue. Many people are active propo-nents of an assessment system and point to the ways in which its presence upholds the standards, values and beliefs of the particular profession of which it is a part. Others would, however, be passionate denouncers of assessment as a tyrannical means of persuasion, coercion and social control, enhancing the power of one group of people – qualified members – over another group – the students (Rowntree, 1987).

Dictionary definitions tend to agree that to assess is to put a value on something. Since the passing of the Nurses Registration Act in 1992, this value, from a nursing viewpoint, has been the status quo and respectability that the qualification of registration carries with it.

Over the years, the traditional views on the purposes of assessment have continued to grow within health-care professions. The fact that students will be assessed is an accepted and welcomed part of the profession's culture. The ways in which that assessment has been inter-preted over the years have, however, changed.

In nursing, for example, the UKCC and the National Boards have long recognized the advantages of continuous assessment. However, only in recent years have the national bodies and colleges been in a position to seriously consider the implementation of such a system in nurse education.

However, it can equally be argued that there is no one definitive system of continuous assessment. Professional and educational bodies may decide to introduce systems which, whilst being principally based on continuous assessment, still retain an element of formal summative assessment.

The system adopted by the National Boards is such a system. Whilst large elements are based on a purist approach to continuous assessment (for nursing practice) it has retained elements of formal unseen assessment for the theoretical component of the course. It could be argued that this creates a gap in the application of theory to practice.

Nurse education challenges: planning for the new culture

Neary (1996) suggested that on completion of each clinical experience the student should have a level of knowledge commensurate with her/his clinical experience, apply aspects of nursing skill according to the principle taught, including aspects of patient/client care, management and teaching and display appropriate professional attitudes. Evidence for this could be gathered through the use of portfolios and learning journals.

The use of a portfolio of practice experience should be extended to demonstrate a student's fitness for practice and provide evidence of rational decision making and clinical judgement. (UKCC, 1999, p.38, Sec. 4.27, Recommendation 14)

The portfolio should be assessed through rigorous practice assessment tools which identify the skills which students have acquired and highlight any deficits which need to be addressed. (UKCC, 1999, Sec. 4.28, Recommendation 15)

Research by Davies *et al.* (1994) and Neary (1996) showed that written process records in the form of journals, portfolios and analyses of clinical situations in the form of critical incidents were required as part of continuous assessment at most colleges. These records frequently revealed awkward, hesitant responses such as 'I was afraid I would say the wrong thing' or 'I just did not know how to answer his [patient's] question'. It could be argued that requiring students to adhere to a list of questions or to address only the list of objectives in the assessment booklet clouds effective communication. A patient's/client's incidental comments may not be explored because they led away from achieving pre-set objectives.

As students progressed through the course they became more receptive and sensitive to incidental remarks and non-verbal cues, their minds being less occupied by singular objective achievements and more open to the interactions and interplay of personalities, perceptions and environments. There also came a point during the varied practice placement allocations at which the student could be expected to have reached an acceptable level of competence having been, up to that point, acquiring the appropriate knowledge and practice to achieve the agreed learning outcomes.

This fact had relevance for the debate concerning when and how frequently assessment should take place and whether assessment of progress should be done intermittently or continuously. In a scheme of intermittent assessment, times for assessment may be identified, implying that in the intervening periods the student had a 'breathing space' during which work would not be formally assessed. In Neary's study, students indicated that with continuous assessment there was no let-up and that any aspect of the students' work was assessed at any time. There was always pressure on the student to maintain an agreed standard of work, which ensured a safe level of competence, to the point of being stressful.

In action, the difference between the two methods of assessment tends not to be as clear-cut as the terms might suggest. The type of assessment carried out depended not so much on the label applied to the scheme as on the criteria identified and their interpretation and implementation. Both types of assessment included some reference to time intervals, aspects of performance to be included and records of assessment made and the degree of formality associated with the occasion of assessment determined some 'staging' of the performance by

BASIC NURSING EXPERIENCE			Comments:			
With the help of the skilled practitioner the student should select suitable patients and demonstrate her ability to:						
1. Competency A:						
Advise the patient on the promotion of health and discuss with the patient the methods that will help to prevent further development of the illness.			Continuous Assessment			
			LEVEL OF PERFORMANCE			
SKILL	**KNOWLEDGE**	**NOTES FOR GUIDANCE**	**SELF-ASSESS**	**1ST ASSESS**	**2ND ASSESS**	**3RD ASSESS**
Enabling Objectives: The student will be able to: Identify the possible causes of this patient's illness Recognize the need for health education within this patient's potential *Critical* *Demonstrate her ability to communicate clearly with the patient	Discuss the meaning of primary, secondary and tertiary health education	Junior students will have limited knowledge of health education but they should be able to communicate some aspect of health education to the patient		·		

Code: A = Achieved; B = Borderline; F = Failed to achieve

the student. The scheme of assessment designed by some colleges resulted in a series of frequent intermittent assessments, to which the term continuous assessment was appropriately applied as shown in Figure 4.1.

It is widely held in education that understanding of the method of assessment is fundamental to its effectiveness, which in our case involves the scheme of clinical progress assessment to be carried out, including the use of continuous assessment booklets and documents, as well as the significance of the grades, scores and comments written by the assessors.

In relation to mainstream education, Smith and Neisworth (1969) suggested that:

The assessment process should not determine what is to be taught and learned. It should be the servant, not the master of the curriculum, yet it should not simply be a bolted-on addition at the

Figure 4.1

Continuous assessment – a sample document.

end. Rather it should be an integral part of the educational process continually providing both 'feedback' and 'feed forward'. It therefore needs to be incorporated systematically into teaching strategies and practices at all levels.

In Neary's study (1996), many assessors agreed that students should have constant feedback. However, not all trained staff carried this through in the clinical area. This was a matter of particular importance because continuous assessment relies on a formative system in which feedback is a key element. Emphasis is laid on the process by which the student arrives at the point at which summative grades or scores are awarded and constructive comments on the student's progress become part of the process. Some assessors, when they had to justify their opinions of students' work by making specific and constructive comments, felt vulnerable. Nevertheless, research data suggest that staff did see the value of their comments and that students considered them to be helpful.

The data indicated that the majority of students were satisfied with the feedback they received on their performance. In general terms, feedback concerns itself with linking a system's output to its inputs, enabling monitoring and control. In an education context, feedback provided by various methods of review and assessment gives information about the student's progress. Being able to give feedback about learning outcomes and achievements was seen as an important skill for all qualified staff.

However, an understanding of the various contexts to which a competence might relate was not clear. Student and assessor interview data highlighted weakness in the assessment documentation in relating the competencies to specific client groups, e.g. mental health and child health, and revealed both student and assessor uncertainty about the 'what' and 'how' of assessment, a somewhat confused understanding of competencies. Many assessors ignored the college-set learning objectives, using instead clinically set objectives agreed on the spot. Davies *et al.* (1994) supported this finding. Both students and assessors found the college-set learning objectives restrictive and ill-fitted to the daily practice in the 'real world' of clinical placement and having more relevance to non-clinical placements, for example in social services, occupational health and factories, to which students were allocated for three- to four-day periods. Assessors felt that it was important that each clinical area should construct learning opportunities, so that each student would know what could be learnt during each clinical placement and speciality. Assessors believed that, with identification of learning objectives, education and service staff could formulate appropriate assessment criteria and the target levels required for each stage of student training. Both students and assessors expressed a need for clearer guidelines, less jargon, fewer objectives and more practice orientation and to be given more opportunities to discuss students' standard of performance, ability and achievements through assessment tools such as contract assignments, practice portfolios and reflective/learning journals.

Activity

Think back to the last time you were assessed.
Write notes under the following headings.

1 What form did the assessment take?
2 How did you feel before the asssessment?
3 How did you feel about the assessment?
4 How did you feel after the assessment?
5 Was the assessment:
   ● one-off or continuous assessment?
   ● product or process?
6 What did you learn from the assessment?
7 What did you learn from the experience itself?
8 What stands out most in your mind as a result of the assessment?

Use this format to complete the above exercise.

1 Assessment	2 Feelings	3 Feelings	4 Feelings	5 Type of assessment	6 Learn from assessment	7 Learn from experience

9 What stands out the most? (Adapted from Race, 1992)

Activity

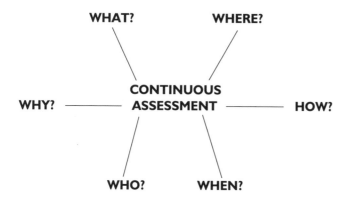

Take each of the six questions above and list the actual and potential responses in the boxes on pages 116–118, giving your rationale.

WHY ASSESS?

List	Rationale

WHAT TO ASSESS?

List	Rationale

WHERE TO ASSESS?

List	Rationale

HOW TO ASSESS?

List	Rationale

WHEN TO ASSESS?

List	Rationale

WHO TO ASSESS?

List	Rationale

CONTINUOUS ASSESSMENT OF PRACTICE

The use of continuous assessment as a method of evaluating progress and learning, both in the academic and clinical situation, is now established in many educational institutions. For some institutions it is early days and requires time for those involved to become familiar with the concept.

The use of this method of assessment in the clinical area demands a high level of enthusiasm and commitment from assessors. It takes time and effort but is viewed as a much preferred method of assessment. It can be stressful for the student; however, if utilized as a teaching tool as well as an assessment tool then some of the stress for students will be alleviated (Neary, 1996).

Aims of continuous assessment

This method of assessment has the following benefits.

Self-assessment

It will encourage the health-care student to assess his/her own performance at the beginning of and during the experience and motivate his/her learning throughout the experience.

Learning action plans

It will act as a guide to the assessor in pinpointing areas of practice where the health-care student needs extra help and tuition.

Assessment process

It will prompt the assessor to give positive feedback at frequent intervals throughout the experience.

Standards of competence

It will help in the promotion of improved standards of professional health care to patients and clients.

Why assess?

For three reasons:

1 to ascertain the level of theoretical knowledge
2 to ascertain the level of practical clinical skills
3 to ascertain insight into the level of professional attitudes.

However, Rielly (1975) argued that: 'Assessment is seen as a positive process whose primary purpose is to assess growth'. This was supported by Satterly (1981) who suggests that assessment is a term which includes all the processes and products of learning. This helps to identify several more reasons why assessment is undertaken, as follows.

Motivation

For both student and practitioner, most students becoming increasingly conscientious about their studies throughout the assessment process.

Attainment

Indicates areas in which further tuition or practice is needed; it also reflects the success of the teaching and the course.

Diagnosis/feedback

Assessment in the clinical areas tends to evaluate more accurately the quality of patient/client care. Moreover, with a clinical-based education programme, the practitioners seem to have more influence on the outcome of students' behaviour than the college-based tutor.

Providing and maintaining standards

This is a means of safeguarding public safety and health by restricting employment in some areas, e.g. hospitals, to those who have demonstrated a knowledge of, and compliance with, safe or hygienic procedures. It is an attempt to ensure adequate standards of work on the part of those who serve the public. It is also a measure of the employability of members of the health service workforce or of persons whom it may consider employing.

Prediction of the future behaviour of a health-care professional

On successful completion of a professional course, most practitioners return to work on the wards, in departments or the community.

Fitness for practice

To enable students to consolidate their education and their competence in practice.

Professional licence to practice

For example, the UKCC (1996) Code of Professional Conduct states:

> As a qualified nurse, midwife or health visitor, you are personally accountable for your practice and, in the exercise of your professional accountability, must:
> - maintain and improve your professional knowledge and competence (Section 3).
> - acknowledge any limitations in your knowledge and competence and decline any duties or responsibilities unless able to perform them in a safe and skilled manner.

Activity

Within your professional career there must have been a time when you have experienced the following thoughts.

- She should never have qualified – her attitude and skills are appalling.
- She is a disgrace to the profession.
- I am ashamed that she calls herself a nurse, doctor, physiotherapist. . .

Reflect on the feelings evoked by the statements above, then suggest the reasons why this professional practitioner was allowed to become registered/qualified.

How could you in your future role as a supervisor/assessor prevent this situation from recurring?

WHO ASSESSES?

In practical settings the teaching, supervision and assessment of students must be the responsibility of an appropriately qualified and experienced

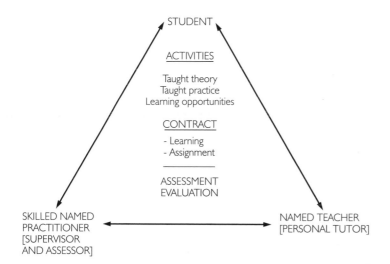

Figure 4.2

Partnership model.

practitioner, e.g. midwife, health visitor, senior medical or other appropriate staff.

Within the context of the nursing team (or other profession) and under the supervision of a skilled practitioner, appropriate significant 'others' may make a contribution to the partnership relationship and to the teaching, supervising and assessing of students at the appropriate level (see Figure 4.2).

All staff concerned with the teaching, supervising and assessing of students must have received appropriate preparation. In addition, all those involved should be familiar with the course structure, organization and content, i.e. the course curriculum.

Practitioners who are enacting the role of assessors are expected to know the process by which the system of continuous assessment is conducted for those students for whom they are responsible. Their knowledge is gained from:

- attendance not only at the preparatory course but at follow-up sessions
- adequate familiarization with the documentation used for the recording of student progress
- continued professional development.

All three partners in the assessment process, i.e. student, practitioner and teacher, have an active role in assessing and learning.

Partnership model

In this model (Figure 4.2) the mentors do not formally assess students. The mentor helps and guides the student and informs the named practitioner of the student's progress.

For the above model to be successful it is recommended that the named practitioner be supernumerary to the workforce in your area of practice, which would give the named practitioner the time and space to teach, supervise and assess the progress of each student in your area.

The role of the assessor

Attributes of the assessor's role include the following.

- Take every reasonable opportunity to maintain and improve professional knowledge and competence.
- Acknowledge any limitations of competence and refuse in such cases to accept delegated functions without first having received instruction in regard to those functions and having been assessed as competent.
- In the context of the individual's own knowledge, experience and sphere of authority, assist peers and subordinates to develop professional competence in accordance with their needs.

Implementation of the role requires the following.

- The named practitioner should receive the health-care student on placement. He arranges exposure to learning opportunities along with any necessary demonstration, instruction or guidance which will enable learning objectives to be achieved. He monitors student

Figure 4.3

Action plan agreed.

| AGREED BETWEEN: |
| DATED: |
| STAGES |
| ACHIEVED | NOT ACHIEVED |
| Signed: .... |
| Date: .... |

performance, ensures safe practice and facilitates the development of continuing skills/practice.

- The assessor has to judge whether a student has achieved the agreed standard in each of the specified objectives. Assessors inform the student of the results and provide reports to the course tutor or mentor as necessary.

A designated associate assessor can be involved with these two processes by supervising and supporting students. The associate assessor should give feedback to the assessor about students' performance.

Where a health-care student is failing to meet identified objectives or progress, it is essential to instigate an appropriate plan of action and procedures as identified in the 'Lack of Progress in Training' documentation (policies may vary from college to college). An example is given in Figure 4.3.

Delegation of supervision

The assessors may delegate limited responsibility for supervision to another skilled practitioner (sometimes called the designated assessor) only when it is clear that the person to whom they have delegated:

- is clear what tasks/skills/practice are to be supervised
- is competent in the tasks/skills/practice to be supervised
- knows what is to be expected of the student in relation to the tasks/skills/practice identified
- has an opportunity to report back on the performance of the student
- is developing and maintaining the acquisition of skills.

Activity_____

Reflect on three students you have assessed to date:

- one at the end of six months
- one at the end of the foundation programme
- one during a branch-specific placement.

What were the differences between each assessment process and why?

The example of assessment criteria on p.125 may prove helpful for this exercise. Think in terms of:

- novice
- advanced beginner
- competent practitioner.

Revisit Figure 1.1 to refresh your memory relating to the different levels.

The role of the student

The development of knowledge and practice is helped by teaching and supervision within the community/clinical setting given by skilled practitioners and by tutorial staff. Young (1999) argued that:

> *Each student has, however, to take on the responsibility of knowing and meeting the desired level of achievement of the enabling objectives as stated for the term of experience and the achievement of an agreed standard.*

The student should complete a self-assessment at the commencement of a clinical experience, in order to identify their perceived strengths and weaknesses. These should be discussed with the practitioner/supervisor at this stage. There should also be a column for a final self-assessment in which the student should assess their performance and knowledge at the end of the experience (see example on p.125).

Because the student self-assesses their own levels of attainment at the beginning and end of the relevant experience, it allows them to be more goal directed and self-critical. It also means that the student is not just passively receiving guidance from the teacher, assessor or mentor but will be actively involved in directing their own learning, which is an essential part of achieving the learning outcomes within a competency-based system. Assessors also assess the student's ability to take responsibility for their own learning (Neary, 1992b).

Self-assessment

All students should become intimately involved in the process of assessing.

1 Self-assessment can be used to help students gain confidence by showing them that they are progressing well before they need to prove this publicly or formally.
2 The act of self-assessing is intrinsically 'learning by doing'. It involves the student in the application of criteria, decision making, judgement and reflection.
3 Self-assessment can allow for a good deal of feedback - far more than could ever be given by the tutor or assessor, which is normally limited due to time and other constraints.
4 Self-assessment can help students make sense of their learning experiences. The time lag between learning experiences and feedback can be less than the traditional methods of assessment.

Activity

All students need to learn the skills of self-assessment.

1 Identify the learning needs required to enable students to self-assess.
2 As the assessor, what can you do to encourage students' self-assessment?
3 Assess your own learning needs and suggest ways to achieve these needs.

Figure 4.4 Assessment criteria: an example.

With the help of a skilled practitioner the student should select suitable patients and demonstrate his/her ability to:

Recognize the significance of the observations made and used to develop an initial 'needs' assessment.

Comments:

By Assessor:

By Student:

NOTES FOR GUIDANCE	RELEVANT KNOWLEDGE	SKILLS (Enabling Objectives)	Self-Assess	1st	2nd	3rd	Final Self-Assess
It is not reasonable to expect a junior learner to be able to undertake a comprehensive assessment.	The student will have some knowledge of:	The student will be able to: Identify level of consciousness/mental state.					
Observations should be taken correctly and recorded accurately. Explanations of abnormal findings will require the assessor to exercise judgement in relation to the level of knowledge shown by the student.	The range of normality for each of these observations and be able to explain why abnormal findings might be related to the patient's condition.	Accurately take and record the following observations: Temperature					
	The nursing care provisions available to maintain the optimum comfort of the individual.	Pulse					
	Why patients who are confined to bed or immobile are at a greater risk of development of pressure sores.	Respiration					
	Pressure sore 'at-risk' assessment tools.	Blood pressure					
	The constituents of the normal urine and the significance of abnormalities found on testing.	Assess the risk of the formation of pressure sores.					
	Students should be able to relate the normal physiology.	Accurately test specimens of urine: (i) through testing (ii) specific tests for glucose, acetone, protein, blood if appropriate					

125

THE 'WHAT' OF ASSESSMENT

What is assessment?

Rowntree (1987) defines assessment in education as:

That of occurring when one person, in some kind of interaction, direct or indirect, with another, is conscious of obtaining and interpreting information about the knowledge and understanding, or abilities and attitudes of that one person. To some extent it is an attempt to know that person.

In education, this 'finding out' about another, this attempt to 'know' a person, is mainly the prerogative of qualified staff, be they clinically or educationally based. However, it is equally important to stress the role of individuals in finding out about themselves, i.e. via self-assessment. Assessment does not necessarily have to be obtained by tests and examinations but can encompass a wide range of informal as well as formal approaches.

The first stage in the finding out, knowing or assessment of individuals is to determine the student's strengths and weaknesses and identify their emerging needs and interests. Assessment can then progress via clearly defined pathways of supervision, support and teaching of the student. This can be accompanied by ongoing assessments which will identify the student's progress or lack of it. In these ways assessments can be continuous and therefore sensitive to an individual's needs whilst upholding the major elements previously considered under the heading of 'Why assess?'

What to assess?

Because of the overall elements identified in 'Why assess?', it is essential that students undergoing an education programme are assessed on the knowledge, skills and attitudes that will satisfy the governing body of nursing, and other professional bodies, that those individuals are indeed suitable and able practitioners.

Example
Rule 18A(1) of the Nurses, Midwives and Health Visitors Approved Order, 1989, No. 1456 (see p.141) identifies the areas in which student nurses need to be competent before they can be admitted to the professional register. (Identify a similar process for your own profession.)

To this end the assessment process, both of theory and practice, should focus upon these items in order to ensure that students are continually and progressively assessed throughout their training.

Competencies, highlighting safety and professionalism, should also be recognized by the curriculum planners and assessor and therefore included in the assessment process (see Appendix 5, UKCC, 1999).

Documentation

Continuous assessment booklets should therefore be written in such a way as to reflect each identified competency. Each booklet could have three headings related to each competency, i.e. notes for guidance, relevant nursing knowledge and nursing practice skills; these clearly identify for the assessor the student's expected level related to their stage of training. Additionally, the level to which the student should be expected to achieve, dependent upon their stage of training, should be stated at the beginning of each booklet (example on p.131).

The booklets should be written in general broad terms to allow their usage within a wide range of clinical/practice placements to which students may be allocated. The example on p.129, Figure 4.5a fits comfortably into the preregistration programme for student nurses. However, other professions can adopt a similar layout for their own programmes.

Making the assessment booklets specific to the clinical/practice area

In order to make the booklets reflect each clinical/practice area, it is necessary for that area to clearly identify the learning opportunities and outcomes that it can offer, respective to each competency. For example:

Under the supervision of a skilled practitioner, advise the patient on the promotion of health and discuss with the patient the methods that will help to prevent further development of the illness.

This is a general statement and in order to make it specific to a particular area, that clinical/practice placement must identify its learning opportunities, outcomes and the methods of health promotion which are pertinent to it.

If, for example, one considers a medical ward which admits patients with cardiovascular problems (CVAs, MIs, etc.), the forms of health promotion identified in the learning opportunities and outcomes may be items related to smoking, stress, diet and exercise, whereas a paediatric ward may identify learning opportunities and outcomes items related to safety in the home, in the hospital, etc.

To enable students' transfer of learning from a similar to a more complex situation, the assessor will initially need to identify learning opportunities which are relevant to each situation, then build these up, making sure they relate to the changing degree of complexity. Students will need to be taught the skills of 'transferability', in both knowledge and skills.

Activity

Select a particular competency from your own profession e.g. *Rule* 18 1999 or UKCC Final Draft, 1999, see page 128.

1   Devise appropriate learning outcomes to translate the chosen compe-
    tency to a particular area of nursing or to other allied professions.

2   Identify the role of the assessor in enabling a student to acquire that
    competency.

3   Identify potential problems and decide on appropriate remedies.

UKCC Rule 18.

1989 No. 1456

The Nurses, Midwives and Health Visitors Approval Order 1989

Preparation for entry to parts 12, 13, 14 and 15 of the Register

18A-(1)
The content of the Common Foundation Programme and the Branch Programme shall be
such as the Council may from time to time require.

(2)
The Common Foundation Programme and the Branch Programme shall be designed to
prepare the student to assume the responsibilities and accountability that registration confers,
and to prepare the nursing student to apply knowledge and skills to meet the nursing needs of
individuals and of groups in health and in sickness in the area of practice of the Branch
Programme and shall include enabling the student to achieve the following outcomes:-

(a) The identification of the social and health implications of pregnancy and child bearing,
     physical and mental handicap, disease, disability, or ageing for the individual, her or his
     friends, family and community.

(b) The recognition of common factors which contribute to, and those which adversely affect
     physical, mental and social well-being of patients and clients and take appropriate action.

(c) The use of relevant literature and research to inform the practice of nursing.

(d) The appreciation of the influence of social, political and cultural factors in relation to health
     care.

(e) An understanding of the requirements of legislation relevant to the practice of nursing.

(f) The use of appropriate communication skills to enable the development of helpful, caring
     relationships with patients and clients and their families and friends, and to initiate and
     conduct therapeutic relationships with patients and clients.

(g) The identification of health related learning needs of patients and clients, families and
     friends and to participate in health promotion.

(h) An understanding of the ethics of health care and of the nursing profession and the
     responsibilities which these impose on the nurse's professional practice.

(i) The identification of the needs of patients and clients to enable them to progress from
     varying degrees of dependence to maximum independence, or to a peaceful death.

(j) The identification of physical, psychological, social and spiritual needs of the patient or
     client, an awareness of values and concepts of individual care, the ability to devise a plan
     of care, contribute to its implementation of evaluation and the demonstration of the
     application of the principles of a problem-solving approach to the practice of nursing.

(k) The ability to function effectively in a team and participate in a multi-professional approach
     to the care of patients and clients.

(l) The use of the appropriate channel of referral for matters not within her sphere of
     competence.

(m) The assignment of appropriate duties to others and the supervision, teaching and
     monitoring of assigned duties.

Common Foundation Programme:		<u>Venue</u>	During a selected branch exposure Adult/Mental Health/Mental Handicap/Children's (delete whichever is not applicable)		
Promotion and Maintenance of Health		<u>Nature</u>	Continuous Assessment		

Elements of Competence	Performance Criteria	Signature of student	Name of assessor	Achieved Not achieved (Signed and dated by assessor)	
The identification of health related learning needs of patients/clients, their families and friends.	Identifies the methods used to teach a health education topic to a patient/client and/or his/her family.				
	Recognizes the ways in which the carer/practitioner helps an individual to accept his/her altered health status.				
	Identifies the factors which can influence the health of an individual.				
	Understands the social factors affecting the patient's/client's perception of health.				
	Identifies legislation, policies and practices designed to maintain a safe environment.				

CONTRACT ASSIGNMENT

<u>FOCUS:</u> The student will produce an assignment (approximately 1500 words) identifying strategies used to help a patient/client promote and maintain his/her health.

Figures 4.5 a and b are examples of how the learning outcomes may be broken down to create learning 'stepping stones' which will enable health care students to develop and achieve the required level of competence to become registered, competent practitioners.

Figure 4.5a

Standard of performance statement.

Activity

Documents you will need for this exercise:

- college scheme of assessment and course curriculum (or other appropriate course documents)
- all appropriate assessment documents.

Work through these assessment documents. The aim is to help you understand what is to be assessed and how that assessment can take place effectively.

NB: A sample of assessment documents can be found in Appendix 3.

UNDER THE SUPERVISION OF A SKILLED PRACTITIONER THE STUDENT IS GIVEN THE OPPORTUNITY TO:

Elements of Competence	Performance Criteria: Learning Outcomes	Date	Student's signature	Comments	Assessor's signature	Comments
(a) Use appropriate communication skills to enable the development of a caring relationship.	Discuss the rights of the individual to be involved in all aspects of his/her care.					
	Discuss the different methods of communications observed and experienced.					
(b) Use appropriate communication skills to initiate and conduct therapeutic relationships with patients/clients and friends.	Communicate the observations made during patient/client interactions.					
	Identify the patient's/client's usual forms of communication and social interaction.					
	Communicate effectively by talking and listening to the individual and his/her family or friends.					
	Identify the patient's/client's communication difficulties.					

CONTRACT ASSIGNMENT

FOCUS: During concurrent learning in each practice placement environment, the student will keep and produce a diary of notable incidents of communication witnessed as part of the self-assessment process.

Figure 4.5b

Standard of performance statement.

PREPARATION FOR PRACTICAL EXPERIENCE AS AN ASSESSOR

During the induction period students are exposed to a variety of learning opportunities. Students are not expected to achieve in all of the Rule 18A outcomes but their progress can be recorded in a 'student's profile' and a statement of progress made on a continuous basis. This process can be viewed in two stages:

1   assessment of student potential
2   assessment of clinical competence.

For both continuous assessment stages, formative and summative assessment are essential aspects.

Assessment statement

When assessment statements have been agreed the assessor and curriculum planning teams should examine each statement and consider the following when developing the assessment tool.

1   Create learning opportunities in order to help the health-care student to develop and progress and to achieve competence in each unit statement.

Days 1 & 2   Student self-assessment
Orientation to the
practice placement

Introduction to ⟨ Assessor/supervisor/named practitioner
➡ Inform student of
arrangements for
supervision and
assessment

Mentor
(guide/supporter/friend)

Close supervision and continuous assessment of practice

1st Interview   Named (assessor)
(Wk 1-2)   practitioner ➡

> Identify strengths and weaknesses
> Identify student's learning needs
> Formulate action plan to meet
> learning needs
> Ensure continuous assessment
> booklet up to date

Continue supervison/teaching
Carry out plan to meet specific learning needs
Continuous assessment of practice and fill in
booklet as appropriate

2nd Interview   Named practitioner
(mid allocation)   (assessor/supervisor) ➡

> Discuss outcome of action plan
> Identify new learning needs
> Formulate new action plan to meet
> learning needs
> Fill in continuous assessment booklet
> where incomplete

Continue supervision/teaching
Carry out new action plan
Continuous assessment of practice and fill in
booklet as appropriate

Final Interview   Named practitioner
(Week prior to end   Supervisor/assessor
of allocation, i.e.   Significant others
penultimate week) ➡

> Discuss outcome of action plan
> Identify learning needs placements
> Complete continuous assessment
> booklet

Figure 4.6

The process of continuous
assessment (from Young, 1994).

2 Break down the assessment statements into related performance
   criteria (RPC) to achieve agreed standards of performance.
3 Identify the process of Continuous Assessment (Figure 4.6 gives an
   example).
4 Decide the status of the assessment: is it a disciplinary event rather
   than an educative process (Bevis, 1990)?

NB: In your organization, learning objectives or enabling objectives may
be used instead of RPC as part of the above exercise. Those terms and
their meanings may need to be clarified.

However, the UKCC report *Fitness for Practice* (UKCC, 1999, p.35)
refers to an outcome-based competency approach to education. It is
important that you understand these terms. (Revisit the section on
Understanding Competencies, p.45.)

Self-development

During your practical experience as a new assessor, observing a skilled
assessor interviewing a student at the various stages can help in the self-
development process. It is also useful to share that experience with
other assessors.

During the process of becoming an assessor, the form in Figure 4.7 can be used as a self-assessment tool which can be completed at the end of the assessment experience.

Follow-up sessions with other assessors can prove useful, where the completed forms can be used to share your experiences. These follow-up sessions could form the basis for an assessor's support group (Neary, 1996).

Formal interviews are times when:

1   individual strengths or weaknesses and learning needs are highlighted, with reference to the student's level in training and previous experience
2   learning opportunities related to patient-centred care are identified
3   action plans are formulated to build on the student's strengths and meet new learning needs
4   the outcomes of agreed action plans are discussed, in relation to their effect on the student's learning and performance
5   the outcome of continuous assessment is discussed
6   the student's general progress is reviewed and feedback given. This should include development of appropriate attitudes, knowledge and skills.

NB: Some students' allocations are less than two weeks, so an assessment of students' competence is not feasible. However, a statement of performance can be recorded and become part of the student 'profile'.

Activity

When planning an assessment process, you must also consider assessment criteria.

1   Write down the criteria you believe are necessary for an effective assessment process.
2   List assessment criteria for your specialist area of practice.

Check your outcomes with p.136.

Figure 4.7

Self-assessment tool.

Teaching & Assessing in Clinical Practice

Supervised Progress Interview

Course Member   _____

Course Number   _____

Mentor/Supervisor   _____

Type of Learner   _____

Stage of Training   _____

1.

Figure 4.7

Continued

COMMENTS	STAGE 1	STAGE 2	STAGE 3
1 Environment used for the interview. (Describe the venue)			
2 Describe how rapport was established.			
3 How was the learner involved in contributing to the setting of learning outcomes?			
4 Learning outcomes reflect the learning opportunities available.			
5 Learning outcomes match the stage of training. (Consider the learner's previous experience)			
6 Existing assessment booklet was discussed, if appropriate.			
7 Competencies to be achieved were agreed, utilizing existing assessment booklet.			
8 An action plan/learning contract was drawn up.			
9 How was the interview concluded?			

SUMMARY OF YOUR OVERALL OBSERVATION

On completing this form, discuss your observations with your mentor and agree an **action plan** for your further development.

2.

OVERALL DISCUSSION (including strengths and weaknesses):

FUTURE DEVELOPMENT ACTION PLAN (including dates):

Signature of agreement:

Mentor _____

Course Member _____

Date _____

3.

Figure 4.7

Continued

Assessment criteria include:

- achievement of aims and objectives
- level of knowledge
- ability to use resources
- ability to apply findings
- presentation skill
- academic rigour
- critical analysis
- evaluation of the process.

RESPONSIVE ASSESSMENT

- Use assessments as a learning opportunity.
- Use learning opportunities in the assessment process.
- Use assessing as a learning process.
- Assess the student's learning process.
- Change the examination culture to continuous assessment of both theory and practice, which should be of equal importance.
- Develop the concept of learning contracts and contract assignments to enhance the assessment of theory and practice as an integrated whole.
- Develop a team approach (see Figure 4.2).
- Create a supervisory post in practice settings for the named practitioner who has the responsibility for supervising and assessing students' clinical competencies.
- Give students a degree of autonomy in the learning and assessment process.
- Use learning contracts to understand your own development needs and negotiate at set points in the course/programme.
- Assess students' performance in situational contexts, i.e. performance related to patients'/clients' health-care needs.

The above list was formalized as a result of a four-year research study (Neary, 1996) which led to the concept of **responsive assessments**. A primary reason for suggesting a responsive assessment model is that responsive assessment changes the assessor role by requiring two actions: description and judgement. Description is the process of providing necessary information about the student. Judgement involves a value component. The assessor is assumed to be qualified to decide the relative value of a student performance. Assessments become a process for both describing students and judging the merit and worth of their performance. Clinical learning objectives are one source of input for determination of the merit of student work, whereas judgement of the worth of that work depends on the interactions between students and patients/clients in selected situational contexts. The use of a 'responsive' model would encourage this judgement. Objective criteria for performance would not then be the sole measure for comprehensive practical assessment.

The focus of nursing care is the client/patient. Teaching and learning cannot be assessed within a void. Unanticipated events occur during clinical practice. These events alter the original situations that were intended to give students the chance to demonstrate behaviour specified in the learning objectives. To be fair to students, situational events need to be considered during the assessment process. Here continuous assessment can come into its own in allowing for such dynamism.

In the real world practice changes constantly, sometimes very quickly. It is at times like these that the skilled practitioner acts not according to the rules or textbook procedures but to the needs of the individual patient/client and 'knows', in that situation, what is necessary, i.e. is responsive to their needs. It was to such situations typically that students in Neary's study were exposed on practice placements, where the pre-set objectives that they bore with them from college proved not very relevant. The data showed assessment strategies to be full of such pre-set objectives which restricted learning opportunities throughout the course. Most students expressed the need to consider the effective as well as cognitive and psychomotor domains of learning as well as to receive 'useful' feedback.

These entirely reasonable aspirations should be met within an assessment framework that allows for consideration of creativity and the emergent along with student, teacher and assessor satisfaction in the teaching and learning process. We could use clinical learning objectives and learning opportunities as realistic measures of growth in the assessment of individual need, rather than for determination of student weakness, in a model for assessment of clinical competence that is dynamic and flexible rather than linear and prescriptive. Stake put it that educational evaluation (in our sense, assessment) of this type 'responds to audience requirements for information' (Stake, 1986, p.14). Stake cautioned that assessors should not assume that only measurable outcomes testify to the worth of a programme.

Another rationale for adopting responsive assessment lies in the style/method of verbal and written reports of student progress to which it gives rise. Instead of reporting specific changes in student behaviour, responsive assessment records performance within a situational context. Each report identifies progress and provides stimulus for the student to develop personal reflection and adjust learning and personal objectives for successive clinical/practical experiences. Such a model might satisfy the assessors who, in response to questions on their performance, said that they would prefer to write or report on student performance on a blank page alongside the pre-set college objectives, rather than tick boxes or simply use scales. This study and others (Davies *et al.*, 1994; Jowett *et al.*, 1994; O'Neill *et al.*, 1993; Powell *et al.*, 1992) have shown that it is common practice for colleges to identify which objectives have and which have not been met, omitting additional experiences that have occurred. Much of this was encapsulated by a Project 2000 student with eight years' experience as a ward clerk, who said:

The learning objectives set for my second placement were the same as for the first placement. I had already achieved these, but I was not credited with this when allocated to my next placement. No allowance was made for my new achievements. It is very frustrating, my progress is bound up by the same set of objectives for the whole of the Common Foundation Programme.

These supplemental experiences, often unplanned, may provide the stimulus for enhanced personal development and opportunities for practice over and above simple behavioural objectives.

In nursing practice, assessing the 'merit' of the intervention can rarely be treated as totally independent of other conditions and desired outcomes. A good example based on student experience was related at a study day. It concerned a student carrying out 'total patient care', including positioning, lifting, moving and handling that in turn required precision and safety for both the patient/client and herself. While it was made clear that assessment of 'merit' of this sequence of action would be positive if the student had followed the correct procedure, assessment of the 'worth' of the interventions to the patient/client, with respect to his/her feelings and student attitudes towards the patient, e.g. having an awareness of discomfort, pain and emotional need, may be different. An assessor ought to consider student–patient interactions before, during and after such an episode when the patient/client may have been in pain and frightened. Should the student fail to minimize pain and fear by explaining the procedure, or provide emotional support, the actions are not of great 'worth' to the patient/client. Yet on the other hand, if the student had minimized pain, explained the procedure and provided emotional support but failed to maintain 'safety procedures', the 'merit' when lifting and handling the patient/client and consideration of the action's 'worth' to the patient and herself are irrelevant. By not adhering to safety procedures, the student may have compromised the safety of them both, as well as patient progress. A good assessment decision could not be made without simultaneous consideration of both 'merit' and 'worth'. In this context, while 'merit' can be assessed using agreed college and placement learning objectives and competencies, 'worth' consists of the unpredicted, unexpected and unintended learning outcomes which need to be assessed 'responsively' so as to allow assessors to enact the two components of this process – description and judgement.

I offer a diagrammatic outline of my conceptual framework for a responsive assessment model in Figure 4.8. It juxtaposes Stake's three stages of antecedents, transactions and outcomes (antecedents are the conditions pertaining before teaching or learning has occurred, e.g. individuals' abilities and willingness to learn; transactions represent all the teaching and learning processes that are engaged in, e.g. teaching methods, contract assignments, assessment strategies etc; outcomes represent the product of the antecedents and transactions, and are characterized *inter alia* by ability and achievement), against Benner's (1984) movement from novice to expert, the skills development required of the reflective practitioner (Schön, 1983, 1987) and Steinaker and Bell's (1979) taxonomy of levels. Benner (1984, p.13) pointed out that:

Stage of training	Knowledge of student (Stake)	Assessment process (Neary)	Level (Steinaker and Bell)	Progress (Benner)
CFP Entry				
Introductory induction period ↓	Antecedents Transaction	Survival kit: practice in safe environment Assessment of student potential (ASP)	Exposure	NOVICE ↓ ↓ ↓
Observation and orientation period	Antecedents Transaction	Aims and intentions identified	Participation Identification	↓ ↓ ↓ ↓
Full participation in practice setting	Transaction	Responsive assessment (RA) Contract assignments (Student set aims, objectives, intentions)	Identification Internalization	COMPETENCE ↓ ↓ ↓
End of CFP				
Entry to branch programme				↓ ↓ ↓
	Transaction	ASP and RA in branch-specific areas	Participation Identification Internalization	↓ ↓ ↓
End of branch programme				
	Outcome	Competent practitioner (has ability and has achieved UKCC Rule 18 (1989) requirement to become a 1st Level Registered Nurse)	Dissemination	↓ ↓ ↓
Required to remain on register				
	Continuous education	Postregistration education and practice (Consolidation and development as expert)	Dissemination continues	EXPERT & REFLECTIVE PRACTITIONER

In acquisition and development of a skill, a student passes through five levels of proficiency: novice, advanced beginner, competent, proficient and expert, and that these different levels reflect changes in the three general aspects of skilled performance. One is a movement from reliance on abstract principles to the use of past concrete experience as paradigms. The second is a change in the student's perception of the demand situation, in which the situation is seen less and less as a compilation of equally relevant bits, and more and more

Figure 4.8

A developmental assessment model for the future.

as a complete whole in which only certain parts are relevant and the third is a passage from detached observer to involved performer.

Some practical knowledge may elude scientific formulation of 'knowing what' and 'know how' that may challenge or extend current theory, can be developed ahead of such scientific formulation. (Benner, 1984, p.2)

Activity

As part of the responsive assessment process reflect on the use of experiential taxonomy and examine how this may be used to assess your performance as an assessor whilst in the clinical placements. Revisit your first attempt at this exercise on p.99.

Experiental taxonomy – assessment methods (Steinaker and Bell, 1979)

Exposure   Observing student reaction to the initial activities to determine attention; understanding of terms, scenes and purpose; and readiness and/or willingness to proceed.

Participation   Examining student choices; signals of understanding or lack of understanding; replications; discussions; questioning to determine understanding; ability to succeed; and, where appropriate, explanation of how the learner would do it if given the opportunity.

Identification   Using criteria, teacher-developed tests or assignments, and mental or actual checklists to assess student progress and teaching or unit effectiveness.

Internalization Using protective measures such as open-ended, anonymous response questionnaires and/or direct measures such as rating scales and interviews; using a pre- and post-test method in which a different test form or assignment is given at a later date and is compared with the original test or assignment to determine retention.

Dissemination   Using student self-assessment instruments; assessing the time devoted to tasks, the variety of techniques employed to promote the learning, and/or the degree of influence achieved.

Activity

To conclude this section and as part of your own self-assessment, turn to p.141 and reflect on your own performance and progress to date.

Assess your competencies

<u>End Competence</u>: The participant is able to apply appropriate assessment procedure and methods. This achievement signifies that the participant has:

STATEMENT OF COMPETENCE	SELF-ASSESSMENT	REFLECTIVE COMMENTS
Identified the purposes of assessment.		
Stated and applied basic assessment design principles.		
Differentiated between the various bases for analysing the outcomes of assessment.		
Selected and justified the procedures for assessing the aims, objectives and learning outcomes of given learning course(s) or provision.		
Selected and justified a range of assessment instruments and procedures in line with intended aims, objectives and/or outcomes.		
Constructed and used a range of assessment instruments.		
Designed marking checks and checklists as appropriate.		
Designed and used assessment procedures for assessing achievements in natural surroundings (such as workplace).		
Interpreted assessment outcomes as a means of making diagnoses and prognoses about learning effectiveness.		
Constructed and/or used mechanisms for recording assessment results (profiles, records of achievement, etc.)		
Communicated feedback to learners regarding the outcomes of assessment.		
Evaluated the assessment strategies and techniques adopted for particular cohort(s) of students.		
Analysed the significance and impact of assessment processes upon equal opportunities and the differential attainments of individual students and groups of students.		

FINAL THOUGHTS ABOUT ASSESSMENTS

Race (1992) advises you to: ask yourselves the following questions.

1   Am I being fair or am I being biased?
2   Are students as involved in the assessment process as they could be?
3   Why don't all students perform the same?
4   Are the criteria for assessing students clear? The right standard, realistic, flexible, achievable?
5   Are assessments used as an integral part of the learning process?
6   Is there a mismatch between assessment and performance opportunities?
7   Am I consistent with my colleagues or am I influenced by other factors?
8   Am I influenced by my previous knowledge of the student's performance?
9   Do I create learning opportunities for the student to follow, succeed and develop?
10 Do students know the assessment criteria? Are the criteria agreed with the student?
11 Do I use the assessment to emphasize the student's failure, weakness, inabilities, insecurities and demonstration?
12 Is the feedback helpful to the students?
13 Are the outcomes I am assessing appropriate?
14 Am I justified to assess the students?
15 Do I need further training to develop into a competent assessor?

Activity

Finally go back to 'Thought on Statements' (p.2).

- Have you changed in your thinking?
- How have you changed?
- Why have you changed?
- What would you do differently?

FURTHER READING

Bradshaw P (ed.) (1989) *Teaching and assessing in clinical nursing practice.* Englewood Clifs: Prentice Hall.

Donabedian A (1982) *The criteria and standards of quality.* London: Health Administration Press.

Jarvis P and Gibson S (1989) *The teacher practitioner in nursing, midwifery and health visiting.* London: Chapman Hall.

Kenworthy N, Nicklin P (1989) *Teaching and assessing in nursing practice: an experiential approach.* London: Scutari Press.

Neary M (1992) Designing, planning and developing an assessment tool. *Nurse Education Today* **12**: 357–367.

Neary M (1996) *An investigation: continuous assessment of students; clinical competence in CFP.* Unpublished PhD thesis, University of Wales, Cardiff.

Rowntree D (1987) *Assessing students: how shall we know them?* London: Kogan Page.

Steinaker N Bell R (1979) *The experiential taxonomy : a new approach to teaching and learning*. New York: Academic Press.

UKCC (1983) *Nurses, Midwives and Health Visitors Rules Approval Order*, 1983, No. 873. ENB Rule 18(1) and 19(1). London: UKCC.

5 EVALUATION OF LEARNING AND FACILITATION

In this chapter, you will learn about, and be encouraged to complete activities in:

- evaluation
- self-assessment and self-appraisal
- individual performance review
- consolidation through reflection and evaluation.

EVALUATION

Introduction

Do not sit in appraisal of others, or your own work will be measured. For in the same way as you apply assessment criteria to others, performance indicators will be defined for you, and against them you shall be appraised. (Professor Phil Race ACETT, University of Glamorgan, Pontypridd, at an International Conference in York, 6 April 1992)

Reflection and evaluation are inherent in the job. It is impossible to meet the demands of teaching without planning, organising, monitoring and evaluating the activites you carry out. (Kyriacou, 1991, p.124)

Evaluation is one of the most important tools available to you in the development of your teaching, and your ability to facilitate your students' learning.

Good quality evaluation requires that you develop and practise a range of techniques.

Evaluation is a dynamic process, by which you exercise and develop skills and qualities of reflective teaching... (Ashcroft and Foreman-Peck, 1994, p.166)

...process that relates to the identification, description and appraisal of the effects and effectiveness of all aspects of teaching. (Heathcote et al., 1982)

What is evaluation?

Having gained teaching, assessing and mentorship experience, we need to ask how good was it, did the learning plan work? How effective has the experience been? Evaluation is a systematic collection and analysis of information about how successful a programme, curriculum, workshop, study days, courses, etc. have been as part of the student's learning and the learning environment. We need to know what it is like to teach, learn and assess within the systems we have created for our students; we need to know what beneficial or disastrous experiences have materialized. An insight gained from evaluations will help to develop and improve the teaching, learning and assessment strategies for both present and future students.

Evaluation is always time consuming but necessary in order to maintain and monitor the process of education. The process of continuous evaluation, if carried out conscientiously, will lead to more effective teaching, assessing and evaluation itself. The spirit of evaluation should inform all our teaching and assessing decisions, whether large or small.

Whilst the teacher is an evaluator, we must not neglect to enlist the students as evaluators. MacKenzie (1970) stated that there are those who want to be entertained, those who want an easy pass, are those who want to cover as much vocationally relevant material as possible, those who want to think deeply and those who want to browse and explore.

Evaluation is an important part of any programme of education. The process is illustrated in Figure 5.1. By the nature of the profession, practitioners and teachers are assessors and evaluators.

The following section is designed to help teachers and assessors with the evaluation process by introducing the following aims.

1   Complete a ward profile and evaluate the status of the learning environment.
2   Revisit your own individual performance review and evaluate your own progress to date.
3   Select and draft objectives to meet learning/education needs.
4   Design a student ward handbook and evaluate it.
5   Examine evaluation forms and comment on their design and purpose.
6   Discuss the relevance and purpose of evaluation.
7   Examine the curriculum for nurse education or allied professions and discuss the importance of a curriculum reflecting the teaching and assessment strategies for students.

The internal course evaluation process (a tabulated summary is shown in Figure 5.2) helps to give focus to the various curriculum components that should be considered in the evaluation process.

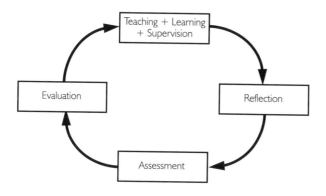

Figure 5.1

Figure 5.2   Internal course evaluation process.

GROUP 1 Organizational Level	GROUP 2 Personnel Involved	GROUP 3 Information Sources	GROUP 4 Items Evaluated	GROUP 5 Further Action
1. Course	Course tutor, students	Students' oral and written critiques, curriculum documents	Relevance of objectives/outcomes, teaching/learning experiences, balance of programme	Report to curriculum planning sub-committee, Board of Study, curriculum monitoring team
2. Curriculum planning development team	Course tutor, students, main lecturers, principal advisory tutor, vice-principal, librarian	Students' oral and written critiques, curriculum documents, teaching staff reports, assessment results, examination results	Relevance of objectives, teaching/learning experiences, balance of programme, relevance of content, curriculum policies	Develop as required within agreed parameters, recommendation for policy change, report to appropriate awarding bodies
3. Academic and administrative	Principals, director, assistant director, all teaching staff, librarian, registrar, administrative assistant	Students' oral and written critiques, curriculum documents, teaching staff reports, assessment results, examination results/reports	Relevance of objectives, teaching/learning experiences, balance of programme, relevance of content, curriculum policies	Recommendation for change to curriculum monitoring team, recommendation for change to Board of Study, report to awarding bodies.
4. Board of education, Board of study, Examination board	Chairman and members	Board of examiners' reports, principal's and director's report, curriculum documents	Any or all aspects of courses	As terms of reference allow

ACTIVITY: Examine each item under identified group headings and reflect on the rationale and relevance of each item in relation to teaching and assessing students.

Activity

Write down what you think these evaluation processes are. Put them into groups. Now check your answers with Figure 5.2.

Course evaluation process

The evaluation of a course will serve two functions. First, it will be a focus for the student. Second, the information obtained through evaluation will assist in the management of current courses and the development of future ones.

Course evaluation consists of three components.

1. Evaluation by students of practical experience. This takes place as soon as possible after completion of each experience.
2. Evaluation by students of theoretical input offered by the college/university. This takes place at the end of each study week (preparation and consolidation) (formative) and at the end of a course (summative).
3. Course tutor's evaluation of the module as a whole, taking into account students' comments, the tutor's self-appraisal and perceptions of the value of the module.

Formative evaluation

Strategies used to evaluate in the early stages of the course will give students an opportunity to review educational experiences personally with peers, tutors and practical supervisors. Students will be encouraged to develop a critical awareness of the education they receive and their involvement in it. At one level these appraisals will be personal because each student will view the course through their own schema of experience. However, it is intended that course evaluation should primarily be a collaborative endeavour involving students, teachers and practitioners. These practitioners will be invited to evaluation sessions to compare and discuss views.

The sharing of experience and appraisal should encourage a high degree of student involvement in the course. This is seen as necessary and beneficial. More specifically, it is hoped that collaboration will enable all those involved to identify learning strengths, needs and problems.

In this climate of shared experience the student will have the formative conditions to assess their development through the course.

The management and development of courses

Free and open communication between students and teachers and practitioners will be necessary for the smooth running of the course. The evaluation strategies used should encourage and aid the identification of learning needs or preferences at group and individual levels. Where practicable, adjustments to current courses will be made.

Summative evaluation

In the long term the information gathered from evaluation should assist in developing the course as a whole. It is fitting that this information be widely disseminated. Relevant parts of the evaluation data should be presented at the meetings of the following, as appropriate.

- Teaching team
- Student representative council
- Curriculum planning team
- Ward/department managers
- Nurse education managers
- Director of nursing services or equivalent
- Examiners and assessors
- Examinations committee
- Board of Studies
- Academic board

Methods of evaluation

Questionnaires can be used throughout the evaluation of the course. These are completed by students and by teaching staff.

Students' questionnaires
- introductory block evaluation
- introduction to module evaluation
- evaluation of practical experience
- consolidation of module evaluation

Teachers' questionnaires
- introductory block evaluation
- introduction to module
- consolidation of module

Use of evaluation tools

Cycles of review
Four 'cycles of review' have been established at different levels of course organization. These will come into play at different times and at different intervals as courses progress.

1   The immediate use of the evaluation is to enable the tutor to make future adjustments to those aspects of teaching and the organization which fall within their sphere of control. This could include items such as lesson content and teaching method plus the reorganization of teaching/learning time within the specific module under review.

2   The teaching team will discuss the evaluation after each module of experience with particular reference to items such as educational visits, practical placements, etc. There may be a need to monitor, more closely, the learning experience of students during future similar modules and decisions on any future action will be made at this time.

3   Where major changes in the curriculum seem necessary these will be

referred to the curriculum monitoring team for action. These could include major changes in allocation of students where, for example, an existing service area was no longer appropriate and alternative placements may need to be found.

Additionally, new resources may be identified by the curriculum monitoring team which may improve the course and action will be initiated by the team in such cases. Final examination results will also be monitored by the curriculum monitoring team and will be considered in conjunction with the evaluations experience previously elicited.

4   The Board of Studies will consider the efficiency of the course both educationally and economically within the context of other courses being organized by the college.

The following is an example of an evaluation tool.

Name: _____ Group No. _____

Module No: _____ Date: _____

The information obtained through this evaluation will assist in the management of current courses and the development of future ones. It is hoped that you will be able to share your views with fellow students, teaching and nursing service staff. The information you provide in this form will *not* be used to formally assess your progress or performance.

Below you will see a number of bipolar scales, each scale representing a continuum. Consider these scales and make a mark (X) where you think it is most appropriate. There are also spaces for your comments. If you think a scale is not applicable, mark (N/A).

1   *Organization and Resources*

1.1   Organization of
the introductory
block was GOOD   _____   Organization of
the introductory
block was POOR

Comments:

1.2   Classroom and
study facilities
were GOOD   _____   Classroom and
study facilities
were POOR

Comments:

1.3   College library
is GOOD   _____   College library
is POOR

Comments:

1.

---

2   Content of Introductory Study Block
Re-read the course programme and objectives before working these scales.

2.1   Generally content
of sessions was
GOOD   _____   Generally content
of sessions was
POOR

Comments:

2.2   Overall,
educational
material was WELL
related to
practical work   _____   Overall,
educational
material was
POORLY related
to practical

Comments:

3   Personal and Group Performance (Course tutor)

3.1   I feel SATISFIED
with my planning and
performance during
this module
                      _____   I feel
DISSATISFIED
with my planning
and performance
during this module

Comments:

3.2   I feel SATISFIED
with how the group
is functioning
                      _____   I feel
DISSATISFIED
with how the group
is functioning

Comments:

General comments:

2.

The questionnaire consists of bipolar scales, each scale representing a continuum. The student completing the form is asked to mark the scale where they think it appropriate and to add comments. The scale itself is a single line 80 mm in length. This form of scale has been used for the following reasons: provides maximum freedom for the marker, within the constraints of the questionnaire; it is hoped that with increased choice (in comparison with predivided scales), students and teachers will be encouraged to consider each scale item carefully; the individual scale gives a range of options when considering analysis. One option is for the scale simply to be viewed and the meaning of the mark construed by the viewer(s). A second option is for a series of divisions to be imposed upon the scale following completion (e.g. dividing the scale into five). This may be useful when contemplating simple statistical analysis or graph formation. A third option would be to measure the mark made upon the scale (i.e. its distance from one pole). This will provide a fine measure of opinion and permit the use of more powerful statistical analysis.

Completing questionnaires

Students will have at least three options open to them when completing the evaluation forms. Students and teachers together will decide whether each student should complete the form by themselves or whether students should complete their forms in pairs. Here it may be beneficial for students to adopt a co-counselling strategy. One student will encourage and facilitate another to complete their questionnaire and give as much information as possible. When the first student has completed the evaluation they can exchange roles and assist the second student to complete their form. Students and teachers could also decide that students could complete their forms during a group discussion.

Group discussion and tutorials

The course evaluation forms provide a framework for, and a record of, course appraisal. The real meaning of these appraisals, however, can best be understood through discussion, either in groups or in tutorial sessions.

Activity

1 Complete evaluation forms 1 and 2 and analyse their effectiveness as an evaluation tool.
2 Design your own evaluation form or scheme.

SELF-ASSESSMENT AND SELF-APPRAISAL

Within nurse education there are other areas which need to be evaluated as part of the total learning environment. Practitioners are also encouraged to self-assess and be involved in their own appraisal.

Activity

1 *Ward profile*

- Complete the ward profile on pp.156–161.
- Evaluate the status of your area of work as a learning environment for your students.
- Consider the purpose of this exercise and agree the rationale for such an exercise in relation to assessment of student clinical competence.

Form I

EVALUATION OF TEACHING, ASSESSING AND EVALUATION COURSE

(Please feel free to comment on the following)

1 How clear were the aims of this course?

....

....

....

2 Did you understand the terminology used?

....

....

....

3 What did we leave out?

....

....

....

4 How useful was it having an experienced assessor to practise with in the clinical area?

....

....

....

5 How can we improve the course/book/guidelines/etc.?

....

....

....

---

2 *Student ward/placement booklet*

- Design a ward/clinical practice placement booklet for health-care students which incorporates learning opportunities (see Appendix 4 for example student placement contract – Ward 12).
- Evaluate the relevance and success of such a booklet.

3 *Individual performance review (IPR)*

IPRs are now used in the NHS and other organizations (in the form of staff appraisal) as a method of management by mutually agreed objectives. This process aims to identify individual development needs and evaluate the process achieved (see p.160–165).

STUDENT EVALUATION SHEET

NAME OF TUTOR: COURSE:

WITH EACH OF THE COMMENTS BELOW, PLEASE TICK THE BOX THAT CORRESPONDS TO YOUR EXPERIENCE

	Totally Agree	Mostly Agree	Mostly Disagree	Totally Disagree
The lecturer captured interest at the beginning of the lesson	☐	☐	☐	☐
The aims and objectives of the lesson were clearly stated	☐	☐	☐	☐
The lesson was well structured, with a clear introduction, development of ideas and conclusion	☐	☐	☐	☐
The lesson was well delivered and interesting	☐	☐	☐	☐
The students were encouraged to participate actively	☐	☐	☐	☐
The lecturer spoke clearly and audibly	☐	☐	☐	☐
The lecturer used good-quality aids, e.g. overheads, handouts	☐	☐	☐	☐
The lecturer used a variety of delivery methods, e.g. input, discussion, group work	☐	☐	☐	☐
The lesson went at the right pace for me	☐	☐	☐	☐
The lecturer explained the subject matter clearly	☐	☐	☐	☐
The lecturer periodically reviewed what we had covered in the lesson	☐	☐	☐	☐
The lecturer checked that students had understood the subject of the lesson	☐	☐	☐	☐
The lecturer gave the opportunity for students to ask questions	☐	☐	☐	☐
The lecturer had a good relationship with the students, e.g. used names, encouragement	☐	☐	☐	☐
The lecturer was enthusiastic about the subject of the lesson	☐	☐	☐	☐
The lecturer was approachable	☐	☐	☐	☐
The lecturer made it clear what work had to be done after the lesson	☐	☐	☐	☐

FURTHER COMMENTS:

- Using the guidelines, select and draft your own objectives (related to teaching and assessing needs) and suggest how these may be achieved to enable you to become a competent teacher and assessor of healthcare students' clinical competencies.
- How would you evaluate your potential progress?

4 *Course evaluation*

Using the guidelines below, draft your own course evaluation form. When you have completed this exercise, answer the questions on page 161.

Guidelines for the review of learning experiences

1. Are the learning outcomes clear, understandable and realistic? Do they describe what the student proposes to learn?

   Low   High
1	2	3	4	5

2. Are there any other outcomes which should be considered?

   Low   High
1	2	3	4	5

3. Do the learning strategies seem reasonable, appropriate and efficient?

   Low   High
1	2	3	4	5

4. Are there other strategies or resources which could be utilized?

   Low   High
1	2	3	4	5

5. Does the evidence of accomplishment seem relevant to the various outcomes and is it convincing?

   Low   High
1	2	3	4	5

6. Is there any other evidence that could be sought?

   Low   High
1	2	3	4	5

7. Are the criteria and means for validating the evidence clear, relevant and convincing?

   Low   High
1	2	3	4	5

8. Are there other ways of validating the evidence that should be considered?

   Low   High
1	2	3	4	5

9. Are the key factors and 'dynamics' explicit in the curriculum and assessment documents?

   Low   High
1	2	3	4	5

Ward profile

Name of Placement...

Address ....

....

....

Brief description of practical experience offered by this placement.

....

....

....

Practical placement – criteria profiles: audit

This document integrates the criteria established for suitable placements, the prospective/actual practical placements and the audit (i.e. establishing suitability) in a simple format intended for use in all areas where student nurses and midwives are placed for practical experience.

The process of carrying out the Profile is intended to enable wards, departments, units and tutorial staff to have greater insight and awareness into facilities and expertise that the practical placements can bring to a student nurse or midwife's training and the requirements of that training with respect to national and local guidelines.

The information upon which the practical placement criteria, Profile and audit are devised has been extracted from:

- English National Board (ENB) Guidelines and Welsh National Board (WNB) 189/003
- the results of a previous pilot scheme
- *A strategy for nursing*
- UKCC Advisory Documents
- curriculum requirements.

In an effort to maintain standardization, familiarity and ease of completion, one universal document is felt to be desirable. Very rarely, some questions within the Profile may not be applicable to all areas.

The minimum standard for each criterion is indicated in the document by a line beyond which the standard is acceptable.

On pages 1–6 of the document a summary of the minimum standard required for a practical area to be considered suitable for the placement of students for experience is indicated. Should any criterion score less than the minimum standard, the placement must not be used unless there are compelling reasons.

In such cases a time limit for action of six months has been agreed. After this time limit has elapsed a further review will take place. Final approval for use by the appropriate director of nurse or midwifery education will also be required.

NB: N/A (not applicable) has been included on the scale for some criteria. Where this is used, supporting comments must be given.

1.

Key statements

1   Importance of criterion is not recognized.
2   Importance of criterion is recognized but not developed.
3   Work towards implementation of this criterion is at an early stage.
4   Working towards implementation of this criterion but further development is required.
5   Optimum achievement of criterion.

CRITERION 1

A statement of the placement's defined philosophy should be present. This philosophy should reflect the beliefs and values that underpin the placement's practice.
    In relation to the stated philosophy of the placement, which of the key statements applies?

1   2 | 3   4   5   N/A

Comments

CRITERION 2

The approach to clients that is practised by the placement should be supported by documentation which illustrates evidence of assessment, planning, implementation and evaluation.
    In relation to the stated philosophy of the placement, which of the key statements applies?

1   2 | 3   4   5   N/A

Comments

CRITERION 3

Quality assurance is seen as a valuable concept in the meeting of the needs of clients and staff.

3.1 In relation to the meeting of needs of clients, which of the key statements applies?

1   2 | 3   4   5   N/A

3.2 In relation to the meetings of needs of staff, which of the key statements applies?

1   2 | 3   4   5   N/A

Comments

CRITERION 4

Relevant research findings and evidence-based practice should be used to address the needs of clients and staff.

4.1 In relation to the meeting of needs of clients, which of the key statements applies?

1   2 | 3   4   5   N/A

2.

4.2 In relation to the meeting of needs of staff, which of the key statements applies?

1   2 | 3   4   5   N/A

Comments

CRITERION 5

The placement must be an environment which upholds the client's privacy, dignity and safety, whilst providing facilities which allow the individual's physical, psychological and social needs to be met.

In relation to placement environment, which of the key statements applies?

5.1 How far are the physical needs met?   1 2 3 | 4 5 N/A

5.2 How far are the psychological needs met?   1 2 3 | 4 5 N/A

5.3 How far are the social needs met?   1 2 3 | 4 5 N/A

5.4 Is safety upheld for clients?   1 2 3 | 4 5 N/A

5.5 Is safety upheld for staff?   1 2 3 | 4 5 N/A

Comments

CRITERION 6

All supervisors/assessors* must be familiar with the assessment strategy for the courses on which they supervise students.

In relation to the familiarity of supervisors/assessors* with the relevant assessment strategy, which of the key statements applies?

1   2 | 3   4   5   N/A

Comments

CRITERION 7

Students must be on duty, when in rostered practice, with their named supervisor/assessor* for an average of at least 60% of the working week.

Which of the following applies?   20% 30% 40% 50% 60%

Comments

CRITERION 8

Each assessor* should not have responsibility for more than two students, whether these students are from the Common Foundation, branch programme or other courses. The aim should be only one student per assessor*.

* May also be called mentors or preceptors.

3.

8.1 No more than two students are allocated to each assessor.

1   2   3 | 4   5   N/A

8.2 What is the maximum number of students this area can supervise per day?   ☐

Comments

8.3 The number of qualified staff in post should be stated together with their grade and qualifications.

Grade   Qualifications   Please state whether *supervisor or assessor*

CRITERION 9
Staff are aware of the need for effective communication.

Is there evidence of effective communication between:

9.1 Staff/staff?	1 2 3 4 | 5
9.2 Staff/clients?	1 2 3 4 | 5
9.3 Clients/clients?	1 2 3 4 | 5

Comments

CRITERION 10
Written details of the standards/policies/procedures applicable to the placement must be available and accessible to the student.

   In relation to availability and accessibility of written details of standards/policies/procedures, which of the key statements applies?

1   2   3   4 | 5   N/A

Comments

CRITERION 11
No unscheduled student movement must occur.

Does unscheduled student movement occur?   Yes/No
If yes, please give details.

Comments

4.

Final outcome of each criterion

Criterion		Score			
1.	1	2	3	4	5
2.	1	2	3	4	5
3.1	1	2	3	4	5
3.2	1	2	3	4	5
4.1	1	2	3	4	5
4.2	1	2	3	4	5
5.1	1	2	3	4	5
5.2	1	2	3	4	5
5.3	1	2	3	4	5
5.4	1	2	3	4	5
5.5	1	2	3	4	5
6.	1	2	3	4	5
8.	1	2	3	4	5
9.1	1	2	3	4	5
9.2	1	2	3	4	5
9.3	1	2	3	4	5
10.	1	2	3	4	5

The result for each criterion is mapped into this score sheet, thus creating a ward profile. The process of carrying out the profile will identify areas which need developing.

The final outcome may look something like this.

Criterion		Score			
1.	1	②	3	4	5
2.	1	②	3	4	5
3.1	1	2	③	4	5
3.2	1	②	3	4	5
4.1	1	2	③	4	5
4.2	1	②	3	4	5
5.1	1	2	3	4	⑤
5.2	1	2	3	④	5
5.3	1	2	3	4	⑤
5.4	1	2	3	④	5
5.5	1	2	3	④	5
6.	①	2	3	4	5
8.	1	2	③	4	5
9.1	1	2	3	④	5
9.2	1	2	3	④	5
9.3	1	②	3	4	5
10.	1	2	③	4	5

5.

Ward profile continued

Recommendations

Is this area suitable   Yes   Yes with   No
for training purposes?   Modifications

....

....

Signature of assessor .... Manager

.... Nurse teacher

Date ....

Date of next review ....

For 'Yes with modifications', signature of appropriate director of education

.... Date ....

6.

1 How useful was this activity?
2 What relevance has this activity for:

- learning assignments?
- learning opportunities?
- teaching and assessing?
- evaluation?
- performance indicators?

INDIVIDUAL PERFORMANCE REVIEW (IPR)

Take some time to read the following pages on IPR, then identify your own learning needs, set your objectives and identify the resources needed to achieve these learning needs.

Guidelines on selecting and drafting objectives, actions and success criteria for staff development

Objectives

Refer to the following when selecting and drafting objectives.

- Be comprehensive, using your job categories and activity headings as a starting point.
- Choose between six and 10 objectives.
- Group related tasks under one objective.
- Ensure that your objectives are all achievable.
- Specify results.
- Include a time scale – either long or short term.
- Phrase your objectives as succinctly as possible.

Actions

Refer to the following when selecting and drafting actions.

- Make sure each objective has 3–5 related actions.
- Specify who, how and when.
- Make sure each action contributes to the objective.
- Ensure that actions fall within the review period.
- Include both your own actions and delegated actions.

Success criteria

Refer to the following when selecting and drafting success criteria.

- Set the criteria in advance.
- Define them as explicitly as possible.
- Make sure you and your manager both know what the success criteria are and agree them.

Activity_____

Job categories

Try this yourself. Using the box below, list the areas of responsibility where you are expected to achieve and draft some objectives.

RESPONSIBILITIES

Service
Responsibility

–

–

–

Organizational/Cultural
Responsibility

–

–

–

Educational
Responsibility

–

–

–

Human resources
Responsibility

–

–

–

ACTIVITY HEADINGS

Activity

1

2

3

4

5

6

7

8

DRAFT OBJECTIVES

Objective

1

2

3

4

5

6

7

8

9

10

Draft actions

Now refer back to two or three of the objectives you have drafted and identify their related actions.

Remember, some actions will be yours; some may be delegated; actions must describe who will do what and by when; actions must relate to the review period in question, even if the objective is long term.

OBJECTIVE 1
Actions   −

                 −

                 −

OBJECTIVE 2
Actions   −

                 −

                 −

OBJECTIVE 3
Actions   −

                 −

                 −

Success criteria

At this point, refer to the objectives for which you have detailed actions and apply appropriate success criteria.

Remember, be as specific as possible and use explicit measures which you can test out.

OBJECTIVE 1
Success Criteria −

                 −

                 −

OBJECTIVE 2
Success Criteria −

                 −

                 −

OBJECTIVE 3
Success Criteria −

                 −

                 −

When completed complete the following questionnaire.

Participant evaluation questionnaire

As a participant in a 'training event', your reflections can provide important information. Your views will be valuable in helping to shape future policy and practice.

To complete the questionnaire, please award a score by marking one box alongside each question. You are invited to add comment at the end.

	Low				High

1. How clear were you about what you wanted from the event?

1	2	3	4	5

2. Did you achieve your objectives?

1	2	3	4	5

3. Did the content of the event match its publicity?

1	2	3	4	5

4. How relevant did you find the content of the event to your anticipated future work/career?

1	2	3	4	5

5. Was the content pitched at a level appropriate to your needs/interest?

1	2	3	4	5

6. How appropriate were the teaching/facilitating strategies used?

1	2	3	4	5

7. Were any materials (including AVA) appropriate and of a satisfactory quality?

1	2	3	4	5

8. Was the nature and range of activities sufficient to sustain your interest?

1	2	3	4	5

9. Was the event well organized?

1	2	3	4	5

10 Were facilities adequate for the purpose?

1	2	3	4	5

11 Do you regard this event as a worthwhile investment of your time?

1	2	3	4	5

12 We would welcome any further comment you might wish to make about this event/ experience/opportunity.

13 Has this event suggested a need for any further staff development courses? (Please specify)

Activity

pre-registration/prequalification education curriculum
For this exercise you will need the course curriculum appropriate to your profession.

1   Using the curriculum in Appendix 2 or a curriculum from your own college, evaluate the curriculum for its content.

   - How does the curriculum reflect the assessment strategy?
   - How could it be improved?

2   Using the assessment documents for the student practice placements from your own college, evaluate the assessment strategy.

   - How does the strategy meet the needs of students?
   - How does it prepare students to be fit for practice?

FORMAL EVALUATION

Neary's study (1996) showed that no formal evaluation of the assessment process was in regular use at any of the three colleges surveyed. College staff depended on the hearsay of students and assessors, neither of whom had complete ownership of their scheme, having been involved in neither its design nor its development. Although two colleges had difficulty in collecting data, the key feature of a formative evaluation instrument used at the third college to produce quantitative information was a form of rating scale which enabled, at the minimum, numerical summation as well as a more elaborate statistical analysis.

Evaluation is arguably the least understood and most neglected element of assessment and curriculum design and development. All too frequently, evaluation has been identified as an afterthought attached to the rest of the curriculum strategy. Lawton (1983) suggested that such an attitude is not unreasonable because it is a fact that issues of evaluation present some of the most difficult problems for curriculum planners.

Examining a number of different evaluation models (James, 1983; Lawton, 1983; Rowntree, 1988; Stenhouse, 1984), Kenworthy and Nicklin (1989, p.128) argued that the 'issues involved in evaluating an educational course as complex as that for pre-service nursing cannot be effectively encompassed by one model'. They summarized various models, as shown in Table 5.1.

It is widely held that all personnel involved both at the planning stage and during implementation ought to contribute to the evaluation of an educational activity. The principal participants in nurse education are teachers, practitioners, students themselves and, most importantly, patients/clients and their relatives. Should there be an opportunity to

Evaluation model	Mode of evaluation	Function of the evaluation	Comments
Classic/experimental	Quantitative	Measurement of behaviour using precise behavioural objectives	An eclectic approach – does not consider broader course values
Illuminative (anthropological)	Qualitative	Description and interpretation based upon observation and interview	Danger of being subjective – role conflict
1. Briefing decision makers	Both quantitative and qualitative	Bureaucratic: consultant	May be seen as providing decision makers with the information they require
2. Briefing decision makers	Both quantitative and qualitative	Autocratic: expert adviser	It is expected that the evaluation results will be acted upon
3. Briefing decision makers	Both quantitative and qualitative	Democratic: information service	Provides a detailed report without recommendations
Teacher as researcher	Both quantitative and qualitative	Dual role of both curriculum developer and evaluator	Use of triangulation? Subjectivity? Role conflict
Case study	Both quantitative and qualitative	Factual reporting	Expensive if using an external agency; may be used to confirm beliefs

Table 5.1

Summary of evaluation models (Kenworthy and Nicklin, 1989)

involve all of these 'principal participants' in evaluation or should advice be sought from 'expert evaluators' not directly involved with health units, e.g. researchers, consultants or advisers?

Quantitative approaches are employed in many questionnaires, attitude scales, observation schedules, interaction analyses and other forms of rating scale. Criticisms of the quantitative approach are that it is restrictive and a possible denial of exposure of important evaluation issues. These problems are sometimes claimed to be lessened by using qualitative methods which 'illuminate' educational experiences and may yield 'richer' information. However, it may be hard to collect and not easily summated for reference.

While qualitative evaluation frequently employs a range of appropriate methods such as interviews, discussion, participant and non-participant observation, diaries, self-reporting and critical incident techniques, Gale and O'Pray (1981) have made the point that it need not be entirely open-ended or unstructured. Many evaluation strategies combine both quantitative and qualitative instruments and evaluation tools which encompass both quantitative and qualitative modes may well constitute a necessary definition of adequacy if results are to be relied upon as an adequate basis for improving the schemes. One such improvement, it is argued by Schön (1994), can be developed through the concept and practices of reflection.

Summary: evaluation

- Evaluation is not assessment.
- Evaluation is central to good practice.
- Honest evaluation will challenge practice.
- Evaluation may serve a variety of purposes.
- Evaluation may be undertaken by 'insiders' or 'outsiders'.
- All aspects of education should be subject to evaluation.
- A range of methods are available for this diversity of purpose.
- Evaluation is important to reflective practice and professional development.
- Evaluation can be 'ad hoc'; done at any time during the programme.
- Involves the systematic collection of evidence:
  - student needs
  - available resources
  - application of a range of teaching/learning methods.
- Evaluation can be a 'painful' process.
- Evaluation challenges assumptions.
- Evaluation redefines problems as opportunities.

What can we evaluate?

'Macro'

- definition of a 'problem'
- require 'instant feedback'
- review teaching as a whole
- end of course
- aspect of whole institution exercise

'Micro'

- aims and objectives
- teaching strategies
- assessment
- course organization
- resources

What techniques are available for the purposes of evaluation?

- questionnaire
- structured interview
- group discussion
- personal reflective diary
- observation by a colleague
- paper/Post-It note comment sheets
- 'wear and tear' of learning

Other forms of 'evidence'

- student assessment performance
- moderator's report

- minutes of course team meetings
- consultation with industry
- consultation with colleagues

Policy context
- student as 'consumer'/quality of student experience
- shift in responsibility of quality assurance from National Boards to the institutions themselves

CONSOLIDATION THROUGH EVALUATING AND REFLECTING

A key feature of any learning is the process of reflection which starts in the first week and continues to the end of the course. This is the linking stage in the learning model.

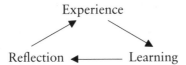

Reflection translates and transforms experience into learning, the kind of learning that can be utilized in the next cycle of experience and reflection. Reflection requires skill and understanding, it requires a non-judgemental attitude (an attitude of empathy and acceptance) and it requires good observational ability. Like all worthwhile skills, the ability to reflect will improve with practice.

Don't think of reflection as an alien or abstract process. It is not something invented by educationalists, it is something that all of us do most of the time. In fact, sometimes we wish we could stop (when we wake up in the middle of the night thinking about an incident the previous day; when we can't concentrate on a good TV programme because our mind drifts off into re-running a bad episode in the classroom, on the ward or assessing a student; or when we go for a walk but take all our 'troubles' with us). This kind of reflection can sometimes take us round in the kind of circles we can't get out of – the kind that can make things worse.

The essence of being a skilled reflector can be summarized as follows.

- Use good information and observation (rather than hearsay).
- Be non-judgemental.
- Look at alternatives.
- Aim for a proposal for action.
- Reflect nearer and nearer to the incident (the experience) itself until reflection becomes part of your way of thinking and working.

Reflections, the Portfolio and the self-assessment

Our reflections are an essential part of our record of achievement through self-assessment (revisit pp.10–18) and of the procedure which follows in achieving outcomes.

DIAGNOSE → PLAN → IMPLEMENT → EVALUATE

Although reflecting is something that takes place at every stage, the resulting reflections are gathered and recorded as part of the fourth stage of evaluation. Self-assessment documents and reflective journals are one way of formalizing reflection.

Reflections on learning activities

In all taught practice placement or programmes, it might be useful to keep a record of learning activities. This would provide a lot of useful data for reflection. We would become more aware of how we operate as learners, on our own, in a group, at work and in the wider social context. Out of this awareness, and out of trying different approaches to learning, we could further improve our learning ability, particularly our ability as an autonomous learner.

Reflections on the achievement of learning outcomes

We are all concerned with the achievement of learning outcomes and could reflect on the processes that underlie this achievement. This process would run in parallel with our diagnosis of learning needs and our planning, implementation and evaluation of that learning.

Reflections on the teaching and assessment experience

During any learning experience we should reflect on at least some of the responses we received from students. A good practice here would be to follow one or more groups over a period of time (a longitudinal study). In this instance, it would be possible and helpful to gain the support of other people (students, mentors, other colleagues, the visiting tutor) to add to our reflections. Video and audio tapes and data from question-naires will also generate new and valuable information on which to reflect.

Reflections on the events

Reflections on events, as they happen, are sometimes part of the way of working in groups. These reflections feed back into the group meeting; sometimes students work in a rota to observe the activities of the group, providing feedback at the end of the day. The aim of these reflections is to develop skills of observation, reflection and giving feedback (it is also a skill to receive and use feedback); they may also be used to improve the dynamics of the group by identifying barriers to learning and other problems.

Activity

In order to consolidate your own learning experience, complete the self-assessment forms on pages 171 and 172.

COMPETENCY UNIT: PROFESSIONAL CONCERNS AND ISSUES

Learning Outcomes: Participants should be able to develop their role as professional specialized educators, on the basis of their developing knowledge and appreciation of current educational and professional trends and developments. This achievement signifies that the participant has:

STATEMENT OF COMPETENCE	SELF-ASSESSMENT	REFLECTIVE COMMENTS
Developed and applied knowledge and understanding in the development of teaching and learning strategies to minimize disadvantages and deprivations with regard to class/race/gender/disability/age.		
Undertaken a sustained enquiry with a focus upon the teaching/learning process in own curriculum area.		
Planned, implemented and evaluated developmental or innovative projects in selected aspects of a teaching and learning programme.		
Identified and, where appropriate, taken on one or more ancillary role(s) associated with the management of teaching and learning.		
Utilized the local environment, community or workplace as a learning site and resource.		
Participated in management and decision-making processes in education or training contexts.		
Identified and/or used the range of opportunities available to teachers for professional development.		
Participated in the management and decision-making process related to: ● clinical effectiveness ● clinical supervision ● internal validation ● assessment of students		

COMPETENCY UNIT: EVALUATION

Learning Outcomes: The participant is able to evaluate the effectiveness of learning encounters and programmes. This achievement signifies that the participant has:

STATEMENT OF COMPETENCE	SELF-ASSESSMENT	REFLECTIVE COMMENTS
Described the principles and purposes of evaluation and justified planning for it in the process of planning learning events.		
Drawn up and justified checklist(s) of criteria for evaluating different types of teaching/learning encounters.		
Employed a range of strategies and investigative methods in conducting evaluations of teaching/learning encounters.		
Designed, justified and implemented a student-centred evaluation of learning events and outcomes.		
Drawn up a procedure and criteria for evaluating a course or programme of study.		
Implemented monitoring and review procedures appropriate to a given course or programme of study.		
Collaborated with colleagues (as appropriate) to utilize the results of evaluations to improve the learning experience and process.		
Asked advice on issues of impartiality, confidentiality and integrity as these apply to the process of evaluation.		
Designed, justified and implemented a self-evaluation checklist and procedure as part of an ongoing concern for appraisal and improvement of teacher/tutor/assessor/evaluator performance.		

FURTHER READING

Allan P, Jolly M (eds) (1987) *The curriculum in nursing education*. London: Croom Helm.

Allen M (1977) *Evaluation of educational programmes in nursing*. Geneva: WHO.

Clark T, Goodwin M, Mariani M, Marshall M, Moore S (1983) Curriculum evaluation. An application of Stufflebeam's model in the Baccalaureate school of nursing. *Journal of Nursing Education* 22(2).

Cronbach LJ (1982) *Designing evaluations of educational and social programmes*. San Francisco: Jossey Bass.

Crotty M, Bignall A (1988) Using a quality assurance model to evaluate ENB course 998 "Teaching and Assessing in Clinical Practice". *Nurse Education Today* 8: 332–340.

Di Florio I, Duncan P, Martin B, Middlemiss M (1989) Curriculum evaluation. *Nurse Education Today* 9: 402–407.

Gallego A (1983) *Evaluating the school*. London: RCN.

Harris D, Bailey J (1981) *Evaluation resource pack*. Bath: School of Education.

Hogg S (1990) The problem solving curriculum evaluation and development model. *Nurse Education Today* 10: 104–110.

Layton Jones E, Bridge W, Chatfield K, Finn B, Rice M (1981) Course evaluation in post basic education. *Journal of Advanced Nursing* 6: 179–188.

Mander R (1989) 'The best laid schemes'. An evaluation of the extension of midwifery training in Scotland. *International Journal of Nursing Studies* 26(1): 27–41.

Neary M (1993) *Study guide to curriculum studies*. Cardiff: Department of Education, University of Wales.

Parfitt BA (1986) Steps in evaluating a programme of nurse education. *Nurse Education Today* 6: 166–171.

Parlett M (1981) Illuminative evaluation. In: Reason P, Rowan J (eds) *Human inquiry*. Chichester: John Wiley.

Patton M (1986) *Utilisation focused evaluation*. Beverly Hills: Sage.

Scriven M (1967) The methodology of evaluation. In: American Educational Research Association (eds) *Perspectives of curriculum evaluation*. Chicago: Rand McNally.

Simons H (1984) In: Adelman C (ed.), *The politics and ethics of evaluation*. London: Croom Helm.

Stake R (1967) The countenances of education evaluation. *Teachers College Record* **April**: 125.

Stenhouse L (1984) Evaluating curriculum evaluation. In: Adelman C (ed.) *The politics and ethics of evaluation*. London: Croom Helm.

Stufflebeam DL (1969) *Evaluating as enlightenment for decision making and improving educational assessment and an invention for measures of affective behaviour*. Washington DC: National Educational Association.

Svenson MM (1991) Using fourth generation evaluation in nursing. *Evaluation and The Health Professions* 14(1): 79–87.

Thompson J (1990) Hermeneutic enquiry. In: Moody L (ed) *Advancing nursing science through research*. Beverly Hills: Sage.

Watson J, Herbener D (1990) Programme evaluation in nursing education: the state of the art. *Journal of Advanced Nursing* 15: 316–323.

APPENDIX 1 TEACHING, ASSESSING AND EVALUATING A COURSE FOR PRACTITIONERS: AN EXAMPLE

OVERALL COURSE AIMS

1 To make course members appreciate their unconscious power as professional role models.
2 To equip course members with the interpersonal skills to create a positive learning environment in their own clinical settings.
3 To equip course members with the skills required to teach and assess effectively in their own clinical areas.
4 To motivate course members to stay up to date, both clinically and educationally, throughout their professional lives.
5 To provide a structured programme to enhance the participant's knowledge and skills related to the principles and practice of teaching, assessing and evaluating in the clinical or community nursing environment.

COURSE CURRICULUM AND STRUCTURE

The course will consist of formal tuition and self-directed and experiential assessing and teaching methods. This will include lectures, discussions, role play, video work, project work and practical experience in the clinical or community setting.

COURSE PLAN AND SEQUENCE (Figure A1.1)

Total length of course will not exceed six months, excluding interview and follow-up review day. Assessor meetings bimonthly to allow practitioners to share their experiences and to receive up-to-date information on changes in assessment strategies.

Selection Interviews	Approximately two months before commencement of course
Briefing Day	Two weeks before commencement of course
Two Weeks Break	
Module 1 (five days)	Interpersonal Skills and the Teacher
Two Weeks Break	
Module 2 (five days)	Principles and Practice of Teaching and Assessing
Two Weeks Break	
Module 3 (five days)	Recent Developments in Nursing Theory, Nursing Education, Research, Assessments and Evaluation

Followed by
Follow-up Review Day
Attendance Requirement

Twelve-week practice period
Three months after course
Course members who miss three days in total from the three modules will have to retake the course. Only two days absence from any one module will be allowed.

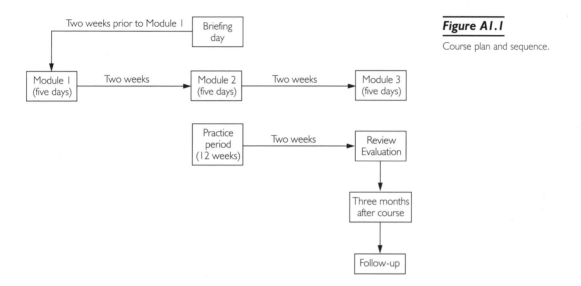

Figure A1.1

Course plan and sequence.

Date started:	Teaching and Assessing in Clinical Practice	Week 1
Monday	Managing change Change theory	Managing the learning environment
Tuesday	Learning theories Adult learning	Learning styles: – Motivation – Questioning in teaching – Essay writing/study skills – Observation
Wednesday	Planning a learning experience	Teaching methods
Thursday	Teaching methods	Feedback on communication and sharing journal reflections
Friday	Consolidation exercise Evaluation and interblock work	Guided study

Date started:	Teaching and Assessing in Clinical Practice			Week 2	
Monday	Criteria/areas/validity, etc./attitudes/qualities/values/ethical/role				
Tuesday	National and local perspectives of nurse education		Curriculum		
Wednesday	Assessment booklet		Action planning. Learning contract using scenarios		
Thursday	Assessment processes in practice setting		Feedback Learning Environment	Progress with learning journals	Evaluation Interblock work
Friday	Midwifery curriculum and others, e.g. school nurse/health visitor and branch		Preparation for supervised assessment		

Date started:	Teaching and Assessing in Clinical Practice			Week 3
Monday	PREPP Preceptorship	UKCC and National Board's Framework & Higher Award CATS	NVQ in nursing in teaching and assessing	
Tuesday	Giving and receiving feedback			
Wednesday	Coursework/practical assessments/tutorials Focus 1: Methods of assessment Focus 2: Methods of evaluation			
Thursday	Open forum for debate How do we assess student's clinical competence?			
Friday	Options: – Microteaching – Seminar – Negotiated other		Evaluation	

FOLLOW-UP WORKSHOPS

Once you have gained practice in assessing students under the super-vision of a mentor, you will be invited to attend a follow-up study day in the form of workshops. The aim of this is to:

- share worries about assessment
- define some performance indicator for 'high-quality' assessment
- define staff development needs in the area of assessments
- pinpoint weaknesses in assessment priorities and devices
- explore alternative ways of assessing
- enhance the learning which can be derived from assessments
- produce 'quality criteria' for assessing
- collect facts and information from experience gained while enacting your role as assessor
- evaluate your role as teacher and assessor
- advise the curriculum planning and moderating team on assessment problems to date.

APPENDIX 2   PRE-REGISTRATION NURSE EDUCATION CURRICULUM: AN EXAMPLE

COURSE STRUCTURE

I YEAR		2 YEARS			TRANSITION PERIOD
Foundation Programme		**Branches**			**Staff Nurse Designate**

Foundation of nursing theory and practice
 	
Basic concept of theory and practice of nursing care
	Summative assessment	Specialist subject applied to branch specific
		
		Advanced nursing product and skills
			Summative assessment	Last 3 months	Professional development
					
					Professional development in the workplace,
					e.g. preceptorship
					       mentorship
					       teaching and assessing
					
					Application of management theory

Formative ►► ►► ►► ►►   ►► ►► ►► ►► ►► ►►   FORMATIVE   ►► ►► ►► ►► ►► ►►

APPLICATION OF THEORY TO PRACTICE
CONTINUOUS ASSESSMENT VIA

LEARNING CONTRACT _____   CONTRACT ASSIGNMENTS _____

OPPORTUNISTIC LEARNING _____   _____

MISSION STATEMENT FOR PART 1 (Adapted from J. North Sheffield/ Doncaster College of Nursing)

Part 1 of the course is concerned with the process of **orientation**. During this part the student will adjust to and align themselves with the course, its contexts and concepts.

As a unique individual, the student will bring to the course life experiences which will enhance their own professional growth and also enrich the educational environment of their peers. Self-awareness and the addressing of interpersonal skills, therefore, provide a medium through which the individual begins to orient towards self.

Orientation towards the peer group is facilitated by an educational approach that values exploration, problem posing, dialogue and equality. This will produce a nurturing environment in which group members feel able to share in the responsibility for learning and to value the contribution made by peers.

Orientation to local, cultural and global issues will be assisted by planned exposure to selected aspects of the neighbourhood. Reflection upon these experiences will illuminate the central concepts.

MISSION STATEMENT FOR PART 2

The second part of the course focuses on the process of **identification**. During this period the student will identify the relationship between previously addressed concepts and their relevance to nursing and health-care provision.

The local and cultural contexts within which the student will operate become increasingly health and health-care centred. They will incorporate both institutional and non-institutional settings; reflection on these experiences will enable identification and recognition of aspects of self and group that will enhance professional development. This process will be facilitated by dialogueand negotiation with the student's academic and placement supervisors.

Previous orientation to the central concepts will enable ideas to be identified, related and adjusted through applying them to real experiences. This process will require the ability to practise, interpret and discuss techniques and knowledge and helps in the acquisition of essential nursing skills and further development of analytical skills.

MISSION STATEMENT FOR PART 3

Part 3 of the course is concerned with the process of **application**. In this part the student will be able to utilize their increasing repertoire of knowledge and skills in relation to the care of a particular client group.

Within the context of hospital and community care, students will engage in the process of nursing and demonstrate flexible responses to meeting an individual's health-care needs.

The intention at this stage is to enable the student to employ conceptual knowledge of health and dysfunction within the practical situation. This will require the student to demonstrate the ability to distinguish and differentiate between care strategies, to be able to apply research findings and to critically analyse their relevance to the individual.

The use of research findings, analysis of specific practice situations and the specialized nature of knowledge input are central to the student's professional development within a specified area of nursing endeavour.

MISSION STATEMENT FOR PART 4

The final part of the course is concerned with the process of **resolution**. During this part, the student will integrate theory and practice to a level whereby situations can be produced and outcomes determined.

The practical experiences at this stage will be within the context of rostered service in NHS hospital provision, enabling the student to contribute in a skilled and meaningful way to the assessment, planning, implementation and evaluation of health care, demonstrating effective observational, communication and caring skills. High-calibre role models, able to assist in disentangling dilemmas and removing uncertainty, will supervise the student's movement towards becoming a registered practitioner able to be innovative and offer creative responses to the changing pattern of health-care demands whilst working within ethical and legal frameworks.

Elucidation of the four central concepts is at a level that will allow the student to demonstrate creative and critical thinking within the activity of critical analysis and reflection.

Resolution will be attained through self and peer reflection, facilitated by the academic supervisor utilizing adult teaching and learning strategies established throughout the course.

During resolution, the student will demonstrate competency in knowledgeably and skilfully meeting the nursing needs of individuals and groups in health and sickness, in a specified area of practice. They will be sufficiently prepared to obtain a qualification which provides eligibility for admission to the Council's Register and to assume the responsibilities and accountability that nursing registration confers.

THE COMMON FOUNDATION PROGRAMME (CFP)

The Common Foundation Programme aims to provide students with a wide range of experience in health care to enable them to participate in and reflect upon care delivery with sensitivity and understanding and thus establish the basis for progression to the branch programme.

Part One in the CFP spans weeks 1–28 and is concerned with the process of orientation. Part Two spans weeks 29–78 and is concerned with that of identification.

Part One

Part One consists of two units:
Unit 1 spans weeks 1–7 and focuses on concepts of Person and Society/Environment.
Unit 2 spans weeks 8–28 and focuses on Health and Nursing.

Part Two

Unit 3 spans weeks 29–51 and focuses on the concepts of Person, and Society/Environment.
Unit 4 spans weeks 52–75 and focuses on Health and Health-care.
Unit 5 spans weeks 76–78 and prepares the student for transition to the branch programmes.

The key components for the CFP are subsumed under the four curriculum concepts, i.e. Person, Health and Health-care, Environment and

Society, and Nursing and are as follows:

Themes		Introduction
Person	1	Biological sciences
	2	Communication/interpersonal skills
	3	Personal development
	4	Philosophy and ethics
	5	Psychology
Environment/	6	Research
Society	7	Sociology
Health and Health-care	8	Health promotion and education
	9	Politics of health
	10	Sociology of health
	11	Therapeutic modes
Nursing	12	Applied biological science
	13	Interpersonal relationships
	14	Philosophy and ethics
	15	Management
	16	Nursing practice (integrated with)
	17	Nursing theory
	18	Professional development/issues
	19	Applied psychology
	20	Applied research
	21	Therapeutic roles

NB: To be developed in the branch, thus presenting a spiral curriculum model.

During the CFP, students will explore the resources and facilities available to meet the health needs of adults, children, parents and clients with a mental health problem and mental handicap/learning disabilities, in a variety of institutional and non-institutional settings.

Integrated contracted assignments

Students will be expected to complete assignments throughout the three-year programme, which will assess their ability to apply theory to practice.

BRANCH PROGRAMMES

Within the branch programmes, nursing becomes the prime concept, subsuming the concepts of Person, Health and Health-care, and Environment and Society. The key components reflect this shift in emphasis:

1 psychology
2 communication and interpersonal relationships
3 biological sciences

4 personal development
5 research
6 sociology of health
7 politics of health
8 health promotion and health education
9 therapeutic modes
10 nursing theory
11 nursing practice
12 ethics
13 professional development and issues
14 management

Part Three

Part Three in the branch programmes spans weeks 79–117 and is concerned with the process of application. Part Four spans weeks 118–156 and is concerned with that of resolution.

Part Three consists of two units:

Unit 6 spans weeks 79–100
Unit 7 spans weeks 101–117

Units 6 and 7 comprise theory-led practice with placements to areas pertaining to the specific client groups of the branch. An elective experience is undertaken during Unit 7.

Elective experience

The elective experience is seen as an integral and important part of the course which demands a high degree of responsibility on the part of the students. It is envisaged that the students will work locally, nationally or internationally. However, it needs to be noted that electives undertaken outside the UK are not recognized as part of the minimum recordable course hours required by the statutory body.

Information regarding the elective will be introduced to the students at the beginning of the Common Foundation Programme and discussed in detail during the CFP in order to allow sufficient time to make appropriate arrangements. It is intended that the elective will offer the students a challenging and fulfilling experience.

The intentions of this elective period are:

1 to allow the students to pursue an interest in an aspect of health-care delivery
2 to promote development of greater autonomy and responsibility and to further develop the ability to direct and control their own study
3 to broaden the student's experience
4 to develop organizing skills
5 to increase critical and evaluative skills
6 to enhance the student's future practice of nursing and delivery of care.

On return from the elective, the students will be expected to produce an evaluative report as well as sharing their experience with the rest of the group.

The area of study will be discussed amongst students, academic supervisors and relevant others in order to negotiate appropriate placements. The student will be responsible for negotiating and/or arranging finances.

Part Four

Part Four consists of three units:

Unit 8 spans weeks 118–133
Unit 9 spans weeks 134–150
Unit 10 spans weeks 151–156

These units contain 1000 hours service contribution in designated areas specific to the branch speciality. Unit 10 brings together students from all four branch programmes during which a formative assignment designed to identify the needs and requirements for professional practice will be undertaken.

Part Five   Transition to professional practice

The notion of bringing all branches together for the theoretical aspects has been retained, but whereas originally the clinical experience would have been gained in an area new to the student, current thinking is that it should be the same environment as that experienced in Unit 9.

This is for a variety of reasons.

- Evaluation of previous courses, where a similar professional transitional period is offered, has strongly indicated that the achievement of outcomes can be maximized if the student is already familiar with the environment.
- As part of the rostered service contribution it would enhance manpower planning and potentially assist in the move towards two intakes a year.
- It will enhance the students' skill acquisition as they will have longer in a known environment where they feel secure and a worthwhile member of the nursing team who is able to make a valuable contribution to care delivery.

Adult Branch Programme

The Adult Branch Programme is designed to continue the themes of the Common Foundation Programme, thus allowing the student to further develop knowledge and skills in order to meet the needs of the adult client/patient. The student will be prepared to work competently and proactively within the context of a service which is responsive to changes initiated by national, local and client need.

It is recognized that individuals are unique, therefore the main thrust of nursing within the branch programme is the study of the provision and management of holistic care. This will ensure that the nursing needs of adults, at any point on the health–illness continuum, through the age range and across the spectrum of health-care settings, will be met.

A developmental approach will continue to be used to facilitate learning. In particular, problem-solving skills will be enhanced during each unit, commencing with emphasis on implementation and planning, moving on to assessment and evaluation. This will enable the student to develop the skills required to deliver care systematically.

The educational process aims to heighten critical awareness of political and professional issues to ensure effective and efficient health-care delivery. Capitalizing upon experiences and opportunities offered within the branch programme will help to instil a sense of personal and professional responsibility which will ultimately enable the person to exercise professional accountability.

Mental Handicap/Learning Disability Branch Programme

The Mental Handicap/Learning Disability Branch Programme seeks to continue the model and themes from the Common Foundation Programme in the context of care for people with a mental handicap/learning disability. It intends to provide the student with knowledge, skills and attitudes they will need in order to fulfil the role and function of a competent nurse. It will also equip them with the flexibility of approach they will require to be able to practise in a variety of situations ranging from a person's own home to the hospital environment.

Throughout the programme, the emphasis is on the promotion of health which can be thought of as the ability to adapt to continually changing demands. Nursing care in this context can be seen as a 'Facilitation to Health' role, where students need to be able to adapt to identified needs, thereby participating in promotion of their own and the client/family health in a partnership. The programme seeks to promote the development of the participants as people, in the context of nursing, and therefore to reinforce the work carried out during the CFP.

A primary skills base will be established, starting with those which enable the practitioners to respond sensitively as a person to the needs of self and others and continuing through those associated with the creation of a positive learning and therapeutic environment in which the student is attached to the client. The importance of the wholeness of care is provided by opportunities to be with the person or the family over a period.

Mental Health Branch Programme

The quest of mental health nurses is the promotion of optimum mental health for all those who come within their sphere of influence. This occurs in many settings and across a broad spectrum of people, ranging from health education through to restorative and rehabilitative strategies or a dignified death. The art, science and craft of mental health nursing are inextricably linked to processes which occur before, during and after human interaction.

The context of mental health care is changing and any course preparing first-level practitioners should reflect this. The increase in care provided in the community, the changing nature of interprofessional work, changes in skill mix and the increasing involvement of other carers are central to these developments.

The content of a course leading to professional registration should not be too precisely prescribed. Indicators of content should be offered so that teachers and students can successfully collaborate in order to develop competence.

Child Branch Programme

The Child Branch Programme grows from and articulates with the Common Foundation Programme, utilizing the same curriculum framework and encompassing the major themes.

The programme recognizes that children are children before they are patients. They are not only individuals but members of families in a pluralistic society, where they adopt differing roles and function within a diversity of groups.

Children have unique needs which comprise varying levels of dependency. Inherent in childhood are the processes of growth and development in all aspects of being.

The concept of child health includes enabling the child and family to reach their optimal health potential. Children and their families have the right to informed participation in all decisions involving their distinct health/health-care needs.

It is acknowledged that, because of their specific needs, children should be nursed, whenever possible, within their home environment. Child health encompasses the implications and consequences of both local and international health-care provision.

The environment in which children are cared for must be safe, enhance growth and development and foster the concept of belonging. Children and their families must have access to appropriate facilities and resources which fulfil their needs as members of society.

The branch programme will provide the student with the knowledge, skills and attitudes they will need in order to competently fulfil the role and function of the child care nurse.

Learning resources and library facilities available

Refer to Part A of the Project 2000 supplementary document for details of library services, funding arrangements and their management and development.

COMMON FOUNDATION PROGRAMME – PLACEMENTS

During Units 2–4 students will gain experience in five placement options encompassing Mental Health, Mental Handicap/Learning Disabilities, Mother and Child, Adult and Child settings. This will facilitate the integration of theory and practice by exposing the students to a wide range of people and resources in both institutional and non-institutional settings.

Placements are not sequenced in a specific order as linkage is provided through the major concepts, thereby providing flexibility in the programme to prevent overload of the circuit at any one time.

Each placement is 10 weeks long and includes two weeks of theory and eight weeks of practice. Six study days are detailed to occur during the placement experience.

The aim of the placements is to enable students to gain insight into the total needs of specific client groups in both institutional and non-institutional settings. Flexibility in the structure of these placements is expected given the restricted availability of experiences in certain areas of practice.

Institutional placements

Placements aim to orientate students to the practice of nursing and address the concepts in terms of integrating theory and practice. During placements the students will identify key issues which embrace the nature of nursing and begin to develop the essential care skills underpinning aspects of health and health-care. Placements will be assessed and information recorded in the specific booklets as outlined in the progressive assessment scheme.

Placements have been chosen as per the Criteria for Placement Areas (pp.191–194), in particular, for their ability to provide a supportive learning environment and appropriate learning opportunities for this stage of the course. These areas will constitute an allocation circuit that will continue to be developed to meet emerging needs. Staff will be prepared according to the agreed strategy within the college.

Placement supervision

Within both hospital and community settings the appropriate supervision of students is crucial to the acquisition of knowledge and skills, the development of analytical and critical thinking and the ability to undertake the roles required of a registered practitioner.

One aspect of ensuring that the supervision is at the right level and calibre is to clarify what is meant by 'supervision' and to set guidelines for recognizing people who could act as supervisors. A substantial amount of this work has been undertaken already within the context of continuous assessment of practice, but the branch planners felt it necessary to supplement this further.

Supervision aims at building up the confidence of the student within a safe environment in order that learning may take place. The support and experience should be such as to enable the level of confidence of the student to increase progressively and to finally empower the student to function as an independent practitioner.

Within the learning milieu, the experience provides exposure to the professional culture, values and behaviours that are considered worthwhile for a qualified nurse to acquire. The professional issues and reality of the work situation will be organized in such a way as to help her/him to reach satisfactory resolution and adjustment.

Through experience, learning, support and debriefing from the supervisor, the whole experience will promote growth and development towards becoming a responsible and accountable practitioner.

Support of the student will be forthcoming from both the supervisor and the link teacher. The student will be encouraged to keep a personal journal of their experience which will become the focus for discussion. Throughout the placement, the student, supervisor and the link teacher should discuss progress in order to monitor performance, discuss the learning programme and give guidance/direction to the student regarding educational and other resources.

During placements the clinical supervisor will discuss the learning outcomes of the student and help to formulate a plan of action to be taken in order to achieve the outcomes. The clinical supervisor will provide the opportunities for learning and the necessary support that the student may require.

Non-institutional placements

Placements enable students to familiarize themselves with the local environment whilst exploring the facilities available for particular client groups. Subsequently course participants will examine the major concepts by investigating the locality to identify issues and influences in a pluralistic society which will positively or negatively affect a person's health status.

A range of experiences are available for placements and/or visits which will enable the students to enhance their knowledge regarding mental health, mental handicap, adult and child clients and aspects of parenting.

While it is envisaged that students will gain a broad insight into the facilities, some may wish to focus on one particular aspect whereas others may choose to enquire into a range of opportunities. Negotiation will be between students and their personal tutor and a nominated non-institutional placement coordinator. The coordinator will be responsible for generating placements, ongoing negotiation of placements and keeping files and directories up to date, to ensure a readily available supply of experiences for the student to choose from. The designated person will act as a resource, receiving information from the personal tutor and students regarding requirements. He/she can then give help and guidance to identify appropriate experiences in order to design a comprehensive placement package.

By negotiating and capitalizing upon experiences, students will gain indepth knowledge of the locality and the society within it. During periods of resolution students will share information, ideas and resources with their peers, thereby gathering relevant data to meet the needs of potential future clients.

During each placement the students will be formatively assessed using the appropriate form and will be required to write a report of their experiences and include supportive material to share with teachers and peers.

Study days

During study days students will pursue issues related to: nursing practice, meeting clients needs, solving problems, and illness entities which are specific to the placements. The study days will be facilitated by relevant teachers and students will be encouraged to organize and lead sessions as part of their personal growth and professional development.

Teaching/learning strategies may include:

- visiting speakers
- placement-related visits
- tutorials
- peer group learning
- seminars
- lectures
- learning contracts
- contract assignments.

APPENDIX 3 CONTINUOUS ASSESSMENT OF STUDENTS: AN EXAMPLE

Additionally, see Appendix 5 from UKCC New Nursing Competencies.

ASSESSMENT OF PRACTICE

The purpose of practical assessment

The purpose of practical assessment is to monitor the student's progress and achievements with regard to course learning outcomes as well as personal and professional development. The process of continuous assessment should maximize learning and enable students to maintain an ongoing awareness of their progress.

The form of practical assessment

Assessment of practice comprises both formative and summative elements which ensures students' learning experiences are planned and structured to suit course and individual needs. A team approach to assessing has been adopted and ongoing dialogue between student, placement and teaching staff is an essential feature of the scheme to establish the relationship between theory and practice and to identify strengths and deficits at the earliest opportunity.

Because of the nature of skill acquisition, it is not desirable to separate the process of formative and summative assessment entirely and the curriculum seeks to reflect this by including both within the same documentation.

The **formative element** consists of a series of interpersonal exchanges which provide the opportunity to establish rapport and a climate in which the individual can explore their strengths and weaknesses. It is the responsibility of the placement named practitioner to ensure these exchanges take place.

The **summative element** consists of a series of contract assignments and a rating scale that enables the named practitioners and personal tutors to accurately plot the student's skill acquisition, culminating in competent practice towards the end of the CFP in readiness for the Branch Programme.

Progressive assessment booklets have been designed to incorporate the assessment of applied theory to practice.

The booklets comprise a section for orientation to the placement, thus ensuring the student is aware of certain vital information as quickly as possible. There are progress interview sheets to record information regarding the student's strengths and needs and space for a plan of action to be formulated which must be agreed and signed by both student and assessor.

Activity statements have been written which are congruent with the course and the Nurses, Midwives and Health Visitors Rules Approval Order 1989.

ROLES AND RESPONSIBILITIES OF STAFF INVOLVED IN PROGRESSIVE ASSESSMENT

Placement mentor

The placement mentor role includes the following activities:

- orienting the student to the learning environment
- assessing learning needs and setting out plans of action to meet those needs
- maximizing the opportunities for learning
- providing or organizing direct supervision and instruction
- undertaking formative assessment of the student's performance.

This role may be shared by more than one member of the placement team.

Placement assessor

The placement assessor role includes the following activities:

- overseeing progress towards fulfilling objectives
- ensuring that relevant learning opportunities are provided
- liaising with the mentor and academic mentor as appropriate
- taking responsibility for the summative aspects assessment.

Academic mentor (personal tutor)

The academic mentor role includes the following activities:

- encouraging the relationship between theory and practice
- supervising academic assignments
- maximizing learning opportunities
- advising on learning activities
- providing academic support in the processes of formative and summative assessment
- participating in the preparation of placement mentors.

This role will be undertaken by a member of the teaching staff.

Learning environment evaluation

The learning environment evaluation will help in the following activities:

- monitor the learning opportunities made available to the student
- monitor the process and outcome of progressive assessment
- delegate the placement and assessor/mentor role to suitably prepared and qualified staff
- prepare placement assessors/mentors (joint responsibility with academic mentor)

- endeavour to provide and maintain educational resources
- maximize on the skill mix of the staff to enrich the student's experience.

The student

Within the process of progressive assessment, this role will include the following activities:

- actively participating in the assessment strategy
- taking advantage of learning opportunities offered
- identifying potential/new learning opportunities
- sharing responsibility for the occurrence of progress interviews
- identifying personal objectives and monitoring achievement
- sharing responsibility for outcomes of action plan
- maintaining a personal portfolio.

CLINICAL PLACEMENTS

There will be a period of clinical practice throughout the CFP. You will undertake each of the following three clinical experiences in rotation.

Community placement

A period spent becoming involved in the care of patients/clients and their families in a community setting. The link person in the community will be a skilled practitioner who will introduce you to the range of work as well as coordinating your involvement with other health-care professionals involved in health services. The written assessment format chosen for this experience is the neighbourhood study (see p.193) because it will focus your thoughts on global organization of health services.

Hospital placement

A period spent becoming involved in the care of patients/clients and their families in a hospital setting. A skilled qualified practitioner will be your link person in the area and will introduce you to their field of work. Opportunities will be offered, and should be sought, to participate in the care of patients/clients and their families in a range of hospital environments. You should find it useful to consistently follow the progress of a small group of patients/clients. The forms of written assessment available – case study via contract assignments – should enhance this.

Critical care placement

A period spent becoming involved in the care of patients/clients and their families in an intensive care setting. A qualified skilled practitioner will be your link person in this area and will introduce you to his/her specialist field of expertise and help to support you in this demanding environment. You should aim to achieve consistent involvement in the care of a small group of patients/clients.

LEARNING OPPORTUNITIES FOR CLINICAL STUDIES

Community placement

Under the supervision of a skilled practitioner, the experience gained during this placement will enable you to:

- examine the delivery of health-care services to clients and their families in a range of settings
- apply a primary, preventative approach to health issues
- gain an appreciation of the client's place in his/her family and society
- examine those factors in their environment which may affect health
- examine, while participating within, the organization of services for promotion, maintenance and improvement of health
- appraise the cooperation between professional groups concerned with health in the community
- examine in detail the interdisciplinary efforts required by a small number of clients with particular needs
- apply facets of current theory and research findings to practical health nursing work.

The skilled practitioner with whom you are linked during this placement will act as your 'guide' for this experience. You will have the opportunity to gain an in-depth appreciation of his/her work while learning about health services in general in the community. In the interests of getting as wide a picture as possible of such services, the skilled practitioner will put you in touch with a range of these services within his/her 'patch'. This will also be important for you in preparing the neighbourhood study.

Hospital placement

Under the supervision of a skilled practitioner, the experience gained during this placement will enable you to:

- explore the philosophy and strategies of nursing practice aimed at minimizing the adverse effects of hospitalization on the patient/client and his/her family
- continue to develop interpersonal skills in a range of clinical situations and begin to act as an advocate for the patient/client and his/her family
- examine the rationale for potential nursing actions using current theory and research findings
- develop further therapeutic skills with the patient/client and his/her family
- organize the environment of care in the acute setting to maximize the physical, psychological and emotional safety of the patient and his/her family

- critically evaluate the use of nursing models and nursing care plans in the organization of care for the patient and his/her family.

Critical care placement

Under the supervision of a skilled practitioner, the experience gained during this placement will enable you to:

- examine the role of health-care professionals involved in the care of the sick
- develop communication skills with the patient and his/her family in a hospital environment
- gain an understanding of the specific problems of the patient with life-threatening illness, chronic or acute, and of the dying and of the families of such patients
- practise the skills of nursing
- consider the stresses for the nurse of working in this environment and reflect on strategies for dealing with these in as healthy a way as possible
- develop the skills of working closely with other health-care professionals to ensure the delivery of high-quality care.

THE NEIGHBOURHOOD STUDY – GUIDELINES

Completing a neighbourhood study will give you the opportunity to carefully analyse the environment of a given geographical area. The focus of this examination will, of course, be on the health of patients/clients and their families who live in the area in question. You should use your own observations, the knowledge of health-care professionals working locally and other local information resources. You should aim to describe as fully as possible all the services working to promote and improve health and well-being as well as factors in the environment which might militate against good health.

From your assessment of the area you should also identify an area of health concern or need and outline a plan of nursing action to address the issue.

The aim of this assignment is to:

- give you a greater insight into the character of the area in which you are undertaking a community placement
- enhance your awareness of the influence of environment on health
- look at potential health-care provisions in terms of available health-care resources.

Having agreed your aims and objectives, the format of this paper should contain the following.

- An assessment of the locality using a framework of your choice. Many textbooks on community nursing suggest frameworks for assessing the needs of a community; include epidemiological and social policy data where appropriate.

- Identification of an area of health concern or need, explaining your choice.
- A plan of community nursing action to address this issue within the realistic confines of the resources available.

Appendix 4   Opportunistic learning: an example

The accident and emergency department

To The Student

It is your own responsibility to ensure that the learning opportunities checklist is completed and signed by yourself.

On completion of your Accident and Emergency experience, you should have had the opportunity to complete all the competencies at the required level, i.e. competency code of 3 (see below).

If for any reason this has not been possible, you will need to indicate which level you have achieved. Arrangements can then be made for you to discuss this with your tutor/assessor/mentor.

You will note that many of the learning opportunities are related to safety, either your own or that of other people. It is therefore of the utmost importance that you endeavour to achieve the level of knowledge and competence which will enable you to function as a safe practitioner.

Competency codes

Student – self-assessment

Code
0 = Have not had the opportunity to gain experience.
1 = Know nothing about the skill.
2 = Have knowledge but doubt my ability to perform the skill safely without direction and supervision.
3 = Could perform safely with full supervision.
4 = Could perform safely with minimum supervision.
5 = Could teach the knowledge and skill to a patient or relative and junior nurse.

Assessor – assessment of student

0 = The opportunity for the experience was not available.
1 = Has no knowledge of the required skill.
2 = Has knowledge but is unable to perform safely even with direction and supervision.
3 = Able to perform safely with full supervision.
4 = Able to perform safely with minimum supervision.
5 = Able to demonstrate and perform skills safely without supervision, and has the knowledge and capability to teach a patient or relative and junior nurse.

Criterion for successful completion

For students gaining new skills and knowledge in the A&E department, a competence *code of 3* is the criterion for acceptable performance during the experience. (Neary, 1992)

NB: This page to be completed by the learner before being assessed by assessor.

Triage areas

Aim

1 To enable the student to understand the need for making the correct initial assessment of the patient and to help the student to recognize the various degrees of urgency and priorities.
2 To enable the student to appreciate the need to know the whereabouts of patients and relatives within the department and relevant support areas.

Learning opportunities
Under the supervision of a skilled practitioner, the student should have the opportunity to:

1 receive patients and relatives into the department and assess their immediate needs
2 care for children accompanying adult patients
3 make an initial assessment and recognize the degree of urgency and/or priorities
4 identify patients and initiate appropriate clinical records
5 show sympathetic attention to and communication with patients and relatives, having regard for possible cultural and religious differences
6 discuss the need for deployment of staff in the department and the need to keep account of patients' whereabouts in the department

Self-assessment

Achieved	Not achieved	Code

	Achieved	Not achieved	Code
7 participate in the teamwork necessary for identifying priorities in patient care			
8 develop high standards of nursing care in respect of both the seriously ill and the more numerous minor casualties			
9 develop an understanding and appreciate that all injuries are always major to a patient, regardless of how they may appear to the nurse			

Resuscitation room

Self-assessment

Learning opportunities
Under the supervision of a skilled practitioner, the student should have the opportunity to:

	Achieved	Not achieved	Code
1 discuss the importance of obtaining a comprehensive history of the incident from the patient, witness or ambulance crew			
2 discuss the need for initial rapid assessment of seriously ill or injured patients in terms of: a) checking airway b) assessing breathing c) monitoring circulation d) safeguarding cervical spine			
3 assist in the preparation of the patient for rapid examination, or treatment, in the resuscitation room			

	Achieved	Not achieved	Code

4 demonstrate the ability to clear a patient's airway

5 demonstrate the ability to assist a patient with his breathing

6 demonstrate the ability to assess and maintain a patient's circulation

7 a) assist in and explain the importance of immobilization of injured limbs
  b) assist in the application of different types of splint:
    i) box splint
    ii) Thomas splint and skin traction
    iii) sandbags
  c) observe the use of cervical collars and sandbags

8 increase her knowledge of the methods of pain control in A&E by observing and assisting a skilled practitioner

9 gain a knowledge of the significance of neurological observation and record a neurological status

10 assist in the care of a patient admitted with chest pain

11 a) observe for and recognize the signs of cardiac arrest
  b) describe the methods of basic life support
  c) participate in a cardiac arrest procedure
  d) identify the cardiac arrest drug box and describe the drugs used in this emergency

STUDENT LEARNING CONTRACT

WARD 12

WARD PHILOSOPHY

TO PROVIDE A SAFE, CARING ENVIRONMENT IN WHICH PATIENTS AND RELATIVES CAN RECEIVE PHYSICAL, PSYCHOLOGICAL, INTERPERSONAL, SOCIAL AND SPIRITUAL (HOLISTIC) HELP WHEN SPECIFIC CONDITIONS NECESSITATE, WITH AN INDIVIDUALIZED MANNER/APPROACH.

WELCOME TO WARD 12

May I and all the staff take this opportunity to wish you a rewarding, interesting and happy allocation with us.

This booklet gives a general outline of the ward and should answer some of your questions.

Both your supervisor* and myself are always available for help and guidance.

Ward Sister

*Mentor or preceptor may be the terminology you are familiar with.

Emergency equipment

During your orientation to the ward, you will be shown the position of the cardiac arrest trolley, defibrillator, portable suction machine, oxygen cylinder, fire escape and fire extinguishers. Please familiarize yourself with these. All beds should have fire evacuation sheets.

Ward reports

All early staff receive a ward report at 7.45 a.m. in the seminar room from the night staff. At 1.30 p.m. a report is given to the late shift. Please feel able to attend and to ask questions and exchange ideas, as this is a very useful teaching time.

Resource centre

Here you will find:

1 a collection of books covering most topics
2 handouts and information packs about the types of conditions nursed on the ward
3 current copies of:
   - *Nursing Times*
   - *Nursing Standard*
   - *Surgical Nurse*
   - *Cancer Nursing*
   - *Care of the Elderly*
   - *Practical Diabetes*
4 a selection of audio and video tapes.

Please do not take any of the above away from the ward without first checking with the nurse in charge.

Progress reports

You are on continuous assessment and your named assessor will work through your booklet as per the guidelines stated.

College policy requires that your preliminary interview is conducted during the first week of your allocation, your mid-term interview about the fourth week and a final interview during the last week. These will be done by your team leader and in consultation with your mentor.

If you have learning objectives that you wish to achieve on the ward, please identify these at your preliminary interview, to allow adequate preparations to be made. Sister A and Staff Nurse A are both assessors and mentors; one will act as your assessor, while the other will act as your mentor.

Ward learning opportunities

You will work within a team of nurses and other health professionals, under the supervision of your designated mentor, and will have the opportunity to:

1   learn, consolidate and extend your basic skills
2   evaluate the effectiveness of individualized nursing through the use of the nursing process (within the framework of the Roper/Henderson nursing model)
3   under the supervision of a qualified nurse, to:
   • take a nursing history
   • assess patients' needs
   • formulate a care plan to meet those needs
   • evaluate the effectiveness of the care plan
   • make recommendations regarding possible changes to the care plan
4   observe the effects of illness on:
   • the patient
   • the patient's family and friends, and note how these are dealt with by experienced nurses.
5   consider the relationship between specific illnesses and the patient's mode of life and the part that health education might play in the prevention of further problems
6   consider the problems which patients might have on returning home, how the nursing team might anticipate these problems and the measures which might be taken to solve these
7   as part of a team of nurses, plan, deliver and evaluate pre- and postoperative care for patients undergoing a variety of surgical procedures
8   as part of the assessment and delivery of care, accompany a patient to other departments for investigations and tests
9   participate in the delivery of continuing care to terminal patients and their families.

Special learning opportunities available on Ward 12

1   During the allocation, to gain insight into the pre- and postoperative care of breast cancer patients. To understand the special needs and requirements of these patients with regard to:
    - psychological care, with particular reference to body image
    - fitting of prosthetics and bras, both temporary and permanent
    - support services available to the patients and their families.

2   To provide insight into the pre- and postoperative care of patients requiring a stoma, colostomy, ileostomy or urostomy. To understand the special needs of these patients with regards to:
    - psychological care, with particular reference to body image
    - the use of the appliances available
    - support services available to the patients and their families.

Appendix 5 UKCC (1999) Nursing Competencies: final draft

FINAL DRAFT

Nursing Competencies

The Council uses the term competence to 'describe the skills and ability to practise safely and effectively without the need for direct supervision' (Fitness for Practice 1999:35)

The pre-registration nursing programme shall be designed to prepare the student: to be able, on registration, to apply knowledge, understanding and skills when performing to the standards required in employment; and to provide the nursing care that patients/clients require, safely and competently, and so assume the responsibilities and accountabilities necessary for public protection.

The development of nursing programmes arises from the premise that nursing is a practice based profession, recognising the primacy of patient/client well being and respect for individuals and is founded on the principles that:

- evidence should inform practice, through the integration of relevant knowledge;
- students are actively involved in nursing care delivery under supervision;
- the Code of Professional Conduct applies to all practice interventions;
- skills and knowledge are transferable;
- research underpins practice and
- the importance of life long learning and continuing professional development is recognised.

The outcomes and competencies expressed will be achieved under the direction of a registered nurse.

The author's view

It is my belief that these competencies and outcomes need to be written in language that identifies the standards, conditions and criteria by which students will be assessed. See pages 57–69 for examples and rationale.

Domain	Outcomes to be achieved for entry to the branch programme
1 Professional/ Ethical Practice	**Discuss in an informed manner, the implications of professional regulation for nursing practice.** • Demonstrate a basic knowledge of professional regulation and self regulation; • Recognise and acknowledge limitations of own abilities; • Recognise situations that require referral on to a registered practitioner. **Demonstrate an awareness of the UKCC Code of Professional Conduct.** • Commit to the principle that the primary purpose of the professional nurse is to protect and serve society; • Accept responsibility for own actions and decisions. **Demonstrate an awareness of, and apply ethical principles to nursing practice.** • Demonstrate respect for patient/client confidentiality; • Identify ethical issues in day to day practice **Demonstrate an awareness of legislation relevant to nursing practice.** • Identify key issues in relevant legislation relating to mental health, children, data protection, manual handling, health and safety etc **Demonstrate the importance of promoting equity in patient/client care by contributing to nursing care in a fair and anti-discriminatory way.** • Demonstrate fairness and sensitivity when responding to patients/clients/groups from diverse circumstances; • Recognise the needs of patients/clients whose lives are affected by disability, however manifest.

Competencies for entry to the Register
1.1 **Manage self, one's practice, and that of others, in accordance with the UKCC Code of Professional Conduct, recognising one's own abilities and limitations.** • Practise in accordance with the UKCC Code of Professional Conduct; • Use professional standards of practice to self assess performance; • Consult with a registered nurse when nursing care requires expertise beyond own current scope of competence; • Consult other health care professionals when individual or group needs fall outside the scope of nursing practice; • Identify unsafe practice and respond appropriately to ensure a safe outcome; • Manage the delivery of care services within sphere of own accountability.
1.2 **Practise in accordance with an ethical and legal framework that ensures the primacy of patient/client interest and well-being and respects confidentiality.** • Demonstrate knowledge of legislation and health and social policy relevant to nursing practice; • Ensure confidentiality and security of written and verbal information acquired in a professional capacity; • Demonstrate knowledge of contemporary ethical issues and their impact on nursing and healthcare; • Manage the complexities arising from ethical and legal dilemmas.
1.3 **Practise in a fair and anti-discriminatory way, acknowledging the difference in beliefs and cultural practices of individuals or groups.** • Maintain, support and acknowledge the rights of individuals or groups in the health care setting; • Act to ensure that rights of individuals and groups are not compromised; • Respect the values, customs and beliefs of individuals and groups; • Provide care that demonstrates sensitivity to patients'/clients' diversity.

Domain	Outcomes to be achieved for entry to the branch programme
2 Care delivery	**Discuss methods of, barriers to and boundaries of effective communication and interpersonal relationships.** • Recognise the effect of own values on interactions with patients/clients and their significant others; • Utilise appropriate communication skills with patients/clients • Acknowledge the boundaries of a professional caring relationship. **Demonstrate sensitivity in interaction with and provision of information to patients/clients.** **Contribute to enhancing the health and social well being of patients/clients by understanding how, under the supervision of a registered practitioner, to:** • Contribute to the assessment of health needs; • Identify opportunities for health promotion; • Identify networks of health and social care services. **Contribute to the development and documentation of nursing assessments by participating in comprehensive and systematic nursing assessment of the physical, psychological, social and spiritual needs of patients/clients.** • Be aware of assessment strategies to guide collection of data for assessing patients/clients and use assessment tools under guidance; • Discuss the prioritisation of care needs; • Be aware of the need to reassess patients/clients as to their needs for nursing care. **Contribute to the planning of nursing care, involving patients/clients and where possible their carers, demonstrating an understanding of helping patients/clients to make informed decisions.** • Identify care needs based on the assessment of a client/patient; • Participate in the negotiation and agreement of the care plan with the patient/client, and significant others under the supervision of a registered nurse; • Inform patients/clients about intended nursing actions respecting their right to participate in decisions about their care.

2 Care delivery (Continued)	**Contribute to the implementation of a programme of nursing care, designed and supervised by registered practitioners.** • Undertake activities that are consistent with the plan of care and within the limits of own abilities **Demonstrate evidence of a developing knowledge base that underpins safe nursing practice.** • Access and discuss research and other evidence in nursing and related disciplines; • Identify examples of the use of evidence in planned nursing interventions. **Demonstrate a range of essential nursing skills, under the supervision of a registered nurse, to meet individuals' needs, which include:** maintaining dignity, privacy and confidentiality; effective communication and observational skills, including listening and taking physiological measurements; safety and health, including moving and handling and infection control; essential first aid and emergency procedures; administration of medicines; emotional, physical and personal care including meeting the need for comfort, nutrition and personal hygiene. **Contribute to the evaluation of the appropriateness of nursing care delivered.** • Demonstrate an awareness of the need to regularly assess a patient's/client's response to nursing interventions; • Provide for a supervising registered practitioner, evaluative commentary and information on nursing care based on personal observations and actions; • Contribute to the documentation of the outcomes of nursing interventions. **Recognise situations in which agreed plans of nursing care no longer appear appropriate and refer these to an appropriate accountable practitioner.** • Demonstrate the ability to discuss and accept care decisions; • Accurately record observations made and communicate these to the relevant members of the health and social care team.

Competencies for entry to the Register

2.1	**Engage in, dvelop and disengage from therapeutic relationships through the use of appropriate communication and interpersonal skills.** • Utilise a range of effective and appropriate communication and engagement skills; • Maintain and where appropriate disengage from professional caring relationships that focus on meeting the patient's/client's needs within professional therapeutic boundaries
2.2	**Create and utilise opportunities to promote the health and well being of patients/clients and groups.** • Consult with patients/clients and groups to identify their needs and desires for health promotion advice; • Provide relevant and current health information to patients/clients and groups in a form which facilitates their understanding and acknowledges choice/individual preference; • Provide support/education in the development and/or maintenance of independent living skills; • Seek specialist/expert advice as appropriate.
2.3	**Undertake and document a comprehensive, systematic and accurate nursing assessment of the physical, psycholo-gical, social and spiritual needs of patients/clients/communities.** • Select valid and reliable assessment tools for the required purpose; • Systematically collect data regarding the health and functional status of individuals/clients/communities through appropriate interaction, observation and measurement; • Analyse and interpret data accurately to inform nursing care and take appropriate action.
2.4	**Formulate and document a plan of nursing care, where possible in partnership with patients/clients/carer(s)/ significant others within a framework of informed consent.** • Establish priorities for care based on individual or group needs; • Develop and document a plan of care to achieve optimal health, habilitation, rehabilitation based on assessment and current nursing knowledge; • Identify expected outcomes including a time frame for achievement and/or review in consultation with patients/clients/carers/significant others and members of the health and social care team.

2.5 Based on best available evidence, apply knowledge and an appropriate repertoire of skills indicative of safe nursing practice.

- Ensure that current research findings and other evidence are incorporated in practice;
- Identify relevant changes in practice or new information and disseminate it to colleagues;
- Contribute to the application of a range of interventions to support patients/clients that optimise their health and well being;
- Demonstrate safe application of the skills required to meet the needs of patients/clients within the current sphere of practice;
- Identify and respond to patients'/clients' ongoing learning and care needs;
- Engage with, and evaluate, the evidence base that underpins safe nursing practice.

2.6 Provide a rationale for the nursing care delivered that takes account of social, cultural, spiritual, legal, political and economic influences.

- Identify, collect and evaluate information to justify the effective utilisation of resources to achieve planned outcomes of nursing care.

2.7 Evaluate and document the outcomes of nursing and other interventions.

- Collaborate with patients/clients, and when appropriate additional carers to review and monitor the progress of individuals or groups towards planned outcomes;
- Analyse and revise expected outcomes, nursing interventions and priorities in accordance with changes in individual's condition, needs or circumstances.

2.8 Demonstrate sound clinical judgement across a range of differing professional and care delivery contexts.

- Use evidence based knowledge from nursing and related disciplines to select and individualise nursing interventions;
- Demonstrate the ability to transfer skills and knowledge to a variety of circumstances and settings;
- Recognise the need for adaptation and adapt nursing practice to meet varying and unpredictable circumstances;
- Ensure that practice does not compromise the nurse's duty of care to individuals or safety of the public.

Domain	Outcomes to be achieved for entry to the branch programme
3 Care management	Contribute to the identification of actual and potential risks to patients/clients and their carers, to self and others and participate in measures to promote and ensure health and safety.
	• Understand and implement health and safety principles and policies;
	• Recognise and report situations which are potentially unsafe for patients/clients, self and others.
	Demonstrate an understanding of the role of others by participating in inter-professional working practice.
	• Identify the roles of the members of the health and social care team;
	• Work within the health and social care team to maintain and enhance integrated care.
	Demonstrate literacy, numeracy and computer skills needed to record, enter, store, retrieve and organise data essential for care delivery.

Competencies for entry to the Register

3.1 **Contribute to public protection by creating and maintaining a safe environment of care through the use of quality assurance and risk management strategies.**

- Apply relevant principles to ensure the safe administration of therapeutic substances;
- Use appropriate risk assessment tools to identify actual and potential risks;
- Identify environmental hazards and eliminate and/or prevent where possible;
- Communicate safety concerns to a relevant authority;
- Manage risk to provide care that best meets the needs and interests of patients/clients and the public.

3.2 **Demonstrate knowledge of effective inter-professional working practices that respect and utilise the contributions of members of the health and social care team.**

- Establish and maintain collaborative working relationships with members of the health and social care team and others;
- Participate with members of the health and social care team in decision making concerning patients/clients;
- Review and evaluate care with members of the health and social care team and others.

3.3 **Delegate duties to others, as appropriate, ensuring they are supervised and monitored.**

- Take into account the role and competence of staff when delegating work;
- Maintain own accountability and responsibility when delegating aspects of care to others;
- Demonstrate the ability to co-ordinate the delivery of nursing/health care.

3.4 **Demonstrate key skills:**

- Literacy – interpret and present information that is comprehensible;
- Numeracy – accurately interpret numerical data and their significance for safe delivery of care;
- Information technology and management – interpret and utilise data/technology, taking account of legal, ethical and safety considerations, in the delivery and enhancement of care;
- Problem solving – demonstrate sound clinical decision making that can be justified even when made on the basis of limited information.

Domain	Outcomes to be achieved for entry to the branch programme
4 Personal/ Professional development	**Demonstrate responsibility for ones own learning through the development of a portfolio of practice and recognise when further learning is required.** • Identify specific learning needs and objectives; • Begin to engage with, and interpret, the evidence base that underpins nursing practice. **Acknowledge the importance of seeking supervision to develop safe nursing practice.**

Competencies for entry to the Register
4.1 **Demonstrate a commitment to the need for continuing professional development and personal supervision activities in order to enhance knowledge, skills, values and attitudes needed for safe and effective nursing practice.** • Identify own professional development needs by engaging in activities such as reflection in and on practice and lifelong learning; • Develop a personal development plan that takes into account personal, professional and organisational needs; • Share experience with colleagues and patients/clients to identify additional knowledge/skills needed to manage unfamiliar or professionally challenging situations; • Take action to meet any identified knowledge and skills deficit likely to affect the delivery of care within current sphere of practice.
4.2 **Enhance the professional development and safe practice of others through peer support, leadership, supervision and teaching.** • Contribute to creating a climate conducive to learning; • Contribute to the learning experiences and development of others by facilitating the mutual sharing of knowledge and experience; • Demonstrate effective leadership in the establishment and maintenance of safe nursing practice.

PSDirect/edpol/competencies/nursing/ncompfinal
29 February 2000

Glossary

Accountability   Being answerable for what you do in carrying out your responsibility. In line management, accountability is to the next higher manager.

Advocacy   Representing a person or putting a case to promote the interests of another. Self-advocacy is the ability to present one's own case.

Appraisal   A review or survey of performance, normally for the purpose of career and/or educational development.

Assertiveness   Dealing with interpersonal conflicts in a firm, clear and positive way. It can be contrasted with aggressiveness, which implies hostile and non-compromising behaviour, and passiveness, which indicates a lack of will to stand up for oneself.

Assessment   Determining the extent to which an individual has reached the desired level of competence in skill, knowledge, understanding or attitudes in relation to a specified goal.

Assessment tool   A method by which a judgement is made of a nurse's competence or a patient's/client's needs.

Assessor (primary)   An appropriately qualified and experienced first level nurse/midwife/health visitor who has undertaken a course to develop his/her skills in assessing and judging the student's level of attainment relating to the stated learning outcomes.

Associate nurse   A member of a nursing care team who takes responsibility for the care of patients in the absence of the primary nurse. (See also **primary nursing**)

Autonomy   The power of authority to make your own decisions.

Care plan   Statement of the goals to be achieved by the patient in overcoming problems and of the nursing interventions to be made if progress is unsatisfactory. It includes the implications of the interventions and information from assessment and evaluation.

Competency   The degree of accomplishment that meets a satisfactory standard of performance.

Construct of nursing   Statement of the philosophy of nursing. It is also sometimes called the definition of nursing.

Contract assignment   An integral part of learning contracts which assesses the student's learning.

Critical incident   A problematic or significant event which is documented and analysed in order to find solutions and gain insights.

Curriculum   The total way in which education or training is put into practice, including objectives, content, teaching and learning methods, and evaluation.

Empathy   The capacity to adopt another person's perspective and so understand their situation as it appears to them.

Ethical   Being in accordance with rules of behaviour that are considered right in a profession such as nursing.

Evaluation   Determining the worth or value of a thing, person or process, for example, of a care plan or a personal learning plan. The process attempts to assess many contributing factors, not just achievement.

Experiential learning   An approach to education and training based on providing students with structured activities and the opportunity to reflect on them, so they can learn by doing.

First-level nurse   A registered nurse, e.g. RGN, RMN.

Formative assessment   Continuing and systematic appraisal to determine the degree of mastery of a given learning task and to help identify and agree the further learning necessary to achieve mastery. (See also *summative assessment*.)

Holistic care   An approach to medical treatment which considers the patient as a whole, physically and psychologically, rather than dealing with isolated symptoms.

Implementation   Putting a plan into practice; in nursing, to provide care from a plan devised for specific needs.

Individualized care   An approach to care that is patient or client centred, determined by individual needs or preferences rather than by pre-set ideas or routines.

Interpersonal skill   A term for the skill used in interacting or communicating with other people.

Intervention   Action taken to alter the course of events and/or to solve a problem when progress is unsatisfactory.

Learning contract   A written agreement between tutor, student and mentor, which clearly states what the student will do to achieve the goals set.

Learning opportunities   A wide range of knowledge, skills and attitudes that the student may be exposed to during a clinical/practice placement.

Learning outcomes   Specific items which all students will have the opportunity to acquire during a clinical placement.

Learning process   A systematic approach to helping students to learn by assessing learning needs, planning, implementing, reassessing and evaluating.

Learning reflection diary   A booklet which is used to record details of the nurse's clinical or practical work and the activities carried out. It is used for reflection on this experience and for identifying and recording learning.

Mandatory   Compulsory. For example, mandatory refresher courses must be taken by registered midwives, and registered nurses may be required to take them in the near future.

Mentor   An appropriately qualified and experienced professional who, by example and facilitation, guides, assists and supports a student nurse.

Model   A diagram or construction that can be used as a frame of reference. (Example *models of health* and *nursing models*.)

Multidisciplinary team   A team of professionals from several disciplines or fields of practice. In health care, a multidisciplinary team might consist of medical, nursing, paramedical and social work staff.

Named practitioner An appropriately qualified and experienced first-level nurse/midwife/HV who has responsibility for monitoring, supervising and assessing students.

Negotiated learning A way of planning learning in which both the student and the tutor or mentor agree what will be covered by the learning programme, in what way and with what help and support from others.

Nursing audit A systematic review and evaluation of nursing care records and other relevant information against agreed standards to assess the quality of nursing care.

Nursing model A comprehensive framework in diagram form of components and criteria and their interrelationships in nursing care. It can be used to make rational decisions about such care.

Nursing process A systematic approach to delivering individualized care, comprising four phases: assessment (see *patient assessment*), planning, implementation and evaluation of the patient's or client's needs or problems and of the care given.

Objectives The planned outcomes of an activity. Objectives should be realistic, measurable, achievable and relative.

Open learning A flexible system of learning which attempts to remove some of the barriers commonly experienced by students, particularly in relation to the time, place and pace of learning.

Opportunistic learning See *practice placement learning programme*

Patient allocation The system by which the total care of individual patients or groups of patients is put in the hands of a specific nurse or team of nurses.

Patient assessment Systematic appraisal of a patient's needs, often linked to a selected nursing model. The outcome is then a care plan.

Performance indicator A pointer which draws attention to whether or not students are competent at carrying out tasks.

Philosophy of nursing A framework of values and beliefs used by a nurse or group of nurses by which they evaluate (see *evaluation*) their practice.

Practice nurse A nurse working in primary health care in a health centre or a GP's surgery and employed by the practice.

Practice placement learning programme A plan drawn up of all the possible learning opportunities that students may encounter on a particular clinical placement, together with the appropriate objectives, which are largely patient/client specific.

Primary nursing A way of organizing nursing in which the individual nurse is responsible for the care of a particular group of patients from admission to discharge, in a particular setting. It should not be confused with primary health care.

Psychomotor skills Acquired skill involving physical coordination. Most sports activities depend on psychomotor skills.

Quality assurance Measuring and evaluating (see *evaluation*) a product or a service against set standards and then taking steps to achieve (assure) the standards. (See also *standards setting*.)

Quality circle A staff group within a department or organization who meet regularly to discuss quality issues and to identify areas where improvement can be made.

Responsibility A charge or duty that arises from one's role or status in a profession and/or an organization. Responsibility requires the person in charge to take appropriate action in given circumstances. (See also *accountability* and *autonomy*.)

Self-assessment A method of self-testing by which individuals measure their own understanding and performance.

Self-awareness The capacity of individuals to recognize and understand their own values, prejudices, goals and so on, and to appreciate the extent to which these contribute to their work and interpersonal relationships.

Significant other The member of a multidisciplinary team whose professional background best meets the needs of the patient or client and who therefore assesses (see *patient assessment*) the patient's or client's needs and plans care, using other members of the team as necessary.

Speciality A defined area of professional work requiring specialized knowledge and skills to cater for the needs of a client group; for example, renal nursing, intensive care of the newborn.

Standards setting The establishment within an organization of a defined level and quality of a specified service that is to be achieved. It is usual to include the resources required (structure), the means by which to achieve the standard (process) and what should be achieved (outcome).

Summative assessment A more general assessment of the extent to which a student has achieved agreed standards of performance for the course as a whole or a substantial part of it. Contributes to the grading of a student, his/her qualification or certification. Summative assessments are normally completed at the end of a learning period.

Supervision The professional overseeing and support of a nurse by appropriately qualified staff in order to facilitate the developing of competence in the practice of nursing.

Supervisor The professional supporter of a nurse who oversees the development of competence. The role is a formal one and is normally defined by the role's responsibilities. Each nurse is required to have a designated supervisor on each shift when on duty. An appropriate qualified and experienced first- or second-level nurse/midwife/health visitor who, by example and facilitation, guides, assists and supports the student in learning new skills, adopting new behaviours and acquiring new attitudes.

Task allocation A schedule of organized tasks which enables nurses to complete work by routine. Underlying this system of patient care is the assumption that all patients experiencing a particular condition will respond to it in the same way. This system of care is no longer in action in today's nursing.

Values In psychological terms, the objectives that people seek. Usually the term is used to describe abstract goals such as social equality, understanding, variety, prestige and so on.

References

Argyris C and Schon D (1974) *Theory into practice: increasing professional effectiveness*. San Francisco: Jossey Bass.

Armitage P, Burnard P (1991) Mentors or preceptors? Narrowing the theory–practice gap. *Nurse Education Today* 11: 225–229.

Ashcroft K and Foreman-Peck L (1994) *Managing teaching and learning in FE and HE*. London: Falmer Press.

Ashworth P, Morrison P (1991) Problems of competence based nurse education. *Nurse Education Today* 11: 256–260.

Ashworth P, Saxton J (1990) On competence. *Journal of Further and Higher Education* 14(2): 3–25.

Barton B (1999) *The Yorkshire competency outcomes for nursing*. Standards for West Yorkshire Education Purchasing Consortia.

Benedum E, Kalup A, Freed D (1990) A competency achievement program for direct caregivers. *Nursing Management* 21(5): 32–46.

Benner P (1982) Issues in competency-based testing. *Nursing Outlook* 30(5): 303–309.

Benner P (1984) *From novice to expert: excellence and power in clinical nursing practice*. California: Addison-Wesley.

Benner P, Tanner C (1987) How expert nurses use intuition. *American Journal of Nursing* Jan: 23–31.

Bevis EO (1990) *Curriculum building in nursing: a process*. London: CV Mosby.

Block JH (ed.) (1971) *Mastery learning: theory and practice*. New York: Holt, Rinehart and Winston.

Boreham NC (1978) Test–skill interaction errors in the assessment of nurses' clinical proficiency. *Journal of Occupational Psychology* 51: 249–258.

Boss LA (1985). Teaching for clinical competence. *Nurse Educator* 10(4) 8–12.

Boud D (1981) *Developing student autonomy in learning*. London: Kogan Page.

Boud D, Keogh R, Walker D (eds) (1985) *Reflection: turning experience into learning*. London: Kogan Page.

Boyd EM and Fales AW (1983) Reflective learning: key to learning from experience. *Journal of Humanistic Psychology* 23:(2): 99–117.

Bradshaw A (1998) Defining "competency" in nursing (Part II): an analytical review. *Journal of Clinical Nursing* 7: 103–111.

Brookfield A (1984) The contribution of Eduard Lindeman to the development of theory and philosophy in adult education. *Adult Education Quarterly* 4(34): 185–196.

Brookfield S (1986) *Understanding and facilitating adult learning*. Milton Keynes: Open University Press.

Brown S, Knight P (1995) *Assessing business in higher education*. London: Kogan Page.

Burnard P (1990) The student experience: adult learning and mentorship revisited. *Nurse Education Today* 10: 349–354.

Burnard P (1996) *Acquired interpersonal skills. A handbook of experiential learning for health professionals*, 2nd edn. London: Routledge.

Carper B (1978) Fundamental patterns of knowledge in nursing. *Advances in Nursing Science* 1(5): 13–23.

Carroll E (1988) The role of tacit knowledge in problem solving in clinical setting. *Nurse Education Today* 8: 140–147.

Cell E (1984) *Learning to learn from experience*. Albany: State University of New York Press, p.177.

Chapman H (1999) Some limitations on competency-based education with respect to nurse education: an Australian perspective. *Nurse Education Today* 19(2): 129–135.

Child D (1981) *Psychology and the teacher*, 3rd edn. London: Holt, Rinehart and Wiston.

Clarke A, Castello A, Wright T (1986) *The roles and tasks of tutors in open learning systems*. Cambridge: Industrial Research Unit.

Clutterbuck D (1985) *Everyone needs a mentor: how to foster talent within the organization*. London: Institute of Personnel Management.

Cohen JA (1993) Caring perspectives in nursing education: liberation, transformation and meaning. *Journal of Advanced Nursing* 18: 621–626.

Crout L (1980) From a learner's point of view. *Nursing Mirror* 150(21): 14.

Darbyshire P (1993) In defence of pedagogy: a critique of the notion of andragogy. *Nurse Education Today* 13: 328–335.

Darbyshire P, Stewart B, Jamieson L, Tongue C (1990) New domains in nursing. *Nursing Times* 86(27): 73–75.

Darling L (1985) Mentors and mentoring. *Nurse Educator* 10(6): 18–19.

Darling L (1986) Cultivating minor mentors. *Nurse Educator* 11(4): 24–25.

Davenport J, Davenport JA (1985) A chronology and analysis of the andragogy debate. *Adult Education Quarterly* 35: 152–159.

Davies BW, Neary M, Philips R (1994) *Final report. The practitioner-teacher*. A study on the introduction of mentors in the pre-registration nurse education programme in Wales. Cardiff: UWCC, School of Education.

Day M (1997) Occupational standards and professional development. *Nursing Standards* 12(21): 39–41.

Dewey J (1938) cited by Boud D, Keogh R, Walker D (1985) *Reflection: turning experience into learning*. London: Kogan Page, p.12.

Donabedian A (1966) Evaluating the quality of medical care. In: Schubberg H, Baker F (eds) *Programme Evaluation in Health Fields*. London.

Dreyfus SE, Dreyfus HL (1980) *A five stage model of the mental activities involved in directed skill acquisition*. Unpublished report supported by the Air Force Office of Scientific Research (AFSC) USAF. Berkeley: University of California.

Eraut M (1985) Knowledge creation and knowledge use in professional context. *Students in Higher Education* 10(2): 117–133.

Fagan E (1984) Competence in educational practice: a rhetorical perspective. In: Short E (ed.) *Competence: inquiries into its meaning and acquisition in education settings*. New York: University of America Press.

Fitts PM, Posner MI (1969) *Human performance*. Belmont, California: Brooks Cole.

Forsythe GB, Williams C, McGuthrie C, Friedman CP (1986) Construct validity of medical clinical competence measures: a multinational multi method. Study using confirmatory factor analysis. *American Educational Research Journal* 23(2): 315–336.

French HP (1989) Educating the nurse practitioner. An assessment of the pre-registration preparation of nurses as an educational experience. Unpublished PhD thesis, University of Durham.

Gale J, O'Pray M (1981) The development and implications of frames of reference in curriculum evaluation programmes. The experience of a British school of medicine. *British Journal of Educational Technology* 1: 49–63.

Gelatly A (1987) *The skilful mind*. Milton Keynes: Open University Press.

Hagerty B (1986) A second look at mentors. *Nursing Outlook* 34: 16–20.

Hartree A (1984) Malcolm Knowles' theory of andragogy: a critique. *International Journal of Lifelong Education* 3(3): 203–210.

Heath H (1998) Keeping a reflective practice diary: a practical guide. *Nurse Education Today* 18: 592–598.

Huddleston P, Unwin I (1997) *Teaching and learning in further education: diversity and change*. London: Routledge.

Hyland T (1992) The vicissitudes of adult education: competence, epistemology and reflective practice. *Education Today* 42(2): 7–12.

Hyland T (1993) Competence, knowledge and education. *Journal of Philosophy of Education* 27(1) 55–66.

James M (1983) Course evaluation and curriculum development. *Nursing Times* 10(8): 83.

Jarvis P (1983) *Professional education*. Beckenham: Croom Helm.

Jarvis P (1984) The educational role of the supervisor in the tutorial relationship. *Nurse Education Today* 3(6): 126–129.

Jarvis P (1985) *The sociology of adult and continuing education*. London: Croom Helm.

Jarvis P (1995) *Adult and continuing education: theory and practice*, 2nd edn. London: Routledge.

Jeeves M, Greer B (1983) *The analysis of structural learning*. London: Academic Press.

Jessup G (1989) Foreword. In: Burke JW (ed.) *Competency based education and training*. Lewes: Falmer Press.

Jessup G (1990) *The evidence required to demonstrate competence*. In: Black H, Wolf A (eds) *Knowlege and competencey: current issues in training and education*. Sheffield: COIC.

Jessup G (1994) *Outcomes: NVQs and the emerging model of education and training*. London: Falmer Press.

Johns C (1994) Nuances of reflection. *Journal of Clinical Nursing* 3(2): 71–75.

Jowett S, Payne S, Walton I (1994) *Project 2000: the final report*. Slough: NFER.

Kemmis S (1985) Action research and the politics of reflection. In: Boud D, Keogh R, Walker D (eds) *Reflection: turning experience into learning*. London: Kogan Page.

Kenworthy N, Nicklin P (1989) *Teaching and assessing in nursing practice: an experiential approach*. London: Scutari Press.

Keyzer DM (1985) *Learning contracts: the trained nurse and the implementation of the nursing process*. PhD thesis, University of Manchester.

Keyzer DM (1986) Using learning contracts. *Nursing Education Today* 6: 103–106.

Knowles M (1975) *Self-directed learning. A guide for learners and teachers*. Chicago: Follett.

Knowles M (1990) *The adult learner*, 4th edn. Houston: Gulf.

Knowles M (1984) *The adult learner: a neglected species*. Houston: Gulf.

Kolb DA (1978) *Learning style inventory: technical manual*. Boston: McBeri.

Kolb DA (1984) *Experiential learning: experience as the source of learning and development*. Englewood Cliffs: Prentice-Hall.

Kolb DA, Fay R (1975) Towards an applied theory of experiential learning. In: Cooper G (ed.) *Theories of group processes*. Chichester: John Wiley.

Kyriacou C (1991) *Essential teaching skills*. Cheltenham: Stanley Thornes.

Lawton D (1983) *Curriculum studies and educational planning*. London: Hodder and Stoughton.

Le Var R (1996) NVQs in nursing and midwifery: a question of assessment and learning? *Nurse Education Today* 16: 85–93.

Long P (1976) Judging and reporting on student nurse clinical performance – some problems for the ward sister. *International Journal of Nursing Studies* 13: 115–121.

Luker K, Carlisle C, Davis C, Riley E, Stilwell J, Wilson R (1996) *Project 2000 Fitness for Practice*. Joint Report of the Universities of Liverpool and Warwick to the Department of Health.

MacKenzie N (1970) State School. London: Penguin.

Marshall K (1991) NVQs: an assessment of the outcomes approach in education and training. *Journal of Further and Higher Education* 15(3): 56–64.

Matthews R, Viens D (1988) Evaluating basic nursing skills through group video testing. *Journal of Nursing Education* 1: 44–46.

McAleavey M, McAleer J (1991) Competence-based training. *British Journal of In-service Education* 17(1): 19–23.

McAleer J, Hamilly C (1997) *The assessment of higher order competence development in nurse education*. Belfast: National Board for Nursing, Midwifery and Health Visiting for Northern Ireland.

McGagaghie WC, Miller GE, Sajid AW, Telder TV (1978) *Competency-based curriculum development in medical education: an introduction*. Geneva: WHO.

Messick S (1975) The standard problem: meaning and values in measurement and evaluation. *American Psychologist* **October**: 955–966.

Messick S (1982) *Abilities and knowledge in educational achievement testing: the assessment of dynamic cognitive structure*. Princeton, New Jersey: Educational Testing Service.

Miller C, Hoggan J, Pringle S, West G (1988) *Credit where credit's due. The report of the Accreditation of Work-Based Learning Project*. Glasgow: SCOTVEC.

Milligan F (1995) In defence of andragogy. *Nurse Education Today* 15: 22–27.

Mocker DW, Noble E (1981) Training part-time instructional staff. In: Gnabowski S *et al*. (eds) *Preparing educators of adults*. San Francisco: Jossey Bass.

Moon J (1999) *Towards purpose, clarity, effectiveness in training, teaching and learning*. Unpublished PhD thesis, University of Glamorgan, Pontypridd.

Moon J (1999) *Reflection for professional development*. London: Kogan Page.

Morle KMF (1990) Mentorship – is a case of the King's new clothes or a rose by any other name? *Nurse Education Today* 10: 66–69.

Neary M (1992a) Contract assignments. An integral part of adult learning and continuous assessment. *Senior Nurse* 12(4): 14–17.

Neary M (1992b) Planning, designing and developing an assessment tool. *Nurse Education Today* 12: 357–367.

Neary M (1993) *Students guide to curriculum studies*. Cardiff: Department of Education (now Social Sciences), University of Wales.

Neary M (1994) Teaching practical skills in colleges. *Nursing Standards* 27: 35–38.

Neary M (1996) *An investigation: continuous assessment of students' clinical competence in CFP*. PhD thesis, University of Wales, Cardiff.

Neary M (1997) Project 2000 students' survival kit: a return to the practical room/nursing skills laboratory. *Nurse Education Today* 17: 46–52.

Neary M (1998) Contract assignments: change in teaching, learning and assessment strategies. *Educational Practice and Theory* 20(1): 43–58.

Nottingham Andragogy Group (1983) *Towards a developmental theory of andragogy*. University of Nottingham.

Ogier ME (1986) *An ideal ward sister seven years on. Nursing Times* 82(2): 52–57.

O'Neill E, Morrison H, McEwen A (1993) *Professional socialisation and nurse education: an evaluation*. Belfast: Queen's University.

Pelosi-Beaulieu L (1988) Preceptorship and mentorship: bridging the gap between nursing education and nursing practice. *NSNA/IMPRINT* **April/ May**: 111–115.

Polanyi M (1958) *Personal knowledge*. London: Routledge and Kegan Paul.

Powell A, Owen L, Hatton N (1992) *Learning in clinical settings. Perceptions of students in nursing*. Sydney: University of Western Sydney.

Race P (1992) *Developing competence*. Professorial inaugural lectures 1991– 1992. University of Glamorgan, Pontypridd, 112–133.

Redford J, Govier E (1980) *A textbook of psychology*. New York: Sheldon Press.

Rielly DE (1975) *Behavioral objectives in nursing evaluation of learner attainment*. New York: Appleton-Century-Crofts.

Rogers C (1969) *Freedom to learn*. Columbus: Merril.

Rogers C (1983) *New directions in educational psychology - learning and teaching*. Basingstoke Press.

Ross M, Carrol G, Knight J *et al.* (1988) Using the OSCE to measure clinical skills performance in nursing. *Journal of Advanced Nursing* 13: 45–56.

Rowntree D (1987) *Assessing students: how shall we know them?* London: Kogan Page.

Rowntree D (1988) *Educational technology in curriculum development*, 2nd edn. London: Paul Chagman.

Runciman P (1990) *Competency-based education and the assessment and accreditation of work-based learning in the context of Project 2000 programmes of nurse education: A literature review*. Edinburgh: National Board for Nursing, Midwifery and Health Visiting for Scotland.

Ryle G (1949) *The concept of mind*. London: Hutchinson.

Satterly D (1981) *Assessment in schools*. Oxford: Basil Blackwell.

Schön DA (1971) *Beyond the stable state*. New York: Norton.

Schön DA (1983) *The reflective practitioner: how professionals think in action*. New York: Basic Books.

Schön DA (1987) *Educating the reflective practitioner*. San-Francisco: Jossey-Bass.

Schön DA (1994) A rather orderly chaos. King's Fund Workshop on the challenge facing the NHS. *Health Journal* **October 6**: 16.

Schön DA, Argyris C (1977) *Theory in practice: increasing professional effectiveness*. San Francisco: Jossey-Bass.

Sheenan J (1979) Measurement in nursing education. *Journal of Advanced Nursing* 4(1): 47–56.

Smith RM, Neisworth JJ (1969) Fundamentals of informal educational assessment. In: Smith RM (ed.) *Teacher diagnosis of educational difficulties*. Columbus: Merrill.

Smyth W (1986) *Reflection in Action*. Victoria, Australia: Deakin University Press.

Snow RE, Frederico P, Montague WE (eds) (1980) *Aptitude learning and instruction*. Hillsdale, New Jersey: Lawrence Erlbaum Associates.

Stake RE (1986) Progress evaluation, particularly responsive evaluation. In: Madaus GF, Scriven M, Stufflebeam DC (eds) *Evaluation models: Viewpoints in educational and human services evaluation*. Boston: Kluwer-Nijoff.

Steinaker N, Bell R (1979) *The experiential taxonomy: a new approach to teaching and learning*. New York: Academic Press.

Stenhouse L (1984) Evaluating curriculum evaluation. In: Adelman C (ed.) *The politics and ethics of evaluation*. London: Croom Helm.

Sternberg RJ (1986) *Beyond IQ: a triarchic theory of human intelligence*. New York: Cambridge University Press.

Tomlinson PC (1988) The teaching of skills: modern cognitive perspectives. In: Sugden DA (ed.) *Cognitive approaches in special education*. London: Falmer Press.

Training Agency (1989) *Development of accessible standards for national certification guidance. Note no.1*. Sheffield Employment Department/Training Agency.

UKCC (1992) *Code of professional conduct for the nurse, midwife and health visitor*, 3rd edn. London: EKCC.

UKCC (1999) *Fitness for practice*. London: UKCC.

Watson SJ (1991) An analysis of the concept of experience. *Journal of Advanced Nursing* **16**(9): 1117–1121.

Whittington D, Boore J (1988) Competence in nursing. In: Ellis R (ed.) *Professional competence and quality assurance in the caring professions*. London: Chapman and Hall.

WNB (1992) *Mentors, preceptors and supervisors: their place in nursing, midwifery and health visitor education*. Guidance letter, GL 2/92. Cardiff: Welsh National Board for Nursing, Midwifery and Health Visiting.

Wolf A (1989) Can competence and knowledge mix? In: Burke JW (ed.) *Competency-based education and training*. Lewes: Falmer Press.

Wood V (1982) Evaluation of student nurse clinical performance – a continuing performance. *International Nursing Review* **29**(1): 11–18.

UDACE (1991) *What can graduates do?* Consultant document. Leicester: UDACE.

Young D (1994 and 1999) *Personal communication*. Nursing and Health Studies. The Monforth University, Leicester.

Zwolski K (1982) Preceptors for critical care. *Focus* **10**: 7–11.

Index

Index entries in *italic* refer to illustrations, those in **bold** to whole chapters.